Dad's Maybe Book

Dad's Maybe Book

Tim O'Brien

4th ESTATE • London

4th Estate
An imprint of HarperCollins*Publishers*
1 London Bridge Street
London SE1 9GF

www.4thEstate.co.uk

First published in Great Britain in 2019 by 4th Estate
First published in the United States by Houghton Mifflin Harcourt in 2019

1

A catalogue record for this book is available from the British Library

ISBN 978-0-00-837245-3 (hardback)
ISBN 978-0-00-837246-0 (trade paperback)

Printed and bound in Great Britain by CPI Group (UK) Ltd, Croydon

MIX
Paper from
responsible sources
FSC
www.fsc.org
FSC™ C007454

This book is produced from independently certified FSC™ paper
to ensure responsible forest management.

For more information visit: www.harpercollins.co.uk/green

For Tad, Timmy, and
Meredith O'Brien

An entry from our babysitter's journal, January 8, 2008: "You have never lived till you see a two-year-old fall in the toilet."

———— .

And there goes Tad, running through a heavy rain on Rue Malar in Paris, clutching a child's umbrella, carefully splashing down in each available puddle. After a time, he lifts the umbrella over Meredith's head and says, "You are my sunshine, even when it's raining."

Contents

Dad's Maybe Book

1

A Letter to My Son

Dear Timmy,

A little more than a year ago, on June 20, 2003, you dropped into the world, my son, my first and only child—a surprise, a gift, an eater of electrical cords, a fertilizer factory, a pain in the ass, and a thrill in the heart.

Here's the truth, Timmy. Boy, oh, boy, do I love you. And, boy, do I wish I could spend the next fifty or sixty years with my lips to your cheek, my eyes warming in yours.

But as you wobble into your sixteenth month, it occurs to me that you may never really know your dad. The actuarial stuff looks grim. Even now, I'm what they call an "older father," and in ten years, should I have the good luck to turn sixty-eight, I'll almost certainly have trouble keeping up with you. Basketball will be a problem. And twenty years from now . . . well, it's sad, isn't it?

When you begin to know me, you will know an old man.

Sadder yet, that's the very best scenario. Life is fragile. Hearts go still. So now, just in case, I want to tell you about your father, the man I think I am. And by that I mean not just the graying old coot you may vaguely remember, but the guy who shares your name and your blood and half your DNA, the Tim who himself was once a Timmy.

Above all, I am this: I am in love with you. Pinwheeling, bedazzled, aching love. If you know nothing else, know that you were adored by your dad.

In many ways, a man is what he yearns for, and while it may never happen, I yearn to walk a golf course at your side. I yearn for a golden afternoon in late August when you will sink a tough twelve-footer to beat me by a stroke or two. I yearn to shake your hand and say, "Nine more holes?"

I yearn to tell you, man to man, about my time as a soldier in a faraway war. I want to tell you what I saw and what I did. I yearn to hear you say, "It's okay, Dad. All that's over."

So many other things, too. Right now, as I watch you sleep, I imagine scattering good books around the house—in the bathrooms, on the kitchen counter, on the floor beside your bed—and I imagine being there to see you pick one up and turn that first precious page. I long to see the rapture on your face. (Right now, you eat books.)

I yearn to learn from you. I want to be your teacher, yes, but I also want to be your student. I want to be taught, again and again, what I've already started to know: that a grown man can find pleasure in the sound of a happy squeal, in the miraculous sound of approaching feet.

I yearn to watch you perform simple acts of kindness and generosity. I yearn to witness your first act of moral courage. I yearn to hear you mutter, however awkwardly, "Yeah, yeah, I love you, too," and I yearn to believe you will mean it.

It's hard to accept as I watch you now, so lighthearted and purely good, so ignorant of gravestones, but, Timmy, you are in for a world of hurt and heartache and sin and doubt and frustration and despair. Which is to say you are in for being alive. You will do fine things, I know, but you will also do bad things, because you are wholly human, and I wish I could be there, always, to offer forgiveness.

More than that, I long for the day when you might also forgive me. I waited too long, Timmy. Until the late afternoon of June 20, 2003, I had defined myself, for better and for worse, by the novels and stories I had written. I had sought myself in sentences. I had loved myself only insofar as I loved a chapter or a scene or a scrap of dialogue. This is not to demean my life or my writing. I do hope you will someday read the books and stories; I hope you will find my ghost in those pages, my best self, the man I would wish to be for you. Call it pride, call it love, but I dare to hope that you will commit a line or two to memory, for in the dream-space between those vowels and consonants is the sound of your father's voice, the kid I once was, the man I now am, the old man I will soon become.

That said, I would trade every syllable of my life's work for an extra five or ten years with you, whatever the going rate might be. A father's chief duty is not to instruct or to discipline. A father's chief duty is to be present. And I yearn to be with you forever, always present, even knowing it cannot and will not happen.

There have been advantages, of course, to becoming a father at my age. I doubt that at twenty-eight or even at thirty-eight I would have fully appreciated, as I do now, the way you toddled over to me this morning and gave me a first unsolicited hug. (You knew I was waiting, didn't you?) I doubt I would have so easily tolerated the din at bedtime, or your stubborn recklessness, or your determination to electrocute yourself, or the mouthfuls of dirt you take from the potted plants in the foyer, or how, just a half hour ago, you hit the delete key as I approached the end of this letter.

You had awakened from your Shakespearian slumber. You were on my lap, squirming, and then you whacked the keyboard and let out a delighted squeal when I muttered a nasty word or two.

I've rewritten what I can remember. And now you are on my lap again, my spectacular Timmy. I'm using your fingers to type these words.

I love you,
Dad

2

A Maybe Book (I)

And then it becomes November 22, 2018.

My son Timmy has grown into a tall, basketball-loving fifteen-year-old. He has a brother, Tad, who is thirteen, and both have a father who, at age seventy-two, is at last approaching the end of this book of love letters to his children, along with a few anecdotes and some tentative words of advice.

I began writing back in 2003, stopped for a while, then resumed near the end of 2004. My intent was to leave behind little word-gifts for Timmy and his yet-to-be-born brother Tad, who had been conceived but was still waiting in the wings. The idea was to dash off a few short messages in a bottle that my kids might find tucked away in a dusty file cabinet long after my death. I was fifty-eight back then, not yet an old man, but the mathematics of mortality were already forbidding. It struck me that by the time the boys reached middle school, their father would almost certainly be mistaken for a grandfather, or maybe a grandfather's elder brother. And I was correct about this. In the years between 2005 and 2019, Walmart cashiers and IHOP waitresses would receive my pissed-off glares, my sullen wags of the head, as I informed them that, no, those two boys were my own personal kids. There was nothing funny about it. There was nothing cute.

Reality is reality.

And so, late in 2004, near the end of October, I resolved to give Timmy and Tad what I have often wished my own father had given me—some scraps of paper signed "Love, Dad." Maybe also a word of counsel. Maybe a sentence or two about some long-ago Christmas Eve. My father had always been a mystery to me, and he remains a mystery, and with this in mind, I wanted to offer Timmy and Tad a few scattered glimpses of their own dad, a man they might never really encounter. There was no literary impulse involved. There were no thoughts about making a book. My audience—if there would ever be an audience—was two little boys and no one else.

In 2004, Timmy was barely a toddler, and his brother Tad was little more than a pinprick of protein awaiting the light. But even so, for the next fifteen years, I talked to them on paper as if they were adults, imagining what they might want to hear from a father who was no longer among the living. I told the boys stories about their youth, and about my youth. I talked to them about books I had loved, writers I had admired, a war I had visited, a woman named Meredith who would become their mother. Along the way, I offered a few pointers about this and that. I admonished them to think for themselves, warned them against hypocrisy, and lectured them about the soul-throttling dangers of absolutism. I conducted home schooling classes. I wrote to the boys—no doubt in way too much detail—about my fascination with the battles of Lexington and Concord, and how, in a great many ways, my own war in Vietnam struck me as eerily similar. Over and over, I told them how very proud I was of their Rubik's Cube speed-solving, their hula-hooping, their report cards, their unicycling, and especially their acts of kindness and human decency. I reminded them of funny things they had said and done. I reminded them of sad things, too—one concussion, two broken legs, my mother's death. I applauded their first intelligible utterances. I used the stories of Ernest Hemingway as a window through which they might glimpse the things that have preoccupied me for more than fifty years— making sentences, making stories. I rhapsodized about my lifelong love for magic, a hobby that later led me to try my hand at performing the sorts of illusions found inside books. And so on.

I did not write to the boys often. Sometimes months would pass between the opening and concluding words of a single sentence. (Twice, an entire year passed.) Eventually, in late 2014, Tad proposed the idea of a maybe book. Meredith overheard. "You don't have to commit to an actual book," my wife said. "Just a maybe book. What you've written about fatherhood might mean something to *other* parents."

"Or their kids," said Tad.

The result is Tad's maybe book.

Like the life I have lived, and probably like anyone's life, these pages suffer from irreparable disunity. The book skips around in time, mostly because time has skipped around on me. It skips around in content, because my life's contents have skipped around on me—terror to grief to rage to broken love to despair to elation to late-night conversations with eternity. In a novel or in a story, the illusion of order can be imposed on a human life. But in a book that remains essentially a compilation of love letters to my sons, the imposition of order would be an artificial disgrace and, worse yet, deceitful. My kids are real kids, I am a real father, and chaotic messiness has been the humbling theme of our time together.

Tad, thank you for the book's title.

Timmy, thank you for your sternly revisionist views in regard to my faulty memory: "Dad, it didn't actually *happen* that way."

"How did it happen?"

"I don't remember. But not *that* way."

3

Row, Row

Timmy is just over two months old, nine weeks to be exact, and he won't stop crying. He seems to hate his brand-new world and all things in it, including his crib and his rattle and his mother and me.

Colic, say the doctors, but the kid hates eating and he hates not eating. He hates sleeping and he hates not sleeping. He hates being held and he hates not being held. He hates light and he hates dark. He hates hot and he hates cold and he hates all temperatures in between. He is full of fury.

I have fathered Jack the Ripper.

At the moment, in these early-morning hours of August 28, 2003, I'm taking a break while my wife Meredith sits in the laundry room with our howling little hater. A pediatrician has suggested placing him in a basket atop the clothes dryer. The machine's warmth and its humming motor have worked their magic, to be sure, but only on my exhausted wife, whom I last saw in a state of semiconsciousness.

Timmy just keeps crying and crying.

I hear him now, three rooms away, and it's not baby-crying. It's hate-the-world crying. It's bloody-murder crying. Something is wrong. This cannot be normal.

Meredith and I are first-timers at the whole baby thing, a pair of rookies, and we are not only incompetent but we're getting scared. I'm scared, in fact, at this very instant. In a few minutes I'll be shutting down my computer and returning to duty, except I have no clue as to what my duty actually is. Do I dump the boy in his crib and hope he howls himself to sleep? Do I try to silence him with coos? Do I sit with him in the laundry room for the next three hours? Right now it's 1:10 a.m. and Timmy has been crying since . . . well, since he was born. Nothing stops him—not for long. We'll pick him up and snuggle him and walk him around the house, and for a short while he may (or may not) settle down. But then he tightens up, fidgets, squirms, and eventually convulses in a deep, full-body shudder, as if electricity has just sizzled through his bones, and then his face goes wrinkly with hatred and he lets out a Frankenstein screech that wakes up the nomads in Libya. We're afraid the police will come. We're afraid neighbors will nail bomb threats to our door. We're afraid, quite literally, that our little boy hates being alive.

———

Our nerves are shot. We're exhausted. We have no family nearby, no wise and experienced relatives, no one to spell us for even a few hours. Worse yet, the pediatricians and their nurses seem fed up with our panicky phone calls. Over and over, they use the word "colic," or the word "fussy," as if we're too dumb to remember that these are the words they've been uttering for weeks on end. They murmur reassurances. They tell us to be patient. They tell us all babies are different. They tell us Timmy is going through a "phase." Both Meredith and I get the impression that we're over-reacting, perhaps exaggerating, and that we should man up and shut up and take our medicine.

We blame ourselves, of course. This morning, I've been sitting here at my desk, listening to the baby-din, wanting to cry, and only a few minutes ago I found myself suddenly horrified by the thought that my own hot temper and occasional rages may have been transmitted to my infant son. More horrifying yet, I worry that during Timmy's womb time he'd somehow absorbed the knowledge that for years prior to his conception I hadn't wanted children. Did his biology know that Meredith and I had nearly broken up over that issue during our courtship days? Did the cytosine in Timmy's DNA, or the proteins of his brain stem, somehow program resentment and disgust and outright fury in a kind of organic reaction to his father's selfishness? The blame game is far-fetched, at least in one sense, but it's painfully real in another. Meredith and I *feel* responsible. More than responsible. We feel guilt. We are older than most greenhorn parents, and although neither of us says so, we're both chewing on the possibility that our crusty, over-the-hill chromosomes combined to produce Timmy's wretchedness. (Would Jack the Ripper have been Jack the Ripper if his parents had not crossed genetic paths?) On her part, more practically, Meredith worries aloud that her type 1 diabetes may have infected her breast milk, or may have poisoned Timmy's pancreas, or may have otherwise caused our son all this unrelieved unhappiness. Also, because she's a type 1 diabetic, Meredith underwent induced labor. "Maybe Timmy needed more time inside," she speculated yesterday. "Being forced to wake up—wouldn't that upset anyone?" (I call this her premature ejaculation theory.) In any event, the blaming goes on and on. We page backward in memory through our health histories; we look for seeds of distress in our family trees; we beat ourselves up over that tiny sip of wine eight months ago and that mushroom soufflé consumed during our college years. Meredith has sworn off animal products. She has excised from her diet all broccoli, asparagus, beans, popcorn, cauliflower, prunes, artificial sweeteners, soda pop, citrus fruits, spices, chocolate, strawberries, pineapples, and caffeine. And the crying gets louder.

———

Last night, during my 2 a.m. baby duty, I hit on what appears to be a miracle. An imperfect miracle, a miracle in need of fine-tuning, but a gift from the gods all the same. It is the song "Row, Row, Row Your Boat." Sing it in the dark, sing it in a rocking chair, sing it long enough—maybe forty-five minutes, maybe an hour—and Timmy stops crying. He sleeps. He sleeps without hatred on his face.

When I mentioned my discovery to Meredith this morning, she looked at me skeptically. "So you put him in the crib?"

"Well, no," I said. "I tried, but he—"

"He woke up crying, right?"

"Right, and that's where the fine-tuning comes in. But at least he settled down for a while. You could feel him unwind. You could feel all that tightness go out of him."

"So now what?" said Meredith.

"Now I perfect it. Figure out how to get him into the crib."

"Lots of luck."

I nodded. She was right. Song or no song, his hatred for the crib was a problem, and there was also the fact that he continued to sleep for no more than fifteen or twenty minutes at a time. Moreover, there was an issue with the song itself. "It'll drive me crazy," I admitted to Meredith. "Last night it almost did. It's short—only four lines—and it's a goddamned *round*. Try singing 'merrily, merrily, merrily, merrily' for a whole hour."

She shrugged. "Why not try some other song?"

"I *did* try other songs. He hates 'Rock-a-bye Baby.' He hates 'Twinkle, Twinkle.' He hates 'Jingle Bells.' God knows what we'll do when Christmas comes."

Tears came to Meredith's eyes.

"Sorry," I said.

It's taken a few days, but I've made progress. Partly deletion, partly rewriting.

Among other things, I've tightened up the title. I now call the song "Row, Row." I've deleted the merrily stuff. I've deleted the boat and the rowing. I've deleted the stream. In fact, I've deleted almost everything but the melody, and as Timmy and I sit in the dark, rocking in our rocking chair, father and son, I invent filthy lyrics to keep myself sane. True, I adore that final line, "Life is but a dream," but it had to go. You don't sing about a pair of horny pigeons and end with "life is but a dream." It does not fit. Not with pigeons.

Tonight, I'll branch out.

Buggering mice, maybe.

Although I haven't written much since Timmy was born, I now sit in the dark and produce some of my best work in years. No pressures to publish. So far no bad reviews. I've finally found my subject.

> Bleep, bleep, bleep like mice,
> Gently up the bleep,
> Verily, verily, verily, verily,
> Firmly bleep the bleep.

———

As I mentioned earlier, Meredith and I had come within a whisker of calling it quits over our deadlock on the children question. She very much wanted kids. I very much did not. And so it happened that on a late night several years ago we exchanged heated words on the subject, each of us digging in, and eventually Meredith announced, wearily but bluntly, that there was no future for us. I was hurt by this. I asked her to leave, which she did, and for a couple of weeks we saw nothing of each other.

Now, singing "Row, Row" in the dark, I recall only bits and pieces from that period of silence and separation—mainly the word "crocodile" slithering through my head. I was appalled that Meredith could love something that did not exist, in fact the *idea* of something that did not exist, more than she loved me. It seemed cold-blooded. It seemed heartlessly reproductive.

In the end we met for drinks on neutral ground, in a Cambridge, Massachusetts, bar, and for several hours we learned a great deal about each other, not only emotional things but also the contents of our personal histories, the biographical facts that had brought us to this bar and to this impasse. Meredith talked about her mother dying. She talked about her father, a good man but sometimes a distant man, a man who too often seemed absent from her life. She talked about her sisters, one of whom had been institutionalized for decades with severe schizophrenia, the other of whom had twice attempted suicide (and would later succeed). She talked about the dream she'd been cultivating since she was a little girl, the dream of a happy, normal family life. "Maybe it's a fantasy," she said, "but don't I get to hope for *something*?"

On my part, I opened up about pretty similar things. An alcoholic father. A father who often scared me and who sometimes didn't seem to like me much. I talked about the tensions in our house, the late-night shouting matches between my mom and dad, the cruel words, the brittle silences that followed for weeks afterward. I also expressed, as best I could, my suspicion that I'd make a far less than ideal father. I was impatient, I told Meredith. I was stubborn. I was absent-minded. I was protective of my time. As a writer—a preposterously slow writer—I feared I'd come to resent the minutes and hours and days spent changing diapers and singing silly bedtime lullabies.

Meredith and I managed to work it out.

In that Cambridge bar, and in the weeks afterward, the realization began to stir in me that I too yearned for a happy, normal family life, even if I remained terrified of failing. There were no promises, exactly. But there was a prospect. Three years went by, and Meredith and I got married, and our son was conceived, and now I sit here in the dark, rocking my precious, life-hating Timmy to sleep, singing an unprintable new edition of "Row, Row."

———

The miracle hasn't panned out. In some ways things seem more hopeless than ever. Although "Row, Row" will eventually put Timmy to sleep, he continues to wake up screaming after a half hour or so, often after only a few minutes. He can't tolerate his crib. He looks pale and angry. He'll often cry while he eats, and without exception he cries immediately after he eats. The crying has become infectious. Meredith is crying—a lot. I've cried. All three of us are ragged with fatigue. If this is normal, normal isn't normal.

A dear and very generous friend named Anne Dolan has flown in from Paris to help out, mainly to spell us as we try to stitch our psyches back together. For three days and two nights, Anne endured exactly what we have been enduring. But on the third night—the night before last—she shook Meredith awake and explained that she was helpless, that she couldn't take it anymore, and that our son would not and could not and probably never would cease crying.

And so once again we call the doctor's office. Once again we hear the dreaded word "colic." Once again we are informed of the astonishing news that "babies cry." Once again we receive advice: babies need to be held. And the opposite advice: put him in his crib, shut the door, and let him cry himself to sleep. Once again we get instructions to check for diaper rash, to bathe him in lukewarm water, and—for the quadrillionth time—to place him in a basket atop the clothes dryer.

Alas, I'm back to "Row, Row."

Not only am I exhausted beyond exhaustion, but I've also exhausted all possible combinations of dirty rhymes. I've turned to politics. By daylight, mostly in my head, I invent catchy verses that will carry me through the coming hours of night. I begin by seeking out a fruitful rhyming pattern, then later I devote myself to the overall artistry. Bush—tush. Rice—advice. Rumsfeld—beheld. Cheney—rainy. First names, I've discovered, are much easier. I have fun with George and Don. I have a shitload of fun with Dick. Condoleezza has proven difficult, but like my poetically minded friends, I have no scruples about cheating with near rhymes. Often, to keep things interesting, and also in the interest of poetic richness, I'll combine my two genres, the political lyric blending into the dirty lyric, a hybrid that may represent a profligate new genre unto itself. My masterpiece is a version of "Row, Row" that I sang to Timmy just last night, a version in which every word but one must be redacted. It goes like this:

Bleep, bleep, bleep Dick's bleep,
Bleepily bleep bleep bleep,
Bleepily, bleepily, bleepily, bleepily,
Bleep Dick's bleeping bleep.

I am going mad, of course, but Timmy doesn't notice.

For a few blessed minutes he sleeps.

And perhaps one day, if he survives his life-is-but-a-nightmare infancy, he will thank his father for this solid foundation in modern dirty-mouthed political discourse.

———

Two and a half weeks pass. Things have changed but not for the better. Our friend Anne Dolan fled back to Paris last Thursday. Timmy has lost a quarter pound of body weight. He blinks away tears as he eats; he chews more than he sucks; he vomits; he hisses at us; he hisses and he shrieks both at once.

Day before yesterday we received new advice from our pediatric nurse. We were instructed to secure the boy in his car seat, bundle him "loosely but warmly," and drive until he settles down.

We've been driving by day and driving by night. We've clocked one hundred and sixty-eight miles.

For all but nine of those miles, Timmy has hissed and shrieked.

The hissing in particular, but especially in combination with the shrieking, has a wild-animal sound—an essential and irreducible beastliness—that chills me. It chills Meredith, too. We'll sometimes glance at each other, neither of us uttering a word, and in that glance we'll read each other's terror. Meredith, I'm almost certain, lies awake wondering if our beloved baby boy has inherited the afflictions of her two disturbed sisters. The hissing and the shrieking reproduce the bedlam of a psychiatric ward in Connecticut in which her older sister has resided since Meredith was in tenth grade.

Inevitably, given what we know of genetics, the blaming has revved up a notch. The guilt has thickened.

I worry not just about Timmy, but equally so about Meredith.

I don't think she can handle much more.

––––

Though I try not to let on, I'm also concerned about the limits of my own tolerance. As I sing "Row, Row" in the dark, my thoughts seem to rattle around without content, or without objective and realistic content. I fantasize sometimes. I pretend none of this is happening. I pretend I'm teaching history to my son as I sing about John Wilkes Booth going merrily down the stream.

––––

This morning I found Meredith sitting outside Timmy's bedroom. She was trembling with . . . I don't know what. She was trembling with all that has been and all that still is.

I had seen her weep before, but never like this.

Behind the closed bedroom door, Timmy was shrieking.

I didn't decide anything; I just did it—loaded all three of us into the car and drove to an emergency room.

Seven hours later we departed with three prescriptions: Xanax for Meredith, Xanax for me, and a drug called Prilosec for Timmy. Our son was found to be suffering from acid reflux disease. His case was severe. We were informed that acid reflux can be difficult to diagnose, especially among infants, who are unable to articulate where things hurt or how things hurt or why things hurt or even *that* things hurt. They can cry. They can shriek and hiss. We learned today, along with a great deal else, that insomnia is a common symptom of acid reflux; we learned that the condition is caused by a relaxation of the lower esophageal sphincter, which in turn permits stomach acids to drain into the esophagus; we learned that those acids can produce intense pain, especially in the sensitive tissues of a baby; we learned that the word "colic" (sometimes called "infantile colic") is descriptive of a set of symptoms (frequency of crying, duration of crying) but is not a diagnosis of organic cause; we learned that we were not to blame; we learned that Timmy hated only the terrible pain, not the world.

All that was today.

Now it's 11:17 p.m., and the house is bizarrely silent. The Prilosec did its magic—not instantly, but very nearly so.

The Xanax also worked. Meredith has been sleeping since late afternoon. I'm feeling extremely fine.

Until two hours ago I had been sitting in the dark with Timmy, even though he no longer needs me. He too is feeling fine. He sleeps peacefully. He is in his crib. In a few minutes I'll get some sleep myself, but for now, as I scribble down these few words, I'm content to sit here listening to the all-is-well hum of our baby monitor, its soothing electric buzz coming from some unpopulated and distant galaxy. I'm riding the jet stream of Xanax, true, but I'm also feeling a kind of nostalgia, the sort of backward-looking, tongue-probing surprise one feels after an aching tooth has been pulled. I don't miss all the horror, of course. But I do miss *surviving* the horror. I miss our rocking chair. I miss holding Timmy in the dark. I miss "Row, Row"—enough to feel acutely what is missing. This sensation, whatever it is, reminds me a bit of what I'd once experienced in Vietnam after a firefight ended, when something that was so excruciatingly present became so shockingly absent.

I had been afraid my son would die.

I am still afraid. I will always be afraid.

It occurs to me that one day, when he is a senior in college, or maybe when he receives his doctorate from Stanford, I'll have to let him take his chances out in the killer world. At that point—or maybe when he is elected to his second term as President—I'll probably allow him to apply for a driver's license and (if he's very careful) use the family car to go out on his first dangerous date, though I'll be singing "Row, Row" in the back seat.

4

Skin

Timmy is an infant. He is on my lap. My nose is pressed to the top of his head. My eyes are closed. I am smelling his skin. And the smell of skin — a baby's skin — becomes, in the instant of smelling, the one and only thing in the universe. Nothing else exists. There is no yesterday and no tomorrow, only the smell of skin, no murder, no turpitude, no unhappy endings, only the smell of skin, for everything else is elsewhere, and the smell of an infant's skin is the smell of light obliterating darkness.

5

Trusting Story

Timmy's first fifteen months mostly evaporated for me. What I have in my head, when I have anything at all, is a jumble of diapers and bottles and strollers and car seats and two or three near-death experiences. Timmy eats, or at least tries to eat, live electrical cords. He enjoys dirt for dessert. Last month I swatted a cockroach from his lips. I am not kidding.

But then an event occurs which I need to capture here, for Timmy's sake, as a small record of his early days on our planet. Sometimes I chuckle at what happened; other times I get angry.

In July of this year, not long after Timmy's first birthday, our family attended the Sewanee Writers' Conference up in the mountains of Tennessee, where I had been tasked with providing advice to people who sought to become better writers. Most often in such circumstances I can think of almost nothing to say: read widely, toughen up your psyche, ration the booze, and don't forget to write a little. I want to be helpful, of course, but I don't know how. I feel like an imposter. Occasionally, in my courageous or whimsical moods, I'll offer to my students the tentative suggestion that fiction writers might do well to trust their own stories. Above all, I'll mumble, to trust a story means to tell it—not to creep up on it, not to postpone the "good" parts, not to hint at it or cleverly foreshadow it or offer the reader periodic promises that a glorious tale will soon be coming. To trust a story is to conquer the fear of plunging headfirst into the surprises and contradictions of being human.

So one afternoon last summer I took the plunge. I'd been asked to deliver a public lecture. Meredith and Timmy were in the audience, which revved up my jitters, and for several seconds I went through a catalog of excuses for getting the hell out of there: I'd contracted encephalitis, I'd eaten cockroaches. But then I did it—I plunged. I explained that Meredith and I had been eagerly awaiting our son's first utterance. One of us had been betting on "Mommy," the other on "Daddy."

Yesterday morning, I told the audience, Timmy finally delivered.

He looked up from a toy rattlesnake (we live in Texas) and said, with hair-raising clarity, "'Tis a tale told by an idiot."

Meredith and I were astonished. We were frightened. Immediately we packed the boy up and hauled him down to the Sewanee health facility. A kindly young nurse was on duty. She enthroned Timmy on an examining table and said, "Okay, what's the trouble, little guy?" Timmy stared at her—suspiciously, I thought—and said, "'Tis a tale told by an idiot." The nurse, like Meredith and I, was taken aback. She checked the boy's vitals, excused herself, and went to a telephone. Apparently a doctor was on call. Over the next several minutes, we overheard bits and pieces of the nurse's end of the conversation, a phrase here, a phrase there, the general tone of which was alarm. I'm quite certain I heard the nurse whisper, "These goddamned writers' conferences." Only minutes later, no doubt sped by curiosity, the doctor himself soon appeared, a white-haired, courtly, convivial gentleman dressed for a game of golf. The man smiled and clapped his hands and said, "So what's the story here?" Timmy muttered, "'Tis a tale told by an idiot." The boy seemed pleased with himself.

Medical procedures ensued, tentative probings of the ear and tongue, but, in the end, the physician seemed as puzzled as any of us. He scratched his head. Our son, he finally told us, was not ill. He explained that one-year-olds were well known to have as their first decipherable bit of language not just a single word, such as "Daddy," but in fact two or three words, such as "Hi there, Daddy," or "Bye-bye, Daddy," or other such simple constructions. "Your son," the doctor said, "has merely tacked on a few additional syllables."

"Well, yes," said Meredith, "but those are *famous* syllables. Those syllables make *sense*."

The physician pooh-poohed this. He assured us that the abnormality, if one wished to call it that, was far from life-threatening. It was not cancer. It was not polio. And thus, after he'd prescribed a sedative for Meredith and me, we departed the dispensary.

That evening, as any parent can well imagine, Meredith and I shot a good many oblique glances at our son—proudly, yes, but also with a measure of anxiety. It was clear that from this point on we would be wise to watch our tongues. If the boy could pick up on a phrase from Shakespeare, he could certainly master the word "cocksucker." Moreover, I must now admit to something infantile in my own character. As the evening wore on, I found myself increasingly disappointed, then outright irritated, that my son's first utterance had originated in the imagination of a competing writer. At one point, while Meredith set up our video camera, I knelt down beside young Timmy and whispered to him, "First Lieutenant Jimmy Cross carried letters from a girl named Martha, a junior at Mount Sebastian College in New Jersey."

At that point in my Sewanee lecture, I glanced over at Timmy, who squirmed and fussed in Meredith's arms. People stared at him. People were laughing. Though the boy was barely a year old, and though his vocabulary was therefore severely cramped, he nonetheless seemed annoyed at the airing of his intimate personal life in a public setting. He emitted what I took to be heckling sounds.

For twenty minutes or so, although now flustered, I did my best—ineptly, I'm sure—to point out that I was making no claims about the literary merit of my little story. In fact, I admitted, it wasn't even a story, certainly not in the sense of richness or depth. It was a trifling anecdote, nothing more. But even so, I said, it was possible that in certain sympathetic hands, perhaps those of a Donald Barthelme or a Woody Allen or any other writer with a sensibility suited to the comically grotesque, an interesting piece of prose might be forthcoming with the application of much time and imaginative energy. In fact, I myself might one day wish to pick up the tale, adding and subtracting, taking what is now a mere sketch off into the world of a full story. What I surely would *not* do is play much longer with Shakespeare. I would take the story elsewhere, virtually to any elsewhere. I'd try to surprise myself. I'd seek some new narrative dimension. And while striving to sustain something of the humor, I would also keep an eye peeled for gravitas—a thematic heft, a moral weight—hoping the tale might elevate itself above the eccentric or the entertainingly slight. I would trust these first paragraphs to carry me toward that next dimension.

What if . . . What if late that same night, Timmy were to cry out in his sleep, "Alas, Babylon"?

Or what if the next morning, perched in his high chair, he were suddenly to bay, "I ain't nothin' but a hound dog"?

Or what if, a month later or a year later, on a sunny beach along the ocean, he were to whisper, "Bye-bye, Daddy," and then toddle off into the water and slip forever beneath the waves?

To trust a story is to trust one's own story, not someone else's. To trust a story is to avoid the predictable, the familiar, the wholly logical, the already written, the movie you saw last week, the bestseller you read last month, and even that classic you nearly finished back in college. To trust a story is to trust your own imagination, not the imagination of some literary predecessor.

Also, if I were to go forward with the Timmy story—and now, having thought about it, why not?—I would soon be fretting over issues of craft. For example, there is the whole matter of writers writing about writers, which for me carries with it a self-congratulatory stink. I would probably end up dispensing with the reference to *The Things They Carried,* although it would be painful to delete one of the anecdote's funnier lines. (Funny to me, anyway.) No doubt I would tinker, perhaps for hours, with ways to recast or defuse the reference to my own work, but still, at the end of the day, the line would almost certainly have to go.

Beyond all else, I would do nothing to explain how a one-year-old came to declaim a famous phrase from *Macbeth.* The utterance would simply *be,* just as Gregor Samsa simply *is* a bug, or just as Grumpy simply *is* a dwarf. Granted, a baby reciting a phrase from Shakespeare is on its face pretty far-fetched and mysterious. But it seems to me no more far-fetched or mysterious than, say, the existence of our solar system, or human love, or Mohamed Atta flying an airplane into a Manhattan skyscraper.

At that point, as I concluded my talk, Timmy lay snoozing in his mother's arms. Yet even that—the fact that I'd now bored him into unconsciousness—had the feel of a rebuke, and for the remainder of the day I was followed by an unsettling cloud of guilt: that I'd exploited my own son for the sake of a few paltry literary observations.

That evening, in the midst of an outdoor cocktail party, I was approached by a middle-aged gentleman dressed in a bow tie, colorful suspenders, and a vintage straw boater of the sort Gatsby might have favored.

"Your fucking kid," the man said, "never quoted Shakespeare."

"No," I said.

"So why did you have to lie?"

"I didn't *have* to," I told him. "I *wanted* to."

This comment (wholly defensible) pissed him off. He had been drinking, I realized, but plainly his wrath was genuine.

Over the next many minutes I received the gist of the man's complaint, which had to do with my failure to acknowledge that Timmy had not spoken, in any form whatsoever, the words I'd claimed he had spoken. It amounted to intentional and gross deception, the man said. It was unfair to the audience. "You made us laugh," he said, "about a complete lie. You made us feel like fools."

"I didn't intend that."

"Well, my friend," he said, "I'm here to tell you that I took offense. I still take offense."

Ordinarily, I would've tried to smooth things over. But he had referred to Timmy as my "fucking kid." He had referred to me as his friend.

I told him he was a monster.

I told him that one day I would write about him.

"In that case," the man said (and I'm paraphrasing here, omitting two very vulgar words), "according to Shakespeare, that would be a tale *told* by an idiot—by a lying idiot—which is you."

I did not hit him.

In fact, much to my karmic credit, I drew a breath and stepped back. Fiction writers always lie, I said—way too gently. They lie for a living. They lie for money. They lie for the fun of it. They invent stuff and try to convince people it actually occurred—that's the job, that's the joy. Besides, aren't the first words of a child *always* miraculous? *Always* beyond belief?

"Maybe so," the man said, "but why not just give us the actual miracle, not some made-up bullshit? Why not give us your kid's *real* first words?"

"Because it would've been dull—you wouldn't have felt anything."

"That's all you can say?"

"Well, no," I told him. "I guess nobody would've believed me—not Timmy's actual first words. So why not invent something amusing?"

"It wasn't in the least amusing," he muttered. "It was manipulative."

"You didn't laugh?"

"Of course I did. That's what *made* it manipulative. And by the way, in case you don't know, your books make my students feel exactly the same way. Totally scammed."

I nodded. "So you teach?"

"Most definitely, and at a very respectable university."

"And do you also write fiction?"

"Certainly so. Superb fiction."

I should've ended it there, but I didn't.

"Well, listen," I said, "have you considered trying your hand at nonfiction? Maybe a book about automotive repair?"

The man glared. "I take that as a condescending assault on my person. I'll be reporting you accordingly—you can count on it. Plus, I suppose you're too much of a liar to tell me what your kid actually said."

"Does it matter?"

"Ha!" he said. "You're asking if *truth* matters?"

"But we're talking about a story, aren't we? Wasn't it clear that the whole thing was—?"

"Fabrication!" he snarled.

I looked around for assistance. People were staring at us without staring at us.

"All right," I said, "I'll tell you the truth, but it won't be funny. Basically, most of it happened just the way I described it, except of course I changed Timmy's dialogue. But the toy rattlesnake, that part was real."

"I *knew* that," the man said sharply.

"The nurse was real, too. Timmy had an ear infection."

"I assumed as much."

"And the doctor—he was *very* real. Courtly, convivial. Dressed for golf."

"Who cares? All that's obvious. Get to what your kid really said."

I was frightened, I'll admit. But I was thrilled by the certainty that someday (which is right now) I would exact revenge on this literal-minded Philistine.

"Okay," I said, "Timmy's first words were—you won't believe this—a full sentence, perfect grammar, clear as a bell. He looked up from his toy rattlesnake and said, 'Daddy, we should go find a guy in a straw hat and tie him up and murder him.' Verbatim quote. First utterance ever. I warned you it wouldn't be funny."

The man peered at me.

"Is that a threat?"

"No. It's a miracle."

The man removed his hat, straightened to his full height, and said, very quietly, "Your son has a terrible, terrible father."

6

First Words

When Timmy began to speak, Meredith was in the habit of calling him "honey," which the boy took to mean that others were also to be called "honey."

The mailman frowned at this.

The Walmart cashier, a humorless Texan, squinted at my son with a touch of irritation.

"Bye, honey," Timmy called over his shoulder.

7

Home School

Timmy, I want you to consider something: George Washington was once declared a terrorist in the halls of Parliament. America's beloved patriot had become King George's detested criminal. It is not just beauty that resides in the eye of the beholder.

Also, Timmy, whenever you glance at a five-dollar bill, I want you to remember that Abraham Lincoln engaged in the sexual act. He had four children, after all, and this required ejaculation, and during those exclamatory moments, Lincoln almost certainly was not contemplating the Gettysburg Address. The man on the five-dollar bill is not the whole man.

I want you to bear in mind that truth has no patience for what is tasteful and what is not.

And I want you to ask: Is one-kabillionth of the truth the truth? Is three-quarters of the truth the truth? In fact, is the whole truth, to which we are pledged in courtrooms, ever truly the whole truth, and if so, how do you know? Can you read minds?

Were you present at the creation? Does sunlight come equipped with earbuds through which it whispers to you, "I am truth, I am truth"? Do wars whisper, "I am righteous, I am righteous"? Or is it mankind who whispers those comforting words about sunlight and the wars we make?

There is no Easter Bunny, Timmy. Although your mother and I will do all we can to make you believe in generous rabbits, please don't forget that you once accepted as perfectly true something that was perfectly false.

As you grow older and wiser, I want you to remind yourself that this true-false thing cuts both ways. What is accepted as false may later be accepted as true. And what is accepted as true may later be denounced as false. Planet Earth is not flat. Planet Earth is not located at the center of the universe.

I want you to remember that your country once went to war to get rid of weapons of mass destruction that did not exist.

I want you to consider that the witches executed in Salem, Massachusetts, were probably not true witches, except in the heads of the people who executed them.

I want you to remember that the word "truth" can kill.

I want you to remember that what is true in one place may not be true in another. Right now, for example, it's Christmas Eve, 11:52 p.m., on Friday, December 24, 2004. That's true, I suppose. But it's not true in Tokyo, is it? Or in Baghdad? Or on Neptune?

Right now you are sound asleep in your crib, dreaming your true dreams, but at 5 a.m. tomorrow, when you awaken, what is true at this instant will no longer be true.

I want you to remember that truths can be contradictory. I

could tell you, Timmy, that you live in a great and good country, and I would be telling the truth. But I could also tell you that ours is a country that once permitted the enslavement of human beings, and that too would be true.

Truth can be fluid, Timmy. People fall in love. People fall out of love. What is true on Thursday may not be true on Friday, or may not be true in exactly the same way.

I want you to remember that Newton was succeeded by Einstein.

I want you to remember that what we call the Vietnam War is called by others the American War.

I want you to remember that God did not receive creation instructions from the authors of Genesis or from the trustees of Oral Roberts University. Presumably the instructional flow went the other way.

I want you to remember that sometimes—in fact, many times—literal truth does not matter in the least, and should not matter. As you sit in a movie theater or lie in bed with a good novel, Timmy, I hope you will not mutter to yourself every few seconds: "That's not true, that's not true, that's not true, that's not true, that's not true." If anything of the sort occurs—if literal truth matters to you that much—please seek counseling.

Along the same lines, I want you to keep in mind that any work of history, though it may contain a great deal of truth, will never contain *the* truth. The daydreams of Alexander the Great will not appear in a work of history, and yet daydreams influence aspiration, and aspiration influences behavior, and human behavior influences history. Did Tojo wake up with a bad headache on a

December morning in 1941? Did Ho Chi Minh dream about riding naked aboard an elephant through the streets of Saigon? At
the Little Bighorn, in his final seconds, did Custer appreciate the
irony that he was about to receive exactly what he had come prepared to deliver? History doesn't know.

Also, Timmy, I want you to remember that Osama bin Laden
is at this instant convinced of certain truths, truths he considers
worth killing for, just as Dick Cheney is convinced of his own precious truths, truths he too believes are worth killing for. Truth
does not come dressed in flags or priestly vestments or classy business suits.

I want you to remember that the word "truth," especially
when it's capitalized, can be used as a tyrant's bludgeon or as a
saint's exhortation or as a con man's invitation to invest your life
savings in a Ukrainian time-share.

Also, Timmy, I want you to know that your first utterance had
nothing to do with Shakespeare. It had nothing to do with mur-
dering people in suspenders and straw boaters. Your first words, in
fact, were these: "This so' is *mine!*" (The word "so'," which is not
quite a word, was your parents' shorthand for "soda pop.") While
few will believe it, your grammar was excellent and your youthful
utterance arrived in the form of a flawlessly constructed sentence.
Who cares if skeptics don't believe this? As Galileo discovered, people often prefer comfortable falsehoods to uncomfortable truths.

As I sit at your crib, Timmy, and as I jot down these things
under the glow of a night-light, I'm caught up in some pretty
serious Christmas Eve sentimentality. I'm here beside you, that
seems true, but it's also true that I'm gliding through the silent,

snow-softened Christmas Eves of my Minnesota childhood, then to a sad and fearsome Christmas Eve in Quang Ngai Province, then to a Christmas Eve in 1994 when I'd come to the conclusion that for me there would be no more Christmas Eves ever again. How untrue that was. But how true it then seemed.

Humility is not a bad idea, Timmy.

There's nothing immoral about the word "maybe." This entire maybe book, like our lives, is full of maybes—all those undiscovered truths, all those forgotten truths, all those unknowable truths—and it's okay to say "maybe" even when you believe you have access to some self-evident, ironclad, miraculous, and eternal Truth.

It's also okay to say "I don't know," even when you're cocksure that you do know.

It's okay to say "It seems" instead of "It is."

And so, please, watch out for absolutism, Timmy. Chipmunks are absolutists.

An apple a day may not always, or ever, keep the doctor away.

An eye for an eye may end up becoming a million eyes for a million other eyes, and some of those eyes may belong to children like you.

Be suspicious of slogans and platitudes and generalizations of any sort, including what I just had to say about chipmunks and apples and eyes. Seek the exceptions. Memorize the fallacy of composition. Remember that even mathematicians demand proofs. Raise your eyebrows when you hear the phrase "courage of conviction." Remember that Adolf Hitler and the executioners at Salem had the courage of lunatic conviction.

You were born, Timmy, in a time of epidemic terror—airliners crashing into skyscrapers, anthrax arriving in the morning mail—and among the casualties of terror is our fragile tolerance for ambiguity and uncertainty and all that is unknown. The word "perhaps" becomes "for sure." The word "probably" becomes "slam dunk." Truth, or what we call truth, becomes as wildly cartoonish as the big bad wolf. I realize, Timmy, that in the coming years you, too, like our country at the moment, will find yourself terrified—of love, of commitment, of madmen, of monsters in your closet, of me—and tonight I'm asking only that you remain human in your terror, that you preserve the gifts of decency and modesty, and that you do not permit arrogance to overwhelm the possibility that you may be wrong as often as you are right.

Listen, I'm afraid, too, Timmy.

I'm afraid to leave you alone in your crib on Christmas Eve. And I'm afraid of leaving you alone forever. There will come a Christmas Eve, maybe in five years, maybe in twenty-five, when I won't be here to look after you, and I guess that's why I'm writing these things down. Not just to offer advice, but to give you the voice of your father.

It's late.

I'm going to bed now, Timmy.

But before I switch off your night-light and close the door, I need to let you know that you will have a brother arriving sometime next June. Set a good example for him. Stop eating cockroaches. Learn to change your own diapers. Do all you can to look after your new brother, Timmy, even if it's true that at the moment you do not have a brother.

8

The Best of Times

After one broken leg, and after a bazillion spills and crashes and near amputations, my daredevil son Timmy collided with his third birthday. A few days later, his brother, Tad, became a stylish one-year-old.

It has been an amazing time in the life of this Johnny-come-lately, fifty-nine-year-old father. So many indelible moments: How last night, as I put Timmy into his pajamas, the boy whispered, "Be gentle with me." (This from a kid who would happily dive headlong from a third-story window.) Or how, not long ago, Tad embarked on his first treacherous steps through the world. Treasures such as these are captured in countless photographs that clutter the surfaces of our house: Timmy with his arms wrapped around his brother's neck in what appears to be a police submission maneuver; Tad gazing at the camera with the eyes of a seasoned fashion model.

The word "amazing" doesn't do it justice.

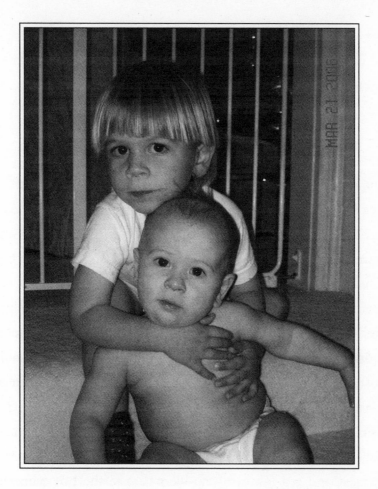

And yet on the dawn of this Father's Day, June 18, 2006, the thought occurs to me that neither boy will remember more than a fragment of our miraculous time together. That which is everything to me will become almost nothing to them. If I were to vanish from their lives at this instant, my sons would have no recollection of their father's face or voice or human presence.

Seems impossible, doesn't it? But even as adults, we salvage precious little from our own lives. Vividly lived-in minutes and hours seem to erase themselves as we scurry toward eternity—the meal we savored, the joke that had us laughing all night, the TV program that held us transfixed. Almost all of it is lost.

———

Right now, as I look back on my own childhood, I'm left with only a handful of interior snapshots. Among them are one or two of my father, who died on August 10, 2004—yesterday, it seems. (My reflective mood on this Father's Day is surely connected to the hole where my dad used to be.) One of those early recollections involves a couple of playmates who had stopped by the house one afternoon while my dad was on the telephone. After hanging up, my father turned and said, "Guess who I was talking to just now? The Man in the Moon!" My friends and I were flabbergasted. "Call him back!" we yelled, and so my dad dialed—or pretended to dial—and for ten or fifteen minutes he carried on a make-believe conversation with the Man in the Moon, relaying our questions and inventing answers that seemed to come from the far reaches of the solar system.

"The Man in the Moon says it's lonely up there," my father told us. "He wants you to pay him a visit."

"He does?" I said.

"You bet," said my dad. "Right away."

We were willing, of course, but the logistics seemed complicated.

"Okay, but how do we get there?" one of us asked.

My father nodded. He passed along the question, listened intently, and said, "The Man in the Moon says you have to visit him in your dreams. You have to dream your way there."

Whether the incident happened just as I've described it or in some other approximate way, I can't be sure. Memory is fallible. What matters on this Father's Day is that I can still see my dad smiling down on me as he spoke into that telephone. And now more than ever I dream my way back to him.

———

Beyond anything, I am struck today by the gap between what is memorable to an adult and what seems to matter to a pair of little boys. Like any young kid, Timmy and Tad live fiercely and absolutely in the moment. A dropped pretzel is a matter of life and death. But an instant later the pretzel is forgotten, succeeded by some other weighty distraction, perhaps a bouncing ball. For children, it seems, everything matters. Yet very little matters for long.

The other day, as one example, I was practicing a magic trick with Meredith, the finale of which was to make her disappear from beneath a white curtain. Timmy, who had been looking on silently, exploded in tears. "You made Mommy go!" he yelled, or screamed, or whatever you wish to call a roof-rattling, bone-melting cry of distress. Here, I thought, was something he would surely remember forever. It occurred to me, in fact, that I might soon have to hustle him off to a child psychiatrist. (Sophisticated young Tad, on the other hand, was distinctly unimpressed by my magic. He crossed his legs, yawned, and pretended to light a cigarette.)

As swiftly as my expertise allowed, I made the boys' mother re-appear. After a tense few moments, Timmy reached for the curtain, studied it closely, and then grinned and said, "Do that again. Make her go for a long time."

The volatile, unpredictable workings of a child's mind will come as no surprise to any parent. What had seemed an enduring trauma turned out otherwise—except perhaps to Meredith. Years from now, my wife and I will still be rehashing the incident, partly laughing, partly wondering. But for Timmy it is already a distant and blurry memory, if a memory at all. Multiply that example by a thousand others, or twenty thousand, and you begin to understand what gives me wistful pause on this Father's Day.

True enough, most of the events of my own early years have gone wherever our lives finally go—maybe into that hole I mentioned. And it's also true that Timmy and Tad will experience the same melting-away process. Still, like my own father, I hope to leave my sons with at least some sense of my enormous love for them. Maybe tonight, before bedtime, I'll lift the boys onto my lap, pick up the telephone, and launch into a conversation with the heavens. Maybe I'll have the wit to invent clever dialogue. And maybe a few decades from now, as my sons begin to feel the cool, insistent press of middle age, they will find comfort in the memory of their father saying, "Sleep well. I'm watching over you. I'm the Man in the Moon."

9

Highballs

It's November 9, 2007. Timmy is four and his brother Tad is two. We are vacationing in the Bahamas, and at the moment it is 3:40 in the morning, still dark outside, and Meredith and the boys are sleeping soundly in the perfumed Bahamian night. I'm sitting on our narrow hotel balcony, gazing out on the lights of Nassau, a town where my father once worked for a hotel called the Royal Victoria. The hotel is gone now, as my father is, but from this balcony I can look across the harbor to the spot where, in the 1930s, the Royal Victoria had for years reigned as one of the world's grand establishments. There, my dad spent many of the happiest days of his life. He was not yet an alcoholic. He did not yet have children. He was young and single, and he had the run of a fashionable hotel on a beautiful and hospitable island, and, knowing my dad, he surely made the most of it. As I sit here now in the dark, it strikes me that, like my father, I've undergone a pretty radical transformation since my younger days. One kind of fun has replaced another. Where before I had taken pleasure in my own well-being, I now take much greater pleasure in the well-being of Timmy and Tad.

As one conspicuous example, the boys are now going through a zealous costume phase, and Meredith and I have spent the bulk of our vacation chasing after Batman and Spider-Man and assorted creatures from outer space. Yesterday, the kids went bodysurfing in their costumes—Timmy was Superman, Tad was a bunny—and more than a few bewildered stares came their way as they emerged from the Atlantic like the survivors of some comic-book shipwreck. They dine at Nobu in their costumes, go down water slides in their costumes, climb rock walls in their costumes, stroll through the casino in their costumes, and high-five puzzled lifeguards in their costumes. The boys are no longer content with store-bought outfits; Meredith devoted the first day of our vacation to manufacturing a pair of unicorn horns, using rolled-up socks, coffee filters, and plenty of ingenuity. Though it's embarrassing to admit, I've sometimes joined the boys in their costumed reveries, patrolling the Bahamian shoreline in my homemade Hulk getup.

What fascinates me, in part, about this costume obsession is the uncompromising earnestness with which Timmy and Tad engage in the fantasies of make-believe. For them, make-believe is the real world, and the real world is make-believe. In one way or another, and to one degree or another, this is how I've led a great deal of my own life for the past sixty-some years. I've dressed up in an Armani suit and pretended I belonged among the rich and famous; I've dressed up in white linens for a cameo role in a movie called *The Notebook,* pretending I was at ease in the presence of

Ryan Gosling and Rachel McAdams; I've dressed up in a helmet and rucksack and pretended I was a competent soldier; I've dressed up in a magician's top hat and pretended I was making miracles happen; I've dressed up in blue jeans and a baseball cap and pretended I was a happy guy.

Two afternoons ago, after I'd lost a hundred bucks at the blackjack table, we took a cab into Nassau, where we spent a few minutes visiting the piece of ground on which the Royal Victoria Hotel had once delivered to my father the only untarnished joy he had ever mentioned in my presence. Meredith snapped a couple of photographs. Timmy and Tad stood nearby, a little impatient, flapping their Batman capes at passing pedestrians. For me, those few minutes were important. I was hoping for . . . Who knows? Nothing revelatory, nothing startling, but maybe some whisper out of history, maybe a tree my father might have climbed, maybe a flowered path down which he might have embarked on a midnight stroll in the company of a highball and a pretty young woman. But time had done its work. Almost all had been obliterated. A small commemorative plaque, mounted on a concrete block along a sidewalk, informed passersby that here had once stood the Royal Victoria, except here was no longer *here,* and the name Bill O'Brien did not appear on the plaque, and after all these years, a kind of shabby, ill-tended dreariness had replaced romantic summer nights and popping champagne corks and tuxedos and fourteen-piece orchestras playing music that could be flirted to and snuggled to and danced to. All that was now a parking lot. The hotel permanently closed its doors in 1971, stood vacant for a time, and was destroyed by fire in the mid-1990s. As with a broken toy, something sad and depressing had subverted not only the Royal Victoria, but also my father's expectations about what the world would offer to him in the years ahead—a glamorous life-long cocktail party that over time turned very ugly. The fantasy became asphalt. My dad ended up hiding vodka bottles in the basement of a small, unstylish house in southern Minnesota.

Now, feeling a pinch in my eyes, I ran a hand across the surface of the Royal Victoria's dismal little plaque. Nothing much happened except the fantasy that something had happened.

After a time, Timmy approached me in his Batman costume.

He took my hand. He asked why I was crying. I told him I was not crying—I was remembering.

"It *looks* like crying," Timmy said.

"I suppose it does," I said, "but *you* look like Batman."

"So what?"

"Well, maybe—" I stopped, composed myself, and lifted the mask from Timmy's face. "Maybe someday you won't be Batman anymore. Maybe someday you won't be a superhero."

"No way," Timmy said. "That can't happen."

"No?"

"Never," he said. "Not to me."

10

Spelling Lesson

Back in second grade—or was it third?—Timmy misspelled the word "utter," replacing the *t*'s with *d*'s, an error to which his teacher responded with the suggestion that spelling matters. "But they sound the same," Timmy told her. "How could anybody except a cow tell the difference?"

11

Home School

Two mornings ago, I came across Tad peeing into a wastebasket. Not only a wastebasket, but a wire mesh wastebasket. And not only a wire mesh wastebasket, but a wire mesh wastebasket situated on a bathroom floor that had been very recently recarpeted.

Tad had been potty-trained; he knew better.

I spoke to the boy sharply—earnestly, you might say. Tad froze. His angle of attack became indecisive. His bull's-eye was no longer the wastebasket, and certainly not the toilet, but instead a point midway between the two. I was furious, as I had every right to be. Scarcely a month earlier, I had selected this new carpet for its lush pile, its regal shade of maroon. ("You'll be sorry," Meredith had said.)

Once Tad finished his business, I told the boy to drop to his knees and begin blotting up the mess with wads of toilet paper.

"Why," I asked, "did you *do* this?"

I asked heatedly—many times—but my son did not look up at me and did not speak. He was frightened, no doubt, by my tone of voice and by a couple of inappropriate words I summoned. Eventually, just as Tad began to cry, Meredith stepped into the bathroom. She gave me a stern, get-out-of-here wag of the head, bent down to console our son, and took over the cleanup operation. I retreated to my office, where for some time I sat muttering to myself.

Maybe a half hour later, Tad came toddling into my office. The boy's lower lip was trembling. He looked at me with a combination of remorse, fear, and ferocious concentration.

"I'm really sorry," he said, "but I have two heads."

"What?" I said.

"Two heads," said Tad.

"*What?*" I said.

"You asked why I did it," said Tad, "and it's because I have two heads. One head told me, 'Daddy won't like this.' The other head said, 'This is gonna be fun.'"

A number of thoughts came to me in a rush. My son was not the budding ax murderer I had envisioned only minutes earlier; my son was smart; my son apprehended the ambiguities of moral choice far better than any talking head on the Fox channel; my son would become a poet one day, or perhaps a psychiatrist, or perhaps need one.

That night, I moved with newfound respect to the boys' bedroom for our usual storytelling session. As a writer, I consider it my responsibility to make up bedtime stories for the kids, little ten-minute tales to escort them into sleep, and that night I began my story this way: "Once upon a time, I actually *knew* a guy with two heads."

"Really?" said Tad.

"Absolutely," I said.

"What was his name?"

"His name," I said, "was Daddy."

Tad and his older brother Timmy fell very quiet. I could sense the boys shifting in the dark, fixing their attention on my neck and shoulders.

"Two actual heads?" said Timmy.

"At least. Sometimes more than two."

"Didn't it hurt?"

"Well, no. Hurt isn't the word. But it made the world pretty complicated."

Tad leaned toward me in the dark, perhaps a bit frightened, perhaps in search of head stumps. "So how did you talk?" he asked quietly. "How did you even think about stuff?"

"Good point," I said. "Thinking wasn't easy. That's what I mean by complicated."

"Boy, I'll bet," said Timmy.

And then, over the next twenty minutes or so, I told my sons the story of what had happened to me in the summer of 1968, the summer I was drafted, the summer I became a soldier. One of my heads—located, let's say, atop my right shoulder—had been fiercely patriotic, loved its country, respected authority, respected tradition, and believed in such things as duty, sacrifice, and service. The other head—teetering precariously above my left shoulder—

had also believed in these things, but at the same time found itself opposed to the war in Vietnam and wanted nothing to do with it, certainly not the killing part and more certainly not the dying part. I was twenty-one years old. I was terrified. And through the summer of 1968 those two heads endlessly confronted each other, challenging, mocking, debating, taunting, cussing, cackling, praying their contradictory prayers, invoking God, invoking the names of LBJ and Richard Nixon and Jane Fonda and Abbie Hoffman and Patrick Henry and Donald Duck. At times the two heads spoke softly and rationally. Other times the heads screamed the most hateful and outlandish obscenities at each other, much as people were screaming in the streets all across our republic during that red-hot summer.

By this point, both Tad and Timmy were asleep. Yet even then, for a long, long while, I lay there in the dark, flanked by these precious little boys, still telling and retelling the story—not aloud, of course—telling it in my thoughts, in the pit of my stomach—just as I have been telling it now for forty-some years and just as I will be telling it and telling it and telling it until I'm gone and cannot ever tell it again—those two heads yapping away across the decades, never shutting up, never at peace, still embittered, still unforgiving and unforgetful. Now and then, the first head will score some sterile rhetorical victory. Other times head number two wins the moment. Sometimes one head might say, "What a coward you were for going to that war," and the other head will shake itself and say, "You did what your country asked you to do," and the first head will let out a bitter chuckle and say, "Yeah, right, and what if my country asked me to blow up Toronto tomorrow? Am

I obligated to do it? Do I saddle up and start killing Canadians?" and the head on my right shoulder will say, "Hey, man, that's totally ridiculous. You live in a good and great country, a country that would never issue such an order," and the other head will say, "What about the Mexican-American War? What about Manifest Destiny? What about the American Indian? What about three million dead Vietnamese? What about those weapons of mass destruction that never turned up?" and the first head will say, "Everybody makes mistakes," and the other head will say, "Exactly my point," and so on and on and on, until eventually one head might say to the other, "Come on, pal, I'm exhausted, let's get some sleep," and the first head will say, "Okay, but I shouldn't have gone to that crummy war, I should've said no," and the other head will say, "You were young, you were afraid," and then off they go again, yapping until dawn, everything slithering back to everything else.

As I lie in the bedroom dark with Tad and Timmy—not only two nights ago but every night—I'm swamped by this ceaseless two-headed bewilderment. I feel so helpless. I feel so hapless. Right and wrong do not announce themselves to me as right and wrong, and if ever they were to do so, I would not know which, if either, to believe. Eat your broccoli, I'll tell the kids, then instantly worry about becoming a broccoli tyrant. Are the vitamins worth the resentment? Who knows? Who knows for sure? Two heads can be a curse. Two heads can lead to late-night second-guessing, wee-hour remorse, endless speculation about prayers not prayed, deeds not done, words of sympathy or love or understanding never uttered. And one day, I'm almost (but never quite) certain, Timmy and Tad will also find themselves entangled in the fearful uncertainties of uncertainty. Should I marry Jane or should I marry Jill? Or should I dump them both and marry Phil? Should I keep plugging away at this hateful job or should I seek a brand-new future in Fiji? Should I march off to war or should I not? Part of being human—as opposed to being, say, a rattlesnake—is the awkward burden of carrying on our shoulders multiple heads, sometimes two, oftentimes many more. And while the load may be heavy, I nonetheless feel an exhilarating, almost explosive happiness to be witnessing the first stirrings of moral awareness in Timmy and Tad. Carrying one or two extra heads through life, however troublesome, however confusing and dispiriting, is to carry a little armor against the soul-killing, people-killing horrors of absolutism.

Mohamed Atta, the hijacker and final pilot of one of the airliners that struck the World Trade Center a few years ago, had but one head—a bonehead, at that—an absolutist of the most consummate and deadly sort. How, I wonder, can a human being be so sure of things? Custer, too. John Wilkes Booth, too. Brutus, too, and Jonathan Edwards, and hooded executioners, and schoolyard bullies, and Joseph Goebbels, and the churchgoing waitress in Tuscaloosa who refuses to deliver French fries to a hungry black man and his hungry children. The bizarre vanity of killer certainty scares me. And now as I watch my children sleep, I can't help but fear that Timmy and Tad may someday become the bloody victims of zealous, self-righteous, I'm-right-and-you're-wrong one-headedness. I also fear that they may become the perpetrators. Through some parenting blunder of my own—an ill-chosen word passing from my lips, an inappropriate chuckle at an inappropriate moment—I worry that I may somehow ignite an inextinguishable fuse of intolerance and hypocrisy in my children. I do not want Timmy and Tad ever to say, or ever to think, "I am so right, and you are so wrong, that I will kill you."

After the events of recent years, I have come to fear that our own nation, as much as any other nation, is endangered by self-righteous, absolutist rhetoric that celebrates our glories while erasing our shortcomings and pooh-poohing our ethical and moral failures—torture, for example.

I love my children. I do not love all they do.

I love my country. I do not love all it does.

Surely any parent or any rational patriot can understand the endless two-headed adjudications we must make between love and moral duty.

We are at war right now. And once again, much like four decades ago in the midst of another war, the contradictions and complications of our universe have been reduced to black-and-white battle cries and a stockpile of pathetic old truisms, none of which is wholly true but each of which is framed in the language of hyperconfident certainty, without qualifiers, without historical amendment, without educative function, without humility, without skepticism, without the tempering tones of doubt or ordinary modesty. No one says, "I think I'm right," or "I hope I'm right," or "Maybe I'm right." Instead, once again, the war rhetoric has the blaring, single-note sound of absolutism.

"No doubt," said George W. Bush about his decision to go to war in Iraq. "I have no doubt."

Similarly, from Dick Cheney: "Simply stated, there is no doubt that Saddam Hussein now has weapons of mass destruction. There is no doubt he is amassing them to use against our friends, against our allies and against us."

No doubt?

No doubt about killing people for a reason that did not then and does not now *exist*?

My point is personal, not partisan. Plenty of Democrats, plenty of liberals, bought into the falsehood (maybe not the outright lie, but very plainly the falsehood) of Cheney's "no doubt" absolutism, and I am sickened by the thought that ten or twenty years from now, as we still try to wiggle our way out of the Middle East, my precious sons, and yours, may be shot in the head or blown to pieces as a consequence of arrogant, one-headed, I'm-right-and-you're-wrong, dead-sure, fear-mongering demagoguery.

Listen, Timmy. Listen, Tad.

It is important to be faithful to your values and to your opinions, but remember that your opinions are opinions. And remember that your values may reorganize themselves over time.

Watch out, in particular, for opinions that involve killing people, because one day you may change your mind, and if that day comes, as it has come for me, I do not want you lying awake at two in the morning wishing to Christ you could wake up a slim, dead, dainty-looking young man sprawled now and forever along a trail in Quang Ngai Province. Your two heads will be heavy. But carry them high. And use them.

12

Hygiene

Near bedtime one evening, when I was complaining to Meredith about still another book banning, Tad overheard and said, "I've got a good idea. Promise them you'll wash out your mouth with soap. But then the book-banning people have to wash all the dead soldiers with soap."

13

The Magic Show (I)

As a kid, through grade school and into high school, my hobby was magic. I liked making miracles happen. In the basement, where I practiced in front of a stand-up mirror, I caused my mother's silk scarves to change color. I used scissors to cut my father's best tie in half, displaying the pieces, and then restored it whole. I placed a penny in the palm of my hand, made my hand into a fist, made the penny into a white mouse. This was not true magic. It was trickery. But I sometimes pretended otherwise, because I was a kid then, and because pretending was the thrill of magic, and because what seemed to happen became a happening in itself. I was a dreamer. I would watch my hands in the mirror, imagining how someday I might perform much grander magic, tigers becoming giraffes, beautiful girls levitating like angels in the high yellow spotlights, no wires or strings, just floating.

It was illusion, of course—the creation of a glorious new reality. White mice could fly, and dollar bills could be plucked from thin air, and a boy's father could say, "I love you, Tim."

What I enjoyed about this peculiar hobby, at least in part, was the craft of it: learning the techniques of magic and then practicing those techniques, alone in the basement, for many hours and days. That was another thing about magic. I liked the aloneness, as God and other miracle makers must also like it—not lonely, just alone. I liked shaping the universe around me. Back then, things were not always happy in our house, especially when my dad was drinking, and the basement was a place where I could bring some peace into my little-boy world, a place where I could make the sadness and terror vanish.

When performed well, magic goes beyond a mere sequence of discrete tricks. As an eight-year-old I was certainly no master magician, but I tried my best to blend separate illusions into a coherent whole, hoping to cast a spell, hoping to create a unified and undifferentiated world of magic. I dreamed, for instance, that someone in the audience might select a card from a shuffled deck —the ace of diamonds. The card might be made to vanish, then a rabbit might be pulled from a hat, and the hat might collapse into a fan, and the fan might be used to fan the rabbit, transforming it into a white mouse, and the white mouse might then grow wings and soar up into the spotlights and return a moment later with a playing card in its mouth—the ace of diamonds.

There were other pleasures, too. I liked the secrecy. I liked the power. I liked showing my empty hands when my hands were not empty. I liked the expression on my father's face when I asked him to slip his head into my magical guillotine.

More than anything, my youthful fascination with magic had to do with a sense of participation in the overall mystery of things. At the age of seven or eight, when I learned my first few tricks, virtually everything around me was still a great mystery—the moon, mathematics, butterflies, my father. The whole universe seemed inexplicable. Why did adults laugh at unfunny things? Why did my dad get drunk? Why did everybody have to die, and why could not the laws of nature permit one or two exceptions? All things were mysterious; all things seemed possible. If my father's tie could be restored whole, why not one day use my wand to wake up the dead?

After high school, I stopped doing magic—at least of that sort. I took up a new hobby, writing stories. But without straining too much, I can say that the fundamentals seemed very much the same. Writing stories is a solitary endeavor. You shape your own universe. You deal in illusion. You depend on the willful suspension of disbelief. You practice all the time, then practice some more. You pay attention to craft. You learn to show your hands to be empty when they are not empty. You aim for tension and suspense, as when a character named Betty slips her finger into a wedding ring, knowing she is not in love and never will be. You try to make beauty. You strive for wholeness, seeking unity and flow, each movement of plot linked both to the past and to the future, always hoping to create or to re-create the great illusions of life. "Abracadabra," says the magician, and a silk scarf changes color. "By and by," says Huck Finn, and you are with him as he boards his timeless raft. "Forgive me," says your father, without ever quite saying it, and you do.

After an intermission of many decades, I've taken up magic again in a pretty serious way. Timmy and Tad live in a house cluttered with birdcages, top hats, wands, explosive devices, floating steel rings, spotlights, dancing canes, and innumerable decks of playing cards.

For the past eight months, a roulette table has occupied a substantial portion of our foyer. It's an illusion I purchased second-hand from a retired Atlantic City magician—a prop that entirely blocks the passageway between our front door and living room. Visitors hesitate. The pizza delivery guy suspects illegal gambling. But Timmy and Tad take it all in stride, as if every father on earth spends his waking hours cussing at candles that fail to appear at his fingertips. (The trick isn't easy. Six candles. Empty hands.) The boys politely take turns vanishing from a chair atop the roulette table; they tolerate the multiple miseries of contorting themselves inside black boxes; they roll their eyes when I tell them it's time to be transformed into a gerbil. Magic bores them, I'm afraid. "If it's really magic," Tad said a few days ago, "why won't you let me stand behind you when you make Mom disappear? Afraid I'll see something?" This ho-hum, slightly hostile attitude sometimes does more than irk me. I get angry. These are children. Children are supposed to *love* magic. In part, I realize, Timmy and Tad have grown up in a household of appearing hotdogs and disappearing parakeets. They've become accustomed to miracles, and over the years, watching me practice, they've discovered the dull realities that make miracles appear to be miracles. They know what back-palming is. They know the technique behind a split-fan production. And from their own experience they know that the roulette table in our foyer is somewhat more than a roulette table. Who can blame them for not wanting to choose still another card —any card at all? Who can blame them for balking at another shuffle that isn't actually a shuffle?

For the most part, the boys suffer in good-natured silence. They seem to understand, or at least intuit, that magic fills up an empty space inside me. Many, many years from now, long after I've vanished from their lives, Tad and Timmy may have a few blurred memories of their dad standing in front of the bathroom mirror, trying to pluck playing cards from the air, mostly failing, but still trying and trying, which is how it is right now as I try to pluck this maybe book from thin air.

———

Meredith and I, along with Timmy and Tad and a group of shang-haied friends, stage an elaborate show in our living room every couple of years. We're amateurs—not great, but getting good. We float tables and children around the house. We appear and we disappear, sometimes in balls of fire, sometimes in large boxes, sometimes right before the eyes of the audience. We dance. We sing. We eat razor blades. A few years ago, we balanced Timmy on the point of a sword, spun him around on it, and then watched the sword penetrate his slim little body. During one disastrous rehearsal, we nearly gave the kid a real-life appendectomy. In other mishaps, we have almost suffocated one of our female magicians, almost decapitated another, and almost burned the house down. Alas, show biz.

As we prepare for each new show, our troupe of amateurs begins practicing about six months in advance, getting together every two weeks, putting in anywhere from three to seven hours of hard work at each session. There is a lot of tedium, a lot of frustration, and a lot of failure. (Again, much like writing stories.) Props stop functioning, threads break, secret doors don't open, Timmy and Tad fall asleep backstage and need to be gently shaken and told it's time to levitate.

In general, the members of our cast have amiably tolerated the long hours and numbing repetition. Some of them, I'm quite sure, don't really care much for magic, but they know I care, and so out of great generosity they've thrown themselves into a pursuit that others might find frivolous, childish, and more than a little bizarre. Real-life teachers dress up as showgirls. A nurse practitioner dresses up as a wealthy casino minx. For months on end, at considerable sacrifice, the members of our troupe gamely toil to master their miracles and to perform them with a measure of grace and elegance. It isn't easy. Angles of vision need to be taken into account. Posture—keeping the shoulders level—can determine success or failure. Too much light, or too little light, can be the difference between applause and grim silence. Despite these stresses, and despite the enormous chunks of time stolen from their lives, the members of our cast have come to appreciate that which I find so beautiful in magic—those moments when a half-dozen colorful parasols appear out of nowhere in swift succession, or when a glass of Beaujolais vanishes beneath a silk cloth, or when the ace of diamonds appears at the tip of a switchblade.

On show nights, as the living room fills up with ninety or so invited guests, our little troupe feels the jittery tension that any professional magician would feel. Backstage, we pace and mumble to ourselves. We rehearse moves in our heads. We feel dread fizzing up inside exhilaration. Although it's only a living room magic show, we might as well be opening on Broadway or in Carnegie Hall or in a gilded theater on the Vegas strip.

And so it begins. The music comes on and we make our way out into a make-believe world, into a dead-end desert casino, where some of us deal blackjack and never lose, and where some of us pull wads of cash from the air, and where a croupier shoots fire from his roulette wheel, and where love is won and lost, and where a cocktail waitress sings to a cowboy doing rope tricks, and where a bartender produces bottles of wine from his bare hands, and where silver balls float to the ceiling, and where Lady Luck sets off her fateful explosions on a long-ago New Year's Eve out in the desert of West Texas. Briefly, at least, it all feels real. The magic is happening.

Sixty-eight tricks later, it's over. We blink and awaken from the dream.

———

Timmy and Tad, if you read this years from now, I want you to understand that my subject here is not magic. Nor is it storytelling. My subject is our longing for miracles. The human journey— yours, Timmy, and yours, too, Tad—is an immersion in all that is unknown and all that is unknowable: the unknown moment from now, the unknown yawn of eternity. Will I live on after I die? Will my children live happy lives? Will mankind survive the final flaring of the sun? Will Alice make her way out of Wonderland? At least in part, it is the mystery of the future that compels us to turn the pages not only of novels but also of our own lives. Unlike the

animals, we conceive of tomorrow—tomorrow *matters* to us—
and we spend a good portion of our time adjusting the present to
shape the future, saving up for that vacation in Europe, heading
off to church each Sunday in the hope that Saint Peter might issue
his precious admission ticket. We yearn for the miracle of a happy
ending. We're human. We can't help it. Likewise, on a less gran-
diose scale, we sometimes ask such questions as: Did Lizzie Bor-
den take an ax and give her mother forty whacks? What happened
to Amelia Earhart on her vanishing voyage over the South Pacific?
What were Custer's last thoughts at the Little Bighorn? Did Lee
Harvey Oswald act alone on that November day in 1963? And
late at night such thoughts can get pretty personal: Where exactly
did things go wrong in my life? How did I end up in this strange
bed, so restless, so shockingly alone? Why am I crying?

In the end, Tad and Timmy, we are mysteries even to ourselves. We may speculate, of course, and we may try to disentan-
gle the microscopic threads of history and conscience and motive,
but who among us really knows why we do the things we do or
why we think the things we think? Is it not guesswork? And beyond that, what about the mysteries of the people all around us
—our fathers and mothers, our children, our lovers, our friends?
Is not each of us encased inside a leaden skull? Are we not all in
solitary confinement? In her novella *The Touchstone,* Edith Whar-
ton writes: "We live in our own souls as in an unmapped region, a
few acres of which we have cleared for our habitation; while of the
nature of those nearest us we know but the boundaries that march
with ours." I cannot read your mind, Timmy, and you cannot
read mine, Tad. Often you surprise me. Often you confuse me.

Often I yearn to crawl inside your heads in search of some elusive ground zero, even knowing there is no ground zero, even knowing that minute by minute we all undergo endless modification. What was true five years ago, or even five minutes ago, is probably no longer true, and almost certainly no longer true in the same way. Yet I keep longing for a miracle. I want to live inside you. I want to swim through your thoughts and sleep in your dreams. What a magic show that would be.

14

Abashment

After a dress rehearsal for one of our magic shows, during which Meredith slithered through the footlights in a sensational show-girl costume, seven- or-eight-year-old Timmy waited a few days before clearing his throat and saying, "Mom, do you think that getup is *appropriate?*"

Meredith smiled and said, "It's only for a magic show."

Timmy said, "But I just called you *Mom*."

15

Sushi

My memory is failing, overburdened by the brain-jangling pace of fatherhood, and now, when I try to survey the past several years, I'm mostly left with tiny, disconnected fragments of my life with Timmy and Tad. Each memory-shot exists in its own dimension. There is no before and no after, just flashes in the dark, as if brilliant pinpricks of light suddenly ignite and then blink out in a vast void of prehistory. Nothing connects with anything else. It would be nice to find shape or some sort of modest unity in my threadbare recollections, but I'm resigned to the sad fact that memory —at least my memory—is less a movie than a scrapbook of moth-eaten images and garbled audio clips.

Here, at 2:37 a.m. on August 13, 2013, is a sampling:

Back in 2010, little Timmy and I were inspecting a suit of armor in an old Belgian castle. "Boy," Timmy said as we moved out into the daylight, "that guy knows how to stand still."

―――――

Tad's first-grade teacher asked the class to write an essay. On a sheet of white paper, Tad carefully wrote: "S. A."

―――――

The year was 2009 or 2010, and in a park near our house Tad was playing a game he called Stop Sign. He circled his arms above his head, approximating the shape of a stop sign, and trotted up to a five- or six-year-old girl playing hopscotch. The girl hopped right past him. Tad turned and watched. After a second, he yelled, "You better not drive till next week."

―――――

And then, somewhere in outer space, a star ignites, and I watch Timmy at age three or four come limping up to me. What he says, exactly, I can't remember―something like, "It hurts." He isn't crying. He's puzzled. His leg is broken.

Time passes, and he turns five or six, and Meredith and I are asking how he broke his leg, and Timmy says, "Spinning," and Meredith says, "Spinning where? How?" and Timmy shrugs as if broken legs are a dime a dozen and says, "On the floor, in the

kitchen, Mommy was doing dishes and I was spinning," and the guilt trip of two parents who never knew how their firstborn broke a leg is partly relieved, partly resolved, though only partly, because there is also the memory of a hospital interview with a kindly social worker whose quizzical expression never changes as we explain, numerous times, that it is all a complete and baffling mystery to us. "Uh-uh," says the social worker, also numerous times.

———

And at some foggy point in history, years and years ago, Tad screamed in his sleep: "Don't hurt me! Don't hurt me!" and two rooms away, as I lay reading a book, I was struck by the terrible certainty that my son was dreaming of his father.

———

Out in the backyard one afternoon, Tad was helping our lawn guy, Jef Pierce, do his weekly mowing. Tad gathered up chunks of firewood and dropped them in front of Jef's oncoming mower. Jef stopped, tossed the logs aside, and kept going. This repeated itself several times. "Okay, look," Jef finally said, "why don't you go get me a glass of water?" Tad stared at him and said, "Why do you want to mow *glass?*"

———

And there in a flash of light stands Timmy at age eight or nine— probably eight—pursuing his bizarre new hobby of sushi preparation. Multicourse sushi. From-scratch sushi. Painstakingly presented sushi. More or less edible sushi. He wears a chef's hat and a white apron. His expression is stern, his hands deep in sticky rice. The floor is littered with bits of crab and avocado and seaweed and cucumber and my son's homemade spicy mayo. Bamboo mats have been carefully flattened and smoothed on the kitchen table. Expensive glass chopsticks have been encased in cloth napkins. This is my child? A prodigy sushi maker? (I do not care for sushi; I applaud people who do.) At one point, after Timmy offered to prepare still another raw-fish feast, I suggested we go outside and toss around a baseball, or kick a football, or try some other all-American little-boy activity. "Sure, maybe tomorrow," Timmy said. "Did Mom buy seaweed?"

————

Of such simple and mundane fragments have the years of my fatherhood been constructed. How little I have influenced my sons' interests. How bravely they dive into their own. How I would chew and chew that sushi.

16

Pride (I)

One constituent of a father's pride is simple astonishment. We expect to instruct our children. We are then surprised to find them instructing us.

An illustration:

Several years back, on his ride home from school, Timmy noticed a man crying on a sidewalk along 15th Street in downtown Austin, Texas. The man was probably homeless, though not certainly, for his appearance and carriage had none of the beaten-down destitution of life on the streets. His clothing seemed clean; he was close-shaven; he wore a new-looking cap with the words "Vietnam Veteran" imprinted on it.

Timmy yelled at Meredith to stop the car, but it was rush hour and stopping wasn't possible. Timmy looked over his shoulder as the crying man receded, and then Timmy himself was crying. He cried all the way home. He cried again at the dinner table. It was more than crying—it was unstoppable, quivering, somebody-has-died wailing. He got out of his chair and lay on the floor and bawled.

Early the next morning, before the sun had risen, I found my son sitting on a kitchen countertop, where he had just finished packing a brown paper bag with little gifts for the crying man on 15th Street. Timmy had packed a yo-yo, a sandwich, a granola bar, a photograph of himself, some fishing line, an apple, and a copy of one of my books. For several weeks afterward, riding to and from school, the boy searched the streets and sidewalks of Austin, but in the end, as anyone might guess, he never again saw the crying man on 15th Street. The sandwich grew moldy. The apple rotted. The granola bar was consumed by Timmy's brother.

No one in our family has forgotten this episode. Certainly, Timmy hasn't.

A year or so after the incident, for his English class, he began writing a poem called "My 15th Street Friend," which is reprinted later in these pages. Though the poem isn't bad for a nine-year-old, its literary merits and defects are not what caused me to look at my son in a new way. Rather, I was surprised—even amazed—that he had been carrying the hurt inside him for more than a year, that he had cared enough to still care, and that I had so wildly underestimated my own child. I would've guessed he might write about Minecraft, or about basketball, or about numerous other interests that appeared to consume him day after day. Not only had he not mentioned his 15th Street friend in many months, but virtually everything else in his life had seemed utterly transitory, here then gone. One moment he'd be clicking a Rubik's Cube, the next moment he'd be watching NBA highlights, the next moment he'd be wrestling with his brother. Until the day he began writing the poem, I'd taken it for granted that his compassion was as short-lived and perfunctory as my own.

As an adult, humbled by my own failures and deficiencies, I have come to expect the worst of myself, almost never the best, and Timmy's compassion for a suffering stranger reminded me of my own pitiful mediocrity: how I donate a few bucks to the United Way but then avoid the eyes of the homeless. I may feel saddened, but I don't cry. Nor do many others. Nor, I guess, do you.

Now, after the passage of several years, what strikes me is the realization that an eight-year-old kid had become a better person that I am, able to feel what I do not. What had years ago been painful to me, seizing me by the throat, has now become little more than nervous embarrassment. What had once been empathy has become what Kafka calls the "frozen sea" of mankind's heart. If a person's humanity is measured by quality of feeling, my inner sea had frozen miles deep. This may be part of growing up, or part of living in an imperfect world, but it is no less depressing and no less despicable.

Timmy's poem, and the incident that generated it, made me want to take Kafka's ax to the frozen sea inside me, and maybe that explains, at least in part, why this maybe book is being written in the first place. I want to hammer away at the ice. I want to yell *I love you, I love you,* with every stroke on this keyboard.

17

Balance

A few days ago, Meredith and I attended Tad's weekly soccer game, which concluded in a rare victory for my son's not-very-talented assemblage of six-year-olds. Tad did not score. He does not believe in scoring. In fact, during the course of the game, Meredith and I could not help noticing that the boy seemed to be intentionally kicking the ball to his opponents, or at least in the general direction of his opponents. At halftime I asked my son about this.

"Well, sure," said Tad, plainly bewildered, "but I was kicking the ball pretty straight, wasn't I?"

"Very straight," I said. "Except straight to the other team."

"Is that bad?"

"Not exactly, but the whole purpose—"

Tad looked up at me as if he were about to cry.

"I felt sorry for them," he said. "I mean, we were really, really clobbering them." His eyes swept back and forth. "I thought you told me sharing is a *good* thing."

———

Timmy plays lacrosse. Not well. He stands motionless at midfield. He balances his lacrosse stick on the middle finger of his right hand, the stick artfully vertical against a blazing-blue Texas sky. He seems to be auditioning for the circus.

Again, I asked about this.

"It's not easy," Timmy said sharply. "I mean, *you* try it."

———

There is nothing in either boy that resembles athletic aggression. Where the competitive instinct might reside, there is instead a very sensible pain-avoidance instinct, or, as Meredith optimistically calls it, a propensity for excessive kindness. Which is not, I suppose, such a terrible thing.

Still, I've suggested that Timmy give some thought to moving his legs during lacrosse games; I've advised Tad to try sharing the soccer ball with his teammates, just for the experience of it.

No luck, I'm afraid.

And so, after some soul-searching, I've become more or less resigned, as fathers must and should, to letting the boys pursue their own visions, athletic and otherwise. But the whole letting-go frame of mind comes very, very hard for me. It's hard to stay silent on the sidelines, hard not to yell pointed instructions to my kids, and hard to be cheerfully encouraging after another midfield balancing act. True, my sons are young, but I want good things for them, happy things, and I've learned that athletic accomplishment can make a boy's life considerably less stressful, especially in the teenage years, and even more especially in this sports-crazy state of Texas. Around here, Scrabble experts don't get elected prom king.

Meredith, of course, jumps all over me when I ramble on like this. "Are you kidding me?" she says. "We're raising a couple of prom kings?"

"Well, no, but—"

"*Prom* kings?"

Swiftly, I cover my tracks, admitting it was a terrible example. But even so, in my head, I can't help flashing back to my high school years. I would've killed to be prom king. I would've eaten salamander guts.

"Okay," I'll say. "What about homecoming king?"

―――

It is February 5, 2012, a Sunday, and Timmy and I have just returned from unicycle practice in the cul-de-sac across the street. The boy has found his sport. Today, after months of false starts, Timmy navigated a complete circle all on his own. What joy on his face, what joy on my face. A unicyclist!

And behold: Tad, too, has blossomed into a whiz-bang athlete. A hula hoop pro!

For many, many months both boys have been pursuing their off-the-beaten-track sporting specialties, and although their feats may never be celebrated in the pages of *Sports Illustrated,* I challenge any high school linebacker to execute a striptease, underwear and all, while simultaneously keeping two hula hoops in motion. I challenge Shaq O'Neal to mount a unicycle.

———

Decades ago, after the publication of my first book, I called my mom and dad to ask how they'd feel if I were to drop out of graduate school and devote myself to becoming a novelist.

"You'll regret it," my mother said. "For sure."

"Oh, for Christ's sake, Harvard is *Harvard,*" said my father. His voice seemed to me uncommonly ardent, a little desperate, as if I were contemplating suicide or bank robbery or both at once. "Listen to me. The world is full of people who think they can be writers. I'm one of them. Look how it turned out. Don't do it."

"All right, thanks," I said, and then I did drop out.

Not immediately: I waited a couple of years. And yet in the midst of that phone call—somewhere between "Listen to me" and "Don't do it"—there was a finality that slammed down on me with the full weight of the future. I remember hanging up the phone. I remember staring down at my hands. I remember how free I felt, how light and happy, and yet a moment later I was struck by a dizzying and unmistakable surge of terror. I knew what was coming. I would be exchanging security for jeopardy, forfeiting a Harvard degree for a degree in advanced uncertainty.

The consequences, whether good or bad, would be with me forever.

Almost certainly what my mother and father had wanted for me was what every parent wants for a child, which above all else is safety. Graduate school was safe; writing novels and stories was not. And now, as a parent myself, I understand the ferocity of that protective instinct. Back during my "Row, Row" days, and over the perilous years afterward, the safety of Timmy and Tad had consumed me, and although I'm far from qualified as a biologist, I'd be surprised if our human DNA were not threaded with a gene or two that chemically wires us to be hypervigilant when it comes to the well-being of our offspring. It is this guardian instinct, I'm almost sure, that makes me worry about lacrosse sticks and soccer balls—a deep-seated, almost reptilian fear that my sons will be at risk in what can be a ruthlessly competitive world. And not just physically at risk. Emotionally, too. Who wants an unhappy kid?

The problem with this sort of thinking, pretty obviously, is that it has the sound of half-baked determinism, a survival-of-the-fittest rigidity that is at odds with the gentling subtleties of modern-day psychology. Even to my own ear, these concerns have the ring of something illiberal and Darwinian, not to mention way too Texan. I should be content with hula hoops. I should let the kids define themselves, each according to his special talents. And no doubt I should celebrate Tad's soccer ball sharing and Timmy's peculiar midfield balancing ballet. I realize all that. Yet when I stroll down high school hallways, as I often do on my travels, there is no mistaking the fact that athletics matter a great deal: the letter jackets, the rah-rah posters, the parent booster clubs, the no-expense-spared gyms and stadiums and locker rooms. And like it or not, ignore it or not, these high school kingdoms are often ruled more by popularity than by probity, more by charm than by charity, and not infrequently more by brawn than by brains.

For boys—and now for girls as well—athleticism remains an important coin of the realm, and like my own parents, I am sometimes drawn to impose my own yearnings on Tad and Timmy. How do I stop *wishing* that they might someday score a goal or two? How do I stop *wishing* for a moment of deftness or speed or strength or competitive spirit? How could I stop *wishing* for some plain old competence?

It isn't that I care about sports—I don't. What I do care about, probably too much, is the happiness and security of my sons, and now, as I sit writing these lines, I envision their coming teenage years and all the stresses that can add up to real pain for a kid. Right now, I suppose, their unaggressive antics seem cute; right now, it's okay—or almost okay—that people chuckle and wag their heads. But in a few years Timmy's and Tad's dogged pacifism may be viewed as considerably less than cute by their coaches and teammates. Chuckles might hurt. Failure might hurt even more. One thing can lead to another: self-esteem problems, a sense of not belonging, humiliation, ridicule, second-class citizenship, and abject defeat in the teenage hierarchy wars.

All this, I realize, could easily be dismissed as a father's obsessive hand-wringing. But cliques *do* exist. Kids *can* be cruel. Every day in this country, 160,000 children skip school because of bullying. The whole popularity imperative is an old and clichéd story, almost a funny story, unless of course you happen to be that unpopular bozo who can't hit a baseball or catch a football, in which case you own the cliché. It's all yours and it isn't pleasant.

Tad and Timmy aren't in that boat yet. They're young. They're still finding their way. They have plenty of time, and so, for now, all I can do is hope for the best. And who knows? Kids develop at different rates, in different ways, and maybe the boys will turn out to be terrific athletes. Maybe prom kings. Maybe Friday-night heroes. In fact, in a decade or two, they may well become headliners at Cirque du Soleil, a couple of sequined superstars, a tightrope-riding unicyclist and a stripping hula-hooper.

In the decades since that phone conversation with my mom and dad, I've often tried to rearrange things in my head. I'll imagine my mother saying, "Of course, do whatever's right," and later my father will come on and listen to me for a while and finally say, "Well, I messed up my own dream. I was too lazy, too scared, too something, and I don't want you to end up like me. Harvard's just a fancy word. Go write your books. I'll pretend I'm you."

It didn't happen that way. But as the years passed I began to feel as if it almost did happen, or as if it could have happened, because my parents were decent and thoughtful people, and because they wanted to protect me from the consequences of failure. Somewhere near the surface of their thoughts, I'm nearly certain, both understood that I was seeking not their permission but a kind of liberation, not their happy hallelujahs but an acknowledgment, however reluctant, that I was ready to weigh the risks all on my own. And of course they were right: the risks were real. I'd be giving up a great deal. By that point I'd completed my Harvard course work, passed my oral exams, and was only a year or so away from a doctorate. Still, I'd known from the start that graduate school amounted to little more than a convenient hideout after Vietnam, a place to put my head together, and my thoughts and ambitions were in no way academic. For more than three years I'd been trooping from class to class, a bit dazed, a bit surprised to find myself alive. I wasn't unhappy, exactly. I'm not quite sure what I was. Bewildered, maybe. Disconnected. I remember thinking how civilized it all seemed, the campus and everyone on it, so peaceful and abstract and decorous, so weirdly *theoretical* in comparison to the boonies of Quang Ngai. I was also aware that the war had done things to me that could not be undone. Partly, I guess, I was full of anger. There was guilt, too, and lots of it. I had betrayed my conscience—my own heart and my own head —by going to a war I considered unjust. I had participated in the killing, and I had done so out of moral cowardice. There were no other words for it. I had been afraid of ridicule and embarrassment. I had been afraid of displeasing others, including my parents and my hometown and my country, and when you do things you believe are wrong because you are afraid not to do them, you cannot call it anything but what it is, and the correct word is cowardice. I needed to confront these things. By daylight I was fine, but at night I was not fine. When I couldn't sleep, which was almost always, I'd get out of bed, sit at my desk, and try to dump the terrible shit on pieces of paper—mortar rounds exploding all around me, a young girl lying dead in a dry rice paddy, her face half gone, one of my buddies telling me to lay off the pity and suck it up and act like a soldier and stop whining about a dead gook.

I'd scribble these things down and go back to bed, and in the morning I'd head for my 9 a.m. class in statistics.

My mother and father knew none of this. For them, Vietnam was history. I'd survived, I'd come home, and it was time now to press forward. They never asked about the war—what did I see, what did I do?—and I never offered much. Each of us, I suppose, was trying to protect the others, which we did with silence, as if to talk about things would pick the scabs and exacerbate the pain and delay the healing. This may seem stupid, or old-fashioned, or callous, or excessively Midwestern, or psychologically illiterate, or emotionally unsophisticated. But they loved me, and I loved them. Not to speak was a kind of speaking, at least in our family, and sometimes it was more powerful speaking than speaking itself.

Surely, though, my parents had to wonder what was eating at me as I considered dropping out of grad school. Surely they were frightened by the prospect. And surely they felt exactly the same helplessness, exactly the same terrified pride, that I feel today as Timmy and Tad begin to move away from what I want toward what they want.

———

Back in second grade, almost two years ago, Timmy had joined a unicycle club that met in his school gymnasium three or four afternoons a week. The club had been founded by an inspired, forward-thinking teacher, Jimmy "Pedals" Agnew, whose dream it was to empower young children with the challenge of mastering an extremely difficult but wholly noncompetitive athletic endeavor. There would be no winners and no losers. There would be no scores and no time clock. There would be no first-stringers and no second-stringers. There would be no 1-A and no 6-A. There would be no getting cut from the team. There would be no water boys and no cheerleaders. There would be no pep rallies. There would be no exclusion. There would be no favoritism by virtue of height or strength or speed or other such common standards of physicality. Instead, as Jimmy gently explained to his second-graders, they were in for a long, frustrating, and repetitive lesson in perseverance, lots of spills along the way, day after day of remounting the unicycle and trying again and then trying once more.

Frustrating was the correct word. Repetitive was also the correct word.

More than fourteen months elapsed before Timmy was able to ride at all, and even then Meredith and I would scamper along beside him, each of us holding one of his hands for balance. Many times, I lost hope. While other kids began pedaling around the gym—some of them simultaneously dribbling basketballs—Timmy spent his time sprawled on the floor or pinned helplessly to a wall. I worried about what appeared to be motor dysfunction. I worried about epilepsy. And yet the idea of the unicycle had somehow seized Timmy's imagination. It was what *he* wanted, not what I wanted. He wouldn't quit. He accepted the scraped knees and the Band-Aids and the sting of iodine. Slowly at first, and then as if awakened by thunder, Meredith and I noticed something emerging in our son that a novelist might call "character." Not so long ago we'd been the parents of an unformed, carefree, almost generalized little boy, but now there was a new and emerging Timmyness, a core of being that seemed to forecast what he would become in the years ahead—an earnest, determined, and intensely focused human being. He had ambition. He had an unsettling hardness in his eyes. He'd mutter to himself, pick himself up, and try again. Both Meredith and I sensed that we were now in the presence of this unfamiliar future Timmy, a Timmy who will one day shed the diminutive name, shed his childhood, shed his parents, and make his way forward without us.

"He's like you with your magic," Meredith said. "Not all that talented, obviously, but stubborn as stone."

"Very true," I said.

"Maybe too stubborn."

"That's the danger."

And so in the cul-de-sac today I let go. Around and around Timmy went, all on his own.

I'm aware, of course, that there is nothing profound in this. Profundity is not the point. All I want is to leave behind a few pages that Timmy might someday find at the bottom of a desk drawer. I want him to know how giddy his father was on February 5, 2012, this eventful winter Sunday, how I yelped with delight as he pedaled away from me. I want him to know that in the midst of my amazed happiness, even as I yelped and chortled, I was struck by the cruel, evil sadness of departure. Why does the world do this to us? Why can't we be together always? A profound man would have a profound answer, but my love is not profound that way. It has no wisdom. It has no intelligence. My love is profound only as snowfall is profound on a chilly night in February.

18

Child's Play

Tad, at age four or five or six, once played with two German-speaking boys in a sandbox in Place des Vosges, directly across the street from our hotel in Paris. Everyone seemed to be getting along nicely. Castles were built. There was excellent teamwork. Later, when I asked Tad if he'd understood the two boys, Tad nodded and said, "They know what sand is."

19

Telling Tales (I)

Timmy and Tad, who at ages five and three are both fans of *Winnie-the-Pooh,* have taken lately to wearing tails. At our local Walmart, and occasionally at church, the boys sport lengths of clothesline dangling from their trousers. They prowl the neighborhood trailing an assortment of ribbons, coat hangers, balloons, telephone cords, belts, blankets, drapery tassels, and electrical extension cords. People notice. Things have gotten out of hand. Alas, we have become a family of tails, and, though I'm embarrassed to make this confession, my wife and I have been persuaded to spruce up our fashion acts. Meredith jogs in a tail. I write in a tail. Yesterday, in a most undignified moment, I answered the doorbell having forgotten the Slinky jiggling restlessly at my buttocks. Imagine the judgments taking shape in the eyes of the UPS man.

Our household seems caught up in a kind of reverse evolution, tumbling backward through the millennia, alighting in an age in which the ancestral tail was as common and quietly useful as, say, the appendix or the tonsil. Like our tree-dwelling relatives, the O'Brien tribe has grown comfortable with its tails. We groom them. We miss them at bath time. We view their absence in our fellow man with pity and suspicion.

Now, as I sit here with my coffee at the kitchen table, I find myself wondering if something about this tail business might smack of the unwholesome, even of the aberrant and fanatical.

Imagination, of course, is a precious human gift. Still, I worry about the future. I entertain visions of Tad awaiting his bride at the marriage altar with a large powdered tail quivering aloft. And I am not alone in such irrational fears. Meredith won't admit to it, but over the past several weeks she has been stealing into the boys' bedroom at night, secretly pulling back the sheets to check for the first hairy sproutings of the real McCoy.

The shadows of childhood can darken our adult lives—that much I know as a certainty—and what parent would not be concerned that present fantasy might somehow influence distant fact? Already the imaginary has embedded itself in the real world. At preschool soccer games, young Timmy is impeded by the awkward mechanics of his "Tigger hop"—four strides and a bounce. Spectators gawk. Coaches squint at me. I feel the chill of silent accusation: what kind of father *are* you?

I've tried, God knows, to reason with the boys. I've used guile and bribery and shameless deceit. (Santa Claus hates tails.) Last night I tried again. "Pretending can be a good thing," I told the boys at bedtime, "but sometimes it can get you in trouble. It can be dangerous."

Tad had already drifted off, but Timmy looked up at me with suspicion. "Is this one of your ridiculous stories?"

"Not ridiculous at all," I said, and then launched into a hastily improvised tale about a little boy who couldn't *stop* pretending —always talking to a make-believe dog, eating make-believe pancakes. After a while, I said, the boy couldn't separate what was real from what wasn't. It landed him in all kinds of trouble.

"But I thought make-believe was supposed to be fun," Timmy said.

"Yes, of course it is," I told him, and then a crucial question occurred to me. "Do you know what pretending *is?*"

For what seemed a long minute I listened to the whir of a five-year-old's mind in motion. "Well, actually," Timmy finally said, using his favorite (and only) four-syllable word, "actually, I guess it's like when you go away on trips. Sometimes I dream about you. I dream about how you'll come home from the airport and bring me surprises and play with me. I get sad when you go away, and so I pretend you're not gone. Is that bad?"

I told him no, it wasn't bad.

"When you go away," Timmy said, "I write your name in the sandbox. I pretend you're pushing me on a swing or making funny faces at me."

I nodded.

The whole issue of tails dissolved into something pale and trivial. The thought struck me that I should begin cutting back on the travel. Fewer airports, more conversations like this one. I kissed the boys good night.

"What about your story?" Timmy asked. "What happened to that little boy who couldn't stop pretending?"

"Nothing bad," I said. "He grew up."

I left the bedroom and went off in search of my old friend Xanax.

———

As I wait for my sons to awaken on this Wednesday morning in July of 2008, and as I still tinker with this piece of writing, I find myself more or less surrendering to tails, at least for the present. As a father, I realize, I have much to learn, or much to relearn, about the power of pretending. Not so long ago, my own father went away on a long trip—went away for good—and, like Timmy, I occasionally get caught up in the world of make-believe. I'll watch my dad toss a baseball to me, or I'll hear him singing a few bars of "I'll Be Seeing You" in his clear, unforced baritone. And in those moments my dad is back home again. Not his body, of course, but whatever it is that abides.

I'm on my second cup of coffee now, a little sad, a little happy, quietly watching the first twinklings of dawn spread out across the panes of glass in our kitchen window.

The human race, I realize, may have lost something when we shed our tails all those eons ago. But we gained something, too. We learned to live not just in the unconscious present, but also in the flow of history and in the possibilities of a miraculous future. True, we cannot bound skyward like Tigger with a thrust of our mighty tails. But we can close our eyes and fly into our fathers' arms. This, I suppose, is why I've become a writer.

Beyond anything, though, the events of recent weeks remind me that Timmy and Tad will themselves need good, strong imaginations in the years ahead. After all, biology is biology. People don't live forever. It's not a morbid thought, really—it's almost joyful—but I'm aware that on some future morning like this one my sons may awaken before dawn, brew up a pot of coffee, and sit dreaming at a kitchen table. Maybe they'll imagine me coming home from the airport. Maybe they'll see me opening up the front door and taking them in my arms and lifting them up high, a Slinky dangling from my faded old blue jeans.

20

Telling Tales (II)

A quick P.S. for Timmy and Tad:

In a few years, one of your English teachers will probably ask you to compose a story of your own, something completely invented, and I hope you tackle the assignment with the same full-throttle imagination you once brought to your make-believe tails. Be a little boy again. Invent your own talking tigers, your own thermodynamics. Forget reality—whatever you need from the real world will wiggle its way into your story all by itself. Be sure not to bore your teacher (or yourselves) with pages of description, pages of explanation, and pages of background information.

Whatever you do, do not begin a story like this:

Batman weighed one hundred and eighty-eight
pounds. His hair was black. His complexion was fair.
Young Batman grew up in Sioux City, Iowa, where

he spent an unhappy and disturbed childhood. His grandfather was well known in town as the man who had invented the machine that lays down lane stripes on highways all across America. Batman's mother was an insomniac. She could sew pretty well. She loved a good pork chop. Batman's father preferred seafood. The church Batman attended was made of limestone. His school was a brick structure. The family car was an Oldsmobile.

You see the problem, right? I could pile on this sort of detail for many, many pages, but eventually something must *happen*—an unusual or surprising or sad or exciting event. Stories are about people (or talking tigers) doing things and feeling things. Pork chops and highway stripes are important only if they fit into the fabric of interesting action.

A better story, although not a great story, might begin like this:

When Batman was six years old, he grew a big bushy tail. Often, it popped right out of his pants. This was embarrassing, especially in a place like Sioux City, Iowa, where tails were very much out of fashion. As a result, Batman had no friends. Kids laughed at him. One day after school, as Batman was walking home, his tail dragging in the mud behind him, he looked back and saw that he had painted a long dark stripe down the center of the road. His grandfather, who happened to be driving by, took note of this, and of how the stripe neatly divided the road into two separate lanes. What a wonderful way to prevent collisions, thought his grandfather. If only that stripe were yellow! And so that night at dinner, Batman's grandfather talked with great excitement about building a machine that would duplicate what he had witnessed on the road that day. "We'll make millions, maybe billions," he said. "We can finally get out of this cruddy town." No one else at the dinner table seemed impressed. ("Pass the pork chops," said Batman's mother.) But the next morning, undaunted, the grandfather tied young Batman to the rear bumper of the family Oldsmobile and handed him a can of yellow paint. "Just dip in your tail whenever it runs dry," said the grandfather. "A nice straight line." And so, for miles and miles, Batman painted a neat yellow stripe up and down the city streets, past limestone churches and brick schoolhouses. Not a month later the city's accident rate had dropped dramatically. Batman suddenly had friends. A parade was held in his honor. Sioux City, Iowa, became known, and is still known today, as the safest city in the safest county in the safest state in America. And young Batman had his first sweet taste of what it is to be a hero, almost a superhero, although to this day his tail remains an appendage he takes great care to disguise. You probably hadn't even noticed it.

I certainly don't claim literary merit for this example. But I do think you would pay attention, Timmy and Tad—a chuckle here, a raised eyebrow there.

"I didn't even know Batman *had* a tail," Timmy might say.

And Tad would say, "Well, *I* did."

21

Pride (II)

Timmy and Tad, here's another story I've made up for you. It goes like this:

You're at a five-hundred-dollar-a-plate fundraising dinner, black ties, ruddy faces, and Karl Rove is over in the corner man-handling a martini, and Don Rumsfeld is explaining to some-body's ex-wife why it is that the First Amendment doesn't apply to denouncing wars, because of course that sort of thing undermines war morale, and what kind of war morale would you have if you didn't have a war? It's not a fun dinner party. Trans fats have been consumed by these people. After a while, to break up the monot-ony, for no particular reason at all, some damned fool mentions his children—an offhand remark, nothing profound, probably just to lighten up the chitchat about waterboarding and electronic eavesdropping and the dangers of probable cause and why ter-rorists don't need trials to determine if they're terrorists, because they obviously *are* terrorists, otherwise why would they be getting tortured at Guantánamo? Right then—at the mention of children —you stop whatever you're doing. You dip into your wallet and pull out a stack of pics and spread them across the dinner table and say, "That's Tad, our five-year-old, he's the wild man," and then, after a rewarding moment or two, you say, "That's Timmy, our gentle soul." Then you wait. You watch Rumsfeld and Rove gaze down covetously at your children. One of them shakes his head and says, "Man, your kids make mine look like slime." You politely agree. You've been expecting this. For the past half hour, in fact, you've been expecting that sooner or later, maybe in a few seconds, maybe after the champagne toasts, somebody like Laura Bush will sidle up to you and whisper, "Listen, what about a trade? Even-steven? My kids for yours?" You aren't surprised by this. Your children are cuter and smarter than everybody else's. And so naturally you've been expecting the President himself to stroll up with the news that Tad and Timmy have been selected as recipients of the Medal of Freedom. Right now, George W. Bush and Cheney are over at the bar, comparing their Vietnam War experiences, but you figure it will take only another heartbeat or two before they've exhausted the topic. So you wait. And, sure enough, a moment later they chuckle and slap hands and make their way toward you with purposive strides. "We heard about your kids," Cheney says, "and we're wondering . . . I'll be blunt about this . . . We wonder if Timmy might give us a few unicycle lessons. George and I, we've been trying like the devil, hours and hours in between WMD briefings—but, well, I hate to admit *any-*

thing, of course, but we simply can't get the hang of it. Same with the hula hoop. The hip action, it's not easy."

The President of the United States frowns quizzically. "Yeah," he says, "especially when you're stripping."

You *expect* all this. Your sons *deserve* this.

True, there's an element of fantasy involved, but these prideful musings about Timmy and Tad are probably recognizable to more than a few other parents. Do not most fatherly hearts flutter during a June graduation ceremony? Is not the breath of most fathers stolen away as a beloved son crushes a ninth-inning homer or as a beloved daughter spikes a volleyball?

————

Pride, of course, is listed among the seven deadly sins. It may be, in fact, that pride reigns as the king of sins, the governing sin of sins, the sin that permits all other varieties to take root in godless man. So, yes, I feel guilty. What a despicable heathen fatherhood has made of me. I have become an obsessive, unrepentant, and joyful celebrant of Timmy and Tad—so prideful that I often take pride in my own pride. The boys may fail at something nine times out of ten, but it is the tenth that I mention to strangers who have had the bad luck to take a seat beside me in a dentist's waiting room. (Both kids, I'll offhandedly point out, have perfect teeth. Never a cavity.)

Another example:

The topic of report cards came up during a recent gathering

with friends. I sat silently for a time, imagining how I would slip in a few remarks about my sons' recent straight A's. The conversation rambled along for two or three minutes, but no one looked at me, no one asked my opinion. I grew impatient, then sullen. Eventually, after a young mother declared that report cards aren't everything, I abandoned my fragile dignity and pointed out, rather forcefully, that although report cards may not be everything, they are certainly *something*, otherwise why were we talking about report cards in the first place? Why bother to hand out report cards? Why give grades at all?

"Well," the young mother said, "just because your kids get straight A's—"

"I didn't say that."

She laughed. "Maybe not, but you said it a week ago. And the week before that."

"I did?"

"And the week before *that*."

My friends fell silent. A couple of them grinned. Most were careful not to look at me.

———

One of the more noticeable aspects of being a father at my age is that almost everything is taken to excess, including prideful thoughts. We are all locked up on death row, to be sure, but now, at age sixty-five, I've found myself trying to squeeze all I can into a rapidly shrinking allotment of days and hours. Where a younger father might tell his children he loves them sixty thousand times over a lifetime, I feel the pressure to cram those sixty thousand I-love-yous into a decade or so, just to reach my quota. A younger father may mete out his I-love-yous two or three times a day. I shoot for ten times a day. This behavior—the imperative for excess—spills over into virtually every crevice of my life with Timmy and Tad. I try not to miss their basketball games, because one day I will not be there for the next basketball game. I kiss the boys on the lips, because one day my lips will not be there to kiss. Although it may seem contradictory, an older father's impulse for excess involves a retreat from the world, a ruthless insularity, a kind of sealing off from what is inconsequential or distracting. More and more, I resent obligations that make me pack a suitcase. I resent answering doorbells and telephones. I resent driving to the bank, speaking invitations, fueling my car's gas tank, and getting dressed for dinner parties. (I resent getting dressed, period.) Anything that pulls my attention away from Timmy and Tad, which is just about everything, comes at the price of squandered time and squandered opportunity.

There is, I realize, something dissolute about these old-man excesses, including the flamboyant pride I take in my sons. I have become excessive in ways that would have bewildered me as a younger man or would have caused me to wag my head in disgust. Boastful fathers once made me chuckle. Boastful *other* fathers still make me chuckle. Yet I've come to believe—probably in defense of my own profligacy—that fatherly pride is an involuntary, maybe even biological state of being, a human condition on the order of what the biblical ancients called original sin. Pride seems to be encoded in the double helix, no more reparable than our need for oxygen. A father's pride can be contained, I suppose, but it cannot be eradicated by the exercise of volition. I've tried to bite my tongue. I *do* bite my tongue. But it heals in an instant.

———

What is the difference between pride and love?

On the one hand, we can surely love someone or something without necessarily experiencing a sense of pride. On the other hand, it is difficult to envision feeling pride without an accompanying sense of love. To take pride in one's work, for example, seems to embrace some degree of love for the work itself, or love for the eventual outcome of one's labor, or love for the challenges and satisfactions found in the attentive pursuit of a particular task. Similarly, to take pride in one's children—to *feel* pride—is also to feel something intimately associated with the complicated emotions we call love. Do we experience the swollen sensation of pride when LeBron James or some other stranger scores a game-winning free throw? Almost certainly not. Do we feel pride when a daughter or son does the same? Almost certainly so. One involves love, the other does not.

With this in mind, I offer an illustration drawn from recent history, an incident that has been keeping me awake at night, sometimes bubbling with pride, sometimes bubbling with love, but mostly bubbling with both at once.

On July 18, 2009, our family was vacationing in southeastern France, in a beautiful but very expensive town called St.-Jean-Cap-Ferrat. Around noon on that sunny July day, Meredith and I had ordered drinks at an outdoor bar on the grounds of our way-too-ritzy hotel, both of us feeling fraudulently upper crust as we watched Timmy and Tad play Ping-Pong on the far side of an expansive green lawn. The hotel was way beyond our means, a miscalculated extravagance, and for two days our family had been immersed in a bizarre, we-don't-belong-here self-consciousness, as if we'd been miscast in an old Grace Kelly or Cary Grant movie. The hotel's clientele was without exception bejeweled, chic, wealthy, and superbly tanned. There was no Burger King on the grounds. The hotel's pizza, at eighteen bucks a slice, tasted like duck liver. Months earlier, stupidly, we had reserved a room here out of misguided romanticism, perhaps in the fantasy that the Prince of Wales might solicit our attendance at a yacht party or that Johnny Depp might invite us for a game of croquet up at his villa in the bluish hills above town. Nothing of the sort had occurred. Virtually no one had spoken to us, including most members of a hotel staff that seemed reluctant to refresh a drink or to provide directions to the men's room. We had walked everywhere, partly to save money, partly to avoid confrontations with what we'd taken to calling "la snootiness de Cap-Ferrat."

Still, we had persevered, grimly faking it, as we were still doing on July 18, 2009, when my cell phone rang midway through a twelve-dollar glass of flat Coca-Cola. It was my sister calling from Texas. My mother had died.

Even as I received the terrible news, I was conscious of the brilliant-blue Mediterranean, the swimmers and seaplanes, my kids playing Ping-Pong on a lawn of green velvet, the flat Coca-Cola in my hand, my irritation at an aggressively unhelpful waiter. I was conscious, too, of France itself, and of how strange it was to be hearing details of my mother's death at such a great remove and in such an unfamiliar place. From the time I was about Timmy's age, six or seven, I had been dreading this moment, wondering how I could possibly hold myself together, and now I sat in an outdoor bar in St.-Jean-Cap-Ferrat with a flat Coca-Cola in my hand, my mother dead on the other side of the world, my children playing Ping-Pong in the ridiculously expensive French sunlight. In those bleak, sickening moments I was made keenly aware of how Minnesotan I was.

After the call, Meredith and I walked across the lawn to the Ping-Pong table.

I told the boys my mother had died.

They were young and had little to say. I did not say much either—almost nothing.

For a long time that afternoon, I played Ping-Pong with Timmy and Tad, not really in France anymore, not really anywhere, and then later in the day, as the sun went down, the four of us headed off for dinner in the town of St.-Jean-Cap-Ferrat, walking down a long, gently sloping hill toward the bay.

I reached out and took Timmy's hand.

We were subdued.

The sky was purply red.

Grace Kelly strolled arm in arm with Cary Grant through the tropical shadows. Soon there would be stars. My mother was dead.

"Are you thinking about Grandma?" I asked Timmy.

"No," Timmy said. "I'm thinking about you thinking about Grandma."

22

What If?

Neither Tad nor Timmy has asked me about Vietnam, not a single question, and for the past year or two, this has been bothering me. Am I that uninteresting to them? Are they not mildly curious?

And so, one evening, after a great deal of thought, I tried to approach the subject through a back door, telling the boys a quick story about my own father's wartime experience, how my dad had been assigned to a destroyer during World War Two, but how the ship ended up sailing without my dad on board. Not long afterward the ship went down with all hands. Or so my father claimed. True? Untrue? Partly true? I don't know. For me, I'll admit, the anecdote has an archetypal quality that seems fishy, too perfectly rounded, too perfectly climactic, more like a fateful parable than a story from the real world.

Timmy and Tad were also skeptical, but truth or falsehood had little to do with it.

"Is this, like, one of your stories with a moral?" Timmy asked. "Like we're not supposed to join the navy?"

"Not at all," I said. "It's just something my dad told me."

A little later Tad said, "It's a cool story, but I think your father was trying to scare you."

"How so?"

"Well," said Tad, "you wouldn't *be* here if your dad got on that ship. I wouldn't be here either."

"That *is* scary."

"And Timmy wouldn't be here. We'd all be nothing. We wouldn't even *know* we're nothing."

"Right," I said.

The conversation soon went elsewhere. Ten or fifteen minutes passed, and then Timmy said, "I just thought of something a lot scarier."

"Such as?" I said.

"What if you and Mom got married while you were in high school? I'd be fifty years old."

"True."

"I'd be almost dead."

Meredith and I looked at each other. Nobody was laughing.

And then, for several days afterward, Meredith and I had trouble erasing the picture from our heads. Two points in time had fused. There was the lasting image of Timmy at age fifty, yet he was also an eighth-grader, a unicyclist, a Rubik's Cube enthusiast, a dreamer, a shy twelve-year-old with false teeth and a potbelly.

"Some things," Meredith said, "I don't want to think about."

23

Home School

I do not know if my sons will ever wish to be professional writers—I hope not—but barring a catastrophic sequence of events, they will certainly *need* to write. In high school and in college, whether they like it or not, they will be called upon to compose clear and effective sentences, and later on, in adulthood, they will discover that precious few pursuits in life involve no writing at all. At the moment, Tad plans to "cuddle bunnies" for a living; Timmy expects to be drafted any day now by the Los Angeles Lakers. Yet even if these unlikely scenarios pan out, the boys will surely find themselves writing letters, text messages, postcards, emails, tweets, and whatever other forms of written communication become fashionable in the coming decades. They will need to express their thoughts with language, for which (at present) there is no substitute, and therefore a few words of advice are in order:

1. Avoid ridiculous, flowery, decorative, long-winded language. Do not write this sentence: "Her neck was like a swan's, long and arched and rubbery and graceful." Instead write: "She honked."

2. Avoid excessive, falsely poetic alliteration. Do not write this sentence: "The red, rollicking river of his tongue rubbed me the wrong way." Instead write: "He kissed me. I gagged."

3. Use active, not passive language. Do not write this boring, passive sentence: "Jack had been happily married for twenty years." Instead write: "Jack turned on the TV, opened up the Cheetos, sat back, and scratched himself."

4. Delete ugliness. It will lighten your heart to strike out a recalcitrantly wooden clause in favor of the breathtaking sunset of a period.

5. Proofread your own writing. There is a difference, for instance, between the word "throng" and the word "thong," and you may not want your readers to imagine a frenzied thong dancing through the purple twilight.

6. When writing fiction, do not be afraid to lie. For a fiction writer, lying is a necessary, noble, and sublime virtue. (Try telling that to a man in a straw boater.)

   The art of fiction is generally, but not always, concerned with that which did not occur, at least not in the so-called real world, but which nevertheless illuminates emotional, moral, and spiritual aspects of the human creature. *Middlemarch* is a sublime lie. *War and Peace* is a noble and necessary lie. As Pablo Picasso put it, bluntly and clearly, "Art is a lie that makes us realize truth." Along similar lines, Ernest Hemingway wrote, "But there is always the chance that such a book of fiction may throw some light on what has been written as fact." Or as Marianne Moore instructed: a true poem should have "imaginary gardens with real toads in them."

Of course, the truths of an invented story are rarely verifiable by empirical means. We cannot prove, for instance, that Thumbelina was a young lady whose stature was, to put it kindly, on the smallish side; in fact, we cannot prove that Thumbelina was a young lady at all, because she never existed as an actual person. The truths of fiction, like the truths of our daydreams and of our nightmares, reside outside history, complementing history, reimagining or manufacturing history, even when the stories we tell have been inspired and midwifed by actual historical events. (*War and Peace* is once again an example.) Art in general and stories in particular live in a kind of twin universe, sometimes reflective of our own, sometimes contradictory. (*Alice's Adventures in Wonderland*, Mickey Mouse, *Slaughterhouse-Five*, and "In Dreams Begin Responsibilities" jump to mind.) In the end, story-truth is only marginally a function of what actually is or what actually was. Rather, as Picasso and Hemingway suggest, a well-told lie might help us realize why Peter Piper picked a peck of pickled peppers, even if we can find no evidence in the real world of the peppers or the peck or a guy named Peter Piper.

Art is not science, and science is not art, but each is keenly informed by aspects of the other: close observation, curiosity, experimentation, coherence, internal consistency, accuracy of expression, and general confidence in the principle of causation. And while a story's "truths" may not be verifiable by the scientific method, they surely can be verified—and *are* verified—in the hearts and bellies and tear ducts of individual readers as a page is turned at the stroke of midnight. A novel may fail as science, but the same novel may succeed brilliantly in providing consolation and encouragement to a sleepless, heartsick, and lonely old woman in Tallahassee. This is not an esoteric defense of fiction. It is a practical defense.

Fiction writers choose to invent things for a reason, otherwise there would be no fiction. There would be no novels, no movies, no short stories, no TV dramas, no Lake Wobegon, no *War of the Worlds,* no *Romeo and Juliet,* no *Ulysses,* no Scrooge, no *Seinfeld,* no Little Red Riding Hood or Rumpelstiltskin or Thumbelina. Broadway would go dark. Hollywood would shut down. Fathers would stop telling bedtime stories to their children. Considering all that, imagine what an impoverished world it would be in the absence of noble falsehoods.

And so I'm urging you, Timmy, and you too, Tad, to tell your lies carefully and vividly and honestly and bravely. This will be difficult. You will lose sleep. But the good news, which I've rediscovered often over the years, is that you will not be required to know anything. You can just make it all up.

7. Express your own thoughts, not thoughts that others may expect you to think or want you to think. If you yearn to cuddle bunnies for a living, say so. If you believe mankind is a failed experiment, say so. However, be sure to carry a copy of Bertrand Russell's *Unpopular Essays* as fortification against those occasions when courage fails. Which it will.

8. The essays of George Orwell may come in handy, too, for the same reason. "If liberty means anything at all," Orwell wrote, "it means the right to tell people what they do not want to hear."

9. Do not impose symbols on your work. Let symbols grow in and from your work. If you write a sentence that contains a symbol merely to insert symbolism, hit the delete key and dip your computer in Clorox.

10. When writing fiction, if you find yourself stuck, write the reverse of what you mean to say. Often the reverse of what you mean to say is what you mean to say. Or, if the reverse of what you mean to say is not what you mean to say, it may turn out to be a great deal fresher and wiser than what you mean to say.

11. Also, if you wish to become writers, it can't hurt to pay heed to the obvious: a writer must write. In this regard, Joseph Conrad describes his daily routine in a letter to a

friend: "I sit down religiously every morning, I sit down for eight hours every day—and the sitting down is all." Religiously, Conrad says. Every day, he says. He sits down not only when he is in the mood, not only when inspiration strikes, and not only when he can think of nothing better to do. A writer performs the act of sitting down to be wholly present, wholly receptive, as the fingers and the mind prepare for those occasions when language and imagination miraculously begin to fuse.

This is not to claim that the sitting down is all good fun. It is almost always painful. You will wait and wait. You will fidget. You will mutter to yourself. You will compose mediocre sentences, repair them, and then throw them away. You will endure tedium and failure and self-doubt as the price to be paid for a few moments of intense pleasure.

In large part, the satisfactions of sitting down each day will be taken in small linguistic accomplishments, word by word: the rush of endorphins, for example, that accompanies the discovery of a perfect adjective, one required by rhythm but one that also gives unique, vital identity to a noun, lifting the noun into bright being, breathing into it the singularity of *thatness*—that house, that sewer, that butterfly and no other—all without sacrificing grace and good sense, a sweet coupling of adjective with noun that brings into the world new beauty and new insight and new music. The musicality of prose, its rhythms and counterpoints and harmonies, is the sea upon which the vessel of fiction always rides and upon which the buoyancy of plot and character always depends. A discordant, graceless sentence will jeopardize the vessel's integrity, and repetitive musical blunders will send an otherwise enchanting story plunging to the ocean's bottom, much as an out-of-tune piano will sink an otherwise gorgeous nocturne. The writer's struggle for linguistic felicity demands an intensity of concentration—a ferocious *listening*—that cannot be achieved without the artist's complete presence. You cannot write while you're bowling.

12. Finally—wake up, Tad!—I conclude today's home school session with Conrad's preface to *The Nigger of the "Narcissus"*: "A work that aspires, however humbly, to the condition of art should carry its justification in every line."

   To this, one might reasonably add: every word, every syllable.

24

Home School

In our previous session, I had cited George Orwell: "If liberty means anything at all, it means the right to tell people what they do not want to hear."

At this point, Timmy and Tad, we must contemplate the consequences of exercising the rights of liberty. It is one thing to applaud George Orwell; it is another thing to summon the courage to tell people what they do not want to hear.

Consider beheading.

For years, Americans have been appalled by gruesome and well-publicized decapitations performed by members of al-Qaeda, ISIS, the Taliban, and other such radical Islamist organizations.

For about the same number of years, Americans have snoozed through the no less gruesome beheadings performed with our own bombs, drones, rockets, artillery, helicopters, naval vessels, and fighter jets.

Does the word "hypocrisy" ring a bell?

If we condemn beheadings by others, should we not condemn our own?

Is one beheading more moral than another?

Are the headless less headless?

Is the gore less gory?

Are we not, as a country, toying with a double standard by refusing to call our beheadings beheadings? Is this not a kind of narcissism?

And is it less sinful, less outrageous, less barbarous, and less disgusting to perform beheadings in the sanitary, well-insulated anonymity of a jet's cockpit than in a squalid alleyway in Kabul?

Does technology make the moral difference?

Do clean hands make clean hearts?

Is it more civilized to ignore our own beheadings—disguising them with neutral language, avoiding ugly photographs, hiding carnage from public scrutiny—than it is to post barbarous, cut-throat videos on YouTube?

Is it an act of Christian decency to denounce "up-close" beheadings, performed with a knife or a sword, while dismissing long-distance beheadings with the techno-shrug of "collateral damage"?

Is intentionality somehow compounded by "in-person" beheading?

Conversely, is intentionality diminished by pushing a launch button at an air force base outside Las Vegas?

Is one an accident and the other not?

When you swing a sword or when you drop a bomb, do you

not realize, Timmy—and you too, Tad—and you too, America— that people will lose their heads?

And which is more cowardly? To slit the throat of Daniel Pearl, drenching yourself in Pearl's blood splatter, or to blow off the head of a sixty-eight-year-old grandmother in Pakistan as you sit drenched in the electronic sterility of a computer trailer in the United Arab Emirates?

Is it not the case that human beings are not only beheaded but also be-armed and be-legged and be-bodied and turned to slush at least as often by drones and jets as by swords and knives?

Is body slush more agreeable to you than throat slush?

Is a Pakistani corpse more agreeable to you than an American corpse?

Do you wish to inspect the corpses to make up your mind?

Do you believe, as pious decapitators and pious body-slushers must, that the Ten Commandments were delivered to Moses as the Ten Suggestions?

In plain English, if not in the original Hebrew and Aramaic, is it not true that beheading is beheading, that killing is killing, that commandment is commandment, and that double standards are the tools of tyrants and madmen?

Why is it, Timmy, that literalists abandon literalism at the drop of a convenient head?

How can it be, Tad, that one man will say to another: "Do as I say, not as I do"?

What happened to decency?

What happened to the Golden Rule?

Enough—you get the idea.

Such questions, which challenge hallucinations of inviolate rectitude, will boost the blood pressure not only of Rush Limbaugh but of a substantial portion of our country's citizenry. You may be viewed as less than wholly American for having raised these and similar matters. You may lose friends. You may be hated. You may be ridiculed. But that's liberty for you.

25

The Old Testament

One evening as we sat watching a televised basketball game, Tad asked, "How old was that guy Methuselah, the one in the Bible?"

"I'm not sure," I said. "Almost a thousand years old, I think."

"Wow," Tad said.

An hour or so later, near the end of a tight and exciting game, Tad said, "What exactly did he eat?"

26

Timmy and Tad and Papa and I (I)

My father had been drinking again, and he no doubt felt some shame about this, and on a hot summer afternoon he entered my bedroom bearing a fat, heavy-looking book. My father had decided, I suppose, to be a father. "Take the book," he said. "It's full of stories. I want you to pick five of them and I want you to read them, and then I want you to talk to me about them." The year was either 1957 or 1958. I was almost, but not quite yet, a teenager. I loved my father very much, but I was afraid of him, and I was embarrassed by the vodka flush on his face and by the thick, too-careful precision in his voice. The word "want" did not mean want. It meant: You will do this, and no arguments.

A few hours later I finished reading. I went in search of my father, feeling a mix of things, mostly apprehension, because I had almost nothing to say about the five stories I'd selected.

I had read "The Killers" because its title promised thrills to a boy of eleven or twelve. I had read "A Clean, Well-Lighted Place" and "Cat in the Rain" because both were short. I had read "Soldier's Home" because I liked playing soldier on the golf course, killing Japanese and Germans, and because I had expected a story called "Soldier's Home" to contain a great deal of gore. I do not remember the fifth story. Almost certainly it was a short one.

I looked for my father in each room of our house, and then I went outside to see if he might be washing his car or mowing grass. His turquoise-and-cream Oldsmobile was no longer parked in the driveway.

For a time, I sat on the back steps and tried not to cry. It was a Saturday, I am almost sure, and the world had the stop-time emptiness of any small-town summer Saturday in the 1950s, when my country and I knew little of irony, when I was old enough to grasp the vocabulary of Ernest Hemingway, his sentence structures and Midwestern syntax, but was far too young to have experienced betrayal or heartbreak or entrapment by my own moral failures.

Eventually I went back inside. Where my father had gone I did not know. I still don't. The month must have been July or August, because the house was very hot and we had no air conditioning then, and because I was clammy with the dread of forgetting even the little I could remember of "Cat in the Rain": A lady looked out a hotel window. She saw a cat in the rain. She went outside to retrieve the cat, but the cat had disappeared, and later a hotel maid brought the lady another cat. Or was it the same cat? Totally unclear.

I felt stupid.

Why, I wondered, would anyone write such a story and think it was a story worth writing? My father would know, of course, and that too scared me. I wanted my father to love me and wanted him to be proud of me, but I had nothing to say about "Cat in the Rain" except that it seemed exceptionally real and exceptionally boring. The same was true, more or less, of the other four stories I had read that afternoon. The exciting and dramatic parts had been left out. It was too bad, I thought, that the cat hadn't drowned. It was too bad that the guy who came home from the war didn't want to talk about all the exciting stuff he must have seen and done. It was too bad the Swedish boxer didn't get out of bed and beat the crap out of those two gangsters who had come to kill him. It was too bad the old waiter couldn't remember the actual words to the Lord's Prayer.

My father must have come home very late that night. What happened then, or the next morning, I can't recall, but in the days and decades afterward he never again mentioned my summer reading assignment. He probably did not remember giving me that fat book. He probably did not remember deciding to be a father. He was a good man and was not to blame. It was alcohol. It was chemistry and sadness.

Nearly six decades have passed. The year is 2016. My father has been dead for a long time.

But when I think about "The Killers," I think first of my father handing me a book and then vanishing into the summer afternoon. "The Killers," for me, is first about booze, then about other things. When I think about "A Clean, Well-Lighted Place," I think of the VFW hall in Worthington, Minnesota, where my father spent many days and many more nights drinking with his friends and playing backgammon and wishing he were in Nassau or Brooklyn and not selling life insurance to farmers in Worthington, Minnesota, the Turkey Capital of the World. When I think now about "Soldier's Home," I think of my father's brooding silence at the dinner table, his dreams rotted, his medals from World War Two scattered in a drawer beneath his socks. When I think about "Cat in the Rain," I think of how much I yearned to come up with smart things to say to my father, so that he would love me, and so that he would stop drinking vodka and explain why a writer would write such a terrible story.

———

Don't forget, Timmy—nor you, Tad—that readers bring their lives to and into other people's books. And someday, if either of you sits down to write a story, please remember that it will become your responsibility to leave room inside the story for your readers' own joys and terrors and lost fathers.

Mediocre stories leave little such room; bad stories leave almost no such room. Bad and mediocre stories explain too much: how the wicked witch became so completely and irreparably wicked— abused as a child, no doubt. Bad and mediocre stories tidy up the world, sorting out the human messes of serendipity and tangled motive. Who among us truly understands the plot of his own life? Do you, Tad? Do you, Timmy? Do you truly understand your own swirling, half-formed, and contradictory motives? Who recalls more than a tiny fraction of his own life—last Tuesday, for example? And if we cannot recall our lives, how can we pretend to explain our lives? It is guesswork. Scantily informed guesswork at that. I think of Hemingway's line in *A Farewell to Arms:* "There isn't always an explanation for everything." Or I think of this line from "The Three-Day Blow": "There's always more to it than we know about." Or I think of "The Devil's Advice to Story-Tellers" by Robert Graves: "Nice contradiction between fact and fact / Will make the whole read human and exact."

The essential object of fiction is not to explain. Explanation narrows. Explanation fixes. Explanation dissolves mystery. Explanation imposes artificial, arrogant order on human contradictions between fact and fact. The essential object of fiction is to embrace and widen and deepen all that is unknown and unknowable —who we are, why we are—and to offer us late-night company as we lie awake pondering our universal journey down the birth canal, and out into the light, and then toward the grave.

In a story, explanation is like joining a magician backstage. The mysterious becomes mechanical. The miracle becomes banal. Delight vanishes. Wonder vanishes. What was once surprising, even beautiful, devolves into tired causality. One might as well be washing dishes.

Imagine, for instance, that Flannery O'Connor had devoted a few pages to explaining how the Misfit became the Misfit, how evil became evil: the Misfit was dyslexic as a boy; this led to that —bad grades in school, chips on his shoulder. Pile on the psychology. Even as explanation, and because it *is* explanation, there would be, for me, something both fishy and aesthetically ugly about this sort of thing, the stink of determinism, the stink of false certainty, the stink of a half- or a quarter-truth, the stink of hypocrisy, the stink of flimflam, the stink of pretending to have sorted out the secrets of the human heart. Moreover, Timmy and Tad, I want you to bear in mind that explanation doesn't always explain. Few dyslexics end up butchering old ladies. Evil *is*. In the here-and-now presence of evil, evil *always* purely is, no matter how we might explain it. Ask the dead at My Lai. Ask the Misfit. "Nome," he says, "I ain't a good man." In the pages of "A Good Man Is Hard to Find," Flannery O'Connor goes out of her way to satirize and even to ridicule such explanation. And for Hemingway, too, explanation is submerged below the waterline of his famous iceberg. In great stories, as in life, we are confronted with raw presence. Events don't annotate themselves. Nightmares don't diagnose themselves. With the first whiff of Zyklon B, with the first syllables of a Dear John letter, with the first ting-a-ling of a dreaded phone call, with the first glimpse of your own nervous oncologist, there is what purely is. There is a cat in the rain.

"Cat in the Rain" and two of the other stories I encountered almost six decades ago have since become great favorites of mine. Each of those dearly loved stories, like all wondrous works of art, presents us with the gift of life's ambiguity, the gift of participation without a guide dog, the gift of fleeting clarity amid overwhelming uncertainty, and the gift of encountering other lives just as random and murky and doomed as our own. Is there a lesson to be drawn from "Indian Camp"? There is not. Read *The Joy of Sex*. Is there wise counsel in "Out of Season"? There is not. Read *Fishing Tips for Freshwater*.

In the years since my father placed that fat book in my hands,

I have returned several times to "Cat in the Rain" and to the numerous other stories and novels of Ernest Hemingway. Recently I finished reading, once again, the 650 pages of the Finca Vigia edition of Hemingway's complete stories, and once again I found myself surprised at how personally I received most of those stories. Which is to say I have my own Ernest Hemingway, just as you, Timmy, have your own Rick Riordan, or you, Tad, have your own Mark Twain. There are, in other words, at least as many Hemingways as there are readers of Hemingway. My father had his Hemingway. My eleventh-grade English teacher had her Hemingway. Gertrude Stein had her Hemingway—rawer and less mature than, say, the Hemingway of Malcolm Cowley. Hemingway's sons had their Hemingway. And of course Hemingway had his Hemingway, and Hemingway's Hemingway almost certainly was not yours or mine or Harold Bloom's.

For better or for worse—by far for the better, I believe—a writer of stories can control only so much, after which a story is completed by vanishing fathers and hot summer days and boys who crave love.

————

For Timmy and Tad, who may one day be curious about their father's interior life, I offer a personal example of what I'm trying to communicate here.

I am a fiction writer. I have written about war. And so, not long ago, I found myself in an auditorium, reading aloud a short piece called "The Man I Killed," which seeks to portray a character's response to viewing the corpse of an enemy soldier he had blown into eternity with a hand grenade. The story's details—emotional and physical—were unpleasant. Memories surfaced. My voice broke. It was hard going. Afterward, in a lobby outside the auditorium, I was approached by a young man of about twenty. "I could tell that was tough for you," he said, "and I appreciate your honesty." I thanked him. He thanked me. The young man began moving away but then stopped and said, "Listen, I've been thinking about joining the Marine Corps. You helped a lot. Now I know for sure I'll be joining."

This was not a singular occurrence. It has happened a dozen or so times over thirty years, virtually the same conversation, occasionally concluding in an awkward hug.

I am always shocked.

I'll go back to my motel room, pull off my tie, look in the mirror, and think: You poor dumb useless yo-yo. I'll feel old and defeated. I'll take a shower and smoke cigarettes and stare at CNN and then finally surrender, as I must, to the space in which reader and writer brush past each other as strangers.

One man's torment is another man's imperative.

———

It is April 12, 2016, and in a few months I will turn seventy. Timmy is twelve, Tad is ten. Basketball has become a problem for me.

I feel the squeeze.

This morning, as I sat trying on these shabby and ill-fitting sentences, my father's urn drew my attention. The urn squatted on its shelf five feet from my desk. Well, I thought, should I try what you tried? There was no answer and there never is. But even so . . . why not?

I got up, went out to the living room, and asked Timmy if he'd mind reading "The Killers."

It wasn't an order—it was barely a request—but Timmy is a nice kid, and he said, "Sure. What is it?" I told him it was a story by Ernest Hemingway, an author he had encountered a few months earlier when his seventh-grade English teacher assigned "A Day's Wait."

Timmy had been lukewarm about "A Day's Wait."

He was lukewarm, too, about "The Killers."

"I don't know, I guess it's okay," he reported.

Timmy is now almost exactly the age I had been when "The Killers" came through my bedroom door. And the words "I don't know" and "guess" and "okay" represent the entirety of what I would've said to my own father if he had not disappeared on that summer afternoon six decades ago.

I asked Timmy if he understood the events of the story. He plainly did. Ole had double-crossed somebody in Chicago, and the somebody had sent two nasty guys to kill him. "The boxer took a fall, I think," said brilliant, literary Timmy, "or else he *didn't* take a fall he was supposed to take." Until that instant I'd had no idea that my son was aware of this uncommon usage of the word "fall." I was delighted. He had swished a three-pointer.

"And what about Ole?" I asked. "I mean, near the end of the story, when Nick goes to warn him, why did Ole say he was done running?"

"I wasn't thinking about that," said Timmy. "I was thinking about something else."

"What?"

"I was wondering why anybody would ever want to be a boxer in the first place. Don't boxers hurt people?"

"They do, yes."

"Don't they get hit in the face?"

"Yes."

"So why be a boxer?"

Timmy has his Hemingway.

———

Almost seventy years old, and it shows, but nonetheless I'm trying to be a decent father. Books are one way. Bedtime stories are another. I throw footballs and baseballs and go dizzy at the Ping-Pong table. Until a couple of years back, I spent a number of afternoons out on the golf course with the boys, just as I'd imagined doing on the day of Timmy's birth, but the romantic notion of bonding with my sons over a tiny white ball did not pan out. Tad and Timmy do not care for golf. They do enjoy driving the golf cart, which can be heart-stopping on water holes, but golf itself seems to them pointless. ("You mean," said Tad, "I'm *not* supposed to hit the ball a lot?") In any case, to the best of my recollection, none of us ever uttered the words "Nine more holes."

Still, I've been present. I haven't vanished. Not yet.

Twelve years ago, like my own father, I decided to be a father. I swore off long days at the computer, swore off making sentences, and as a result, my most recent novel was published in the faraway year of 2002.

There was nothing heroic in this silence. It was in no way a sacrifice. By the early autumn of 2002, when Timmy was conceived, I had come to resent the twelve-hour days that were the price for a half page of passable prose; I resented the loneliness and aloneness; I resented the pitiless subjectivity of it all. What had once been fun for me—tedious fun, frustrating fun—had hardened into something edging up on hatred. At this very instant the hatred bubbles. Should the word "hardened" be replaced by the word "evolved"? Yes? No? Screw it—keep going. Is the word "awaken" too poetic, too precious? Yes. Probably. No. Probably. With every syllable I try to talk myself out of writing the next syllable. Yet here I am, back at it after a long vacation. Five hours a day, not twelve. Plenty of time for checking homework. Plenty of time for soccer and birthdays and Rubik's Cube speed-solving competitions.

My loathing for making sentences remains a big problem, but still, at least on occasion, some of the old writerly passion is back. The buzz of imagination now startles me awake at three in the morning. I roll out of bed. I make coffee. Scraps of dreamland language come and go, sometimes affixing themselves to other scraps. As I clean the kitchen counters, still groggy, a swarm of bumblebee thoughts buzz through my head, reminders of all the things I want to tell Timmy and Tad about their father's time on this planet: a childhood magic trick, a lover's sit-on-your-lap fare-well forever, a booted ground ball, a tambourine jangling at mid-night, a war, a dead little girl of not quite and not ever nine.

Even with writing hell still looming ahead of me over the next few hours, there is again a zippy excitement at three in the morn-ing. This is how it once was, two sons ago.

When I was a kid, I had viewed "Soldier's Home" as a willful and malevolent choice by the author to write the dullest and most uneventful story he could possibly write, with the glaring excep-tion of "Cat in the Rain." Where were the machine guns? Where were the thrills? That nifty contraction—soldier's home—had gone unnoticed, along with its purposeful pun, but even if by some impossible act of precocity I had noted any of this, my yawn would've been wide and my verdict identical.

Squeal "Dear Jesus" and learn.

The "Soldier's Home" of my youth is certainly not the "Sol-dier's Home" I carry inside me today. I've had my own trouble finding words for the horror. "Horror" doesn't do it. Nothing does it. Silence makes sense. (Timmy and Tad have come to ac-cept my sudden silences, although they are also very careful to avoid me on those occasions. They look elsewhere. They go silent themselves. They wait for the mood to change. Dad's bad-time, Tad calls it.)

For people who have killed other people, and for people who have in other ways been immersed in the crankcase evil of war, there is a mute helplessness that comes on hard afterward. Vonnegut's Billy Pilgrim had it. Hemingway's Harold Krebs had it. Heinemann's Paco Sullivan had it. Homer's Odysseus had it. O'Brien's O'Brien had it: "And then for a long time you lie there watching the story happen in your head. You listen to your wife's breathing. The war's over. You close your eyes. You take a feeble swipe at the dark and think, Christ, what's the point?"

Was Hemingway's "Soldier's Home" an influence? Yes, almost for sure. No, almost for sure. My discomfort with the word "influence" is no doubt rooted in the knowledge that Hemingway got there before I did. In fact, he not only got there, he got there *right*—the dense, deep ice beneath a soldier's silence. But still, as I wiggle with irritation, I'll sometimes ask the ceiling: Did Hemingway give thought to the notion that he was crossing terrain navigated centuries ago by war-weary Odysseus? Did Dos Passos sometimes irritate Vonnegut? Did Crane irritate Remarque?

Not long before his death, at an event in Austin, Texas, I was introduced to Norman Mailer, who looked up at me from his wheelchair, first with puzzlement, then with half-formed recognition, and then with an aggressive stare. Forcefully, without solicitation, he said, "Are you that Vietnam writer?"

I nodded at him. I did not care for the words "Vietnam writer."

Mailer kept staring, still aggressively, and then he said, "Well, we all stand on one another's shoulders."

I understood, of course. He had written *The Naked and the Dead*.

But for a half hour afterward, and over the years since, I found myself wondering what had brought on the rebuke in Mailer's eyes, the sharpness in his voice. I'm not a mind reader. Maybe the comment was benign. But we do have to interpret signals—posture, eyes, tone of voice—and I could not and I still cannot ignore the impression that I was in the presence of annoyance bordering on the dangerous. It may have been the annoyance, I sometimes suspect, of a violated proprietorship, of encountering a trespasser, of an author's understandable sense of forfeiture as others begin to stride across a staked literary claim. It goes both ways. Whether one is the influencer or the influenced, there is an instinct to defend one's own. I've felt such irritation myself, many times: I'll pick up a book, scan a page or two, and yell, "That's mine!"

Mailer was right. We do stand on one another's shoulders. Yet as we stand on those shoulders, we also try to hold aloft something new and unique to the world—an A&W root beer stand, a shit field, a woman in pedal pushers, an elusive Silver Star. We build our spanking-new houses on seized ground.

I cherish "Soldier's Home." It is as perfectly made as art can get. And in this respect, the story was a formidable and enduring influence—the controlled tensions, the controlled hurt, the controlled language, the controlled interior, the controlled action, the controlled mood, and most especially the controlled—barely controlled, desperately controlled—hero of the story, Harold Krebs. Could form and content, style and theme, event and character be more masterfully unified? Could the aesthetic bar be higher? Still, at least for me, it's also true that "Soldier's Home" was as much an impediment as it was an influence, partly because it was and is so wonderful a story, partly because it was and is so beloved by me and by others, and partly because it just *was* and just *is*.

What does a writer do?

I cannot unlive my life. I was a soldier. I came home. I learned more than I wanted to learn about the boil of silence.

Despite those brawny shoulders beneath me—among them the shoulders of Ernest Hemingway and Norman Mailer, a couple of *boxers,* for Christ's sake—I yearned to express my own helplessness in the face of memory, my own fear of telling patriotic lies, my own desire to be polite in the company of family and friends, my own everlasting guilt, my own scared-shitless voice still squealing "Dear Jesus" as people try to kill me in my sleep, my own reluctance to re-visit evil, my own moral failings, my own embarrassments, my own inability to utter the word "no" to a war I despised—these were my yearnings and not those of Vonnegut or Homer or Ernest Heming-way. In the end, the most powerful influence on my work was not a literary one. It was the fucking war. It was the replay afterward. I wrote my stories to interrogate my own nightmares, my own fro-zen and inarticulate memory, even if—not because—Mailer and Vonnegut and Hemingway had earlier interrogated theirs.

———

When I think about "Soldier's Home," I most often think very unliterary thoughts. I think about my own homecoming from war, the emptiness in my head, the dreamy haze where Vietnam once was, and after a while I'll circle back to poor, silent Harold Krebs. I'll wonder if he ever discovered language for it all. Did he find peace, I'll wonder, or did he end up with a bullet in his head? This sort of thinking goes sailing down a thousand late-night streets—how this war stuff just will not end—how we never run out of reasons to kill one another, always such wonderful reasons, never bad ones—and how daughters and sons and mothers and wives and lovers must also be counted among the mutilated as they pass by in endless parade—and how wars do not cease with the signing of a peace treaty, how they go on and on at the dinner table, at the VFW hall, and how last night in Orlando an old lady jerked awake and whispered, "Where's my baby? Where's my baby?" even though her baby had been blown into a tree four decades ago in Quang Ngai Province. I think about my father coming home from the South Pacific, dumping his medals in a drawer, and spending the next thirty-five years selling life insurance in the Turkey Capital of the World. I think about how ridiculously trivial the matter of influence is. We are influenced, if we are human, by all that is around us, including a beautiful story called "Soldier's Home," but also including the beautiful stories of Kurt Vonnegut and Homer, and including—don't forget—the neglected bric-a-brac of English teachers and untied shoelaces and voices on intercoms and missed phone calls and an encounter with bad oysters in Tripoli and a little boy named Tad, my son, who only a second ago asked if I could quit writing—please!—and play Monopoly.

———

It's a dead horse, but one last thought about influence. Among the most potent of influences, in literature as in life, are models of what to avoid. Student manuscripts are an influence. "Dear Abby" is an influence. The potholes on the road to a line of decent prose are many, and it is good to be reminded of them. Cliché. Walmart language. Predictability. Sentimentalism. Grammatical error. Gracelessness. Wordiness. Staleness. Contrivance. Disunity. Beating dead horses. Although shining exemplars can be one kind of influence—do this!—mediocrity can often be another—don't do that! I mention this as a reminder, especially to myself, that when we talk about literary influence, we must not overlook the Hardy Boys or underestimate the first-love influences of *The Cat in the Hat, The Boxcar Children,* and *Larry of Little League.* With a full heart and without apology, I can declare that Frank and Joe Hardy made reading fun for me. In the absence of those two resourceful guides, I may not have so eagerly hopped aboard Huck's raft, and may not have later found my way to Paris and Spain and *The Sun Also Rises.*

And so, Timmy and Tad, that is why I have been feeding you book after book all these years, and why I will keep feeding books to you even after I'm gone. I have prepared lists. I have drawn up lesson plans to be consulted when you turn thirty or forty or fifty. I want to be there for you. I want you to receive the pleasures I have received. I want you to think about what you read, and I want you to read things that incite hard thinking.

I remember that as a young boy, no older than six, I had been distinctly uneasy with a slim little volume called *Busy Timmy*. I took it personally. How, I wondered, could the author of *Busy Timmy*, a complete stranger, know so much about me: that I was able to tie my own shoes, that I was able to walk to school all by myself? With the same surprised uneasiness, now, I often wonder how Erich Maria Remarque could understand me so well, and Hemingway, too, and many other writers whose stories seem to expose to the world the secrets of my own heart. So, of course, *Busy Timmy* was an influence—a magical and lasting influence. *Bambi* was an influence. Daffy Duck was an influence. The influences, literary and otherwise, entwine and modify and abridge and qualify and finally fuse with one another. Updike modifies Hemingway, who modifies Shakespeare, who modifies "Hansel and Gretel."

Also, because it's important, I must mention that it was my father—a good man who himself was sometimes hard to find—who delivered *Busy Timmy* into my hands at an outdoor birthday party in the early fifties. It was my father who had taught me to tie my shoes. And it was my father who, in the years ahead, would fill me with mystery and dread of a much greater magnitude than anything inside "Hansel and Gretel." As clearly as I see the words I am typing at this instant, right now, I can see my father as he was sixty-some years ago. He is seated in a chair in our living room. Dark is approaching. Behind him is a lighted lamp. He's reading a book, and on his face there is such peace, such shocking contentment, that he seems to have become the younger and happier man I know only from yellowed photographs—an assistant hotel manager in Nassau, a clerk at the 1939 World's Fair, a chief petty officer looking lean and confident aboard a destroyer off Okinawa in 1945. The living room is still. It's winter, I think. It's twilight. My father is wholly focused on the pages of whatever that book might be. But not just focused, he is elsewhere, he is wherever the book has taken him, and he's delighted to be there, he's relaxed and half smiling and sober, and for a few seconds, as this image captures my attention and then forever impresses itself on me, I am seized by a fierce and impossible desire to *become* that book. I want to *be* those words. I want to *be* those pieces of paper. I want my father to look at *me* that way.

Do you not sometimes wish, Timmy and Tad, for a restore button on your life? I would take the risk. I would squeeze between the covers of that magical book.

Books themselves—the physical artifacts, the objects—are an influence.

———

A few months back, Meredith and I took our sons to an evening of modern dance. It was an outdoor performance, in a horse paddock on a ranch in central Texas, and the dance involved nine young women and a very large horse. There was a great deal of spinning in the dirt. There was swift running, much kicking, many horse-like movements of the head and shoulders. It was strange and very beautiful. At one point, midway through the performance, Meredith leaned over to Timmy and asked if he understood what the dancing was all about. Timmy said no. Meredith said, "Well, right now, for instance, that dancer over there, she's like a baby horse—a foal—trying to stand up for the first time. Can you see that?"

Timmy nodded. He looked puzzled.

"Well, yes," he said, "but what about all the *other* shenanigans?"

That word "shenanigans" caught my ear. I laughed. I'm still laughing. I vowed to deploy the word, somehow, someday, in a piece of writing. I have just done so.

For a writer, the word "shenanigans"—its sound, its sense, its collision against the artistry and spectacle of modern dance—is the sort of utterance that will occasionally find its way from lived life into a character's mouth, or will even sometimes lead to an entire story or novel. Out of nowhere a word will catch a writer's eye or ear—a common noun on a passing billboard, an unexpected epithet in a dispute overheard aboard a train. "All my life I've looked at words," Hemingway says, "as though I were seeing them for the first time."

In exactly this way, as I return to Hemingway's stories and novels, I am often stopped—in awe, in surprise, in confusion, in recognition, in delight, in contention, in envy—by a single word or phrase. For instance, in "The Short Happy Life of Francis Macomber," the writer in me is stopped by the word "plunging." Plunging—"the steady plunging gait" of a galloping bull buffalo. Plunging—"the plunging hugeness of the bull." Plunging. It is a conscious word choice; it appears three times on the same page. It is also a miraculous word choice. Search through a thesaurus, look diligently for that just-right adjective, and you will not type the word "plunging" unless by some similar miracle. It is, of course, the miracle of memory and imagination and close observation—that repetitive downward-forward motion of bone and muscle as the beast thunders across your field of vision. I stop and stare. I think: Forget the damned thesaurus. I think: Make the animal *your* animal and not someone else's. I think: Oh, Christ, I cannot under any circumstances, in any novel or in any story of my own, use the word "plunging."

That same limitation applies to the words "old sport," and to the word "fine," and to the words "by and by," and to the word "phony," and to the word "yes" if used more than three times in a sentence.

Similarly, in "The End of Something," I am stopped by the word "it" in this scrap of dialogue from Nick Adams: "It isn't fun any more." The "it" to which Nick is referring is his relationship with Marjorie. But "relationship" is a sterile and ugly word. And so too are other such nouns—affair, romance, togetherness, liaison, intimacy. (Imagine Nick saying, "Our togetherness isn't fun any more.") The pronoun "it," partly because it *is* a pronoun, seems to my ear entirely in harmony with the evasive, guilt-ridden, and slightly frightened sound of a young man telling a young woman "it" is over. The word "it" relieves pressure on Nick's tongue; the pronoun lightens the burden. If you have been in love, and if one day you are no longer in love, you understand—as Marjorie instantly does—all the beauty and horror that is embraced by a single heartbreaking pronoun.

To read as a writer is to read not only with attention to artistry.

It is also to read with jealousy, with ambition, with disputation, with rivalry, with fellowship, with fear, with hostility, with celebration, with humility, with proprietorial vigilance, with embarrassment, with longing, with despair, with anger, with defensiveness, with pity, and with a wolf's steady contemplation of its next meal.

It is true that a writer's reading will often have a keen aesthetic component, but it is also true that aesthetics will be amended by the ferociously personal and the ferociously human. In just this way, as I return for the sixth time in a week to "Cat in the Rain," I am confronted by bits of language that jerk me back sixty years, back to the image of my father reading a book by lamplight on a late winter afternoon. I'll look up from "Cat in the Rain" and then I'll look down again and read this: "She had a momentary feeling of being of supreme importance." Supreme importance! *That's* what I craved as a young boy! And then I'll read this: "George was not listening. He was reading his book." I admire the undecorated bluntness of this language. I admire the trust Hemingway places in his reader. I admire Hemingway's confidence in himself and in the declarative sentence. But what freezes me is this: I am a cat in the rain.

For everyone, I think, a single word can carry enormous power. If F. Scott Fitzgerald were to encounter the proper noun "Julian," surely a rusty floodgate would swing open in his stomach. Julian would not mean Julian. Julian would mean betrayal and fury and hurt. Or if one day you were to receive a postcard from San Francisco, where the love of your life is enjoying a two-week honeymoon with your old college roommate, I'm pretty confident that "San Francisco" will never again mean San Francisco, and that the word "postcard" will stop your heart as swiftly as any lethal injection.

Only a few sentences ago my own heart stopped. I had typed the word "confidence." My father's face flashed before me. And there he is. He stands aboard a destroyer off Okinawa, half smiling, so youthful, so sober and lean and confident. He's thirty-one years old. He will never die. Not at Okinawa, not ever. He's confident. He's confident in the way youth is confident. There is a scheme of things. There is tomorrow. There is the prospect of joy just down the street, foreverness just off the edge of the calendar. There is a heaven or a samsara or a patterned physics or an Oz or a never-never land or a "Somewhere over the Rainbow" or a something of the sort, and although my dad is in no way religious, in most ways profane, his youthful confidence in the year 1945 contains within it elements of faith and belief and a sense of purposive destination. It all *means* something.

In "A Clean, Well-Lighted Place," Ernest Hemingway uses the words "confidence" and "confident" five times within about two inches of printed text. As someone who frets over word choices with the neurosis of a scab picker, I'm confident that Hemingway was confident about the word "confident." I'm even more confident that he was far, far more confident than I will ever be when it comes to trusting one's own instincts with vocabulary. "Confidence" is the right word. It embraces, but is not limited to, the theological. It is inclusive, also, of an ordinary sense of personal worth. A confident chief petty officer. A confident insurance salesman. A confident young waiter in a well-lighted café. And beyond that, the word also comprehends negligence and forgetfulness; in youth, after all, it is easy to ignore the coming dark. And beyond that, the word implies at its very center some vague, ill-formed notion of truth, for without truth, or without some wispy approximation of truth, how could one have confidence in oneself or in the proposition that one plus one equals, and will forever equal, two?

All those decades ago, in the summer of 1957 or 1958, I took no notice of the words "confidence" or "confident." And if I had taken notice, which I did not, it would have been the sort of notice one gives to a relaxed, self-assured shortstop.

Now, with birthday number seventy near at hand, I'm beginning to understand what that waiter in Hemingway's story meant when he said, "An old man is a nasty thing." Confidence is eroded, and eroded confidence is unpleasant indeed. I awaken at three in the morning. I put on a baseball cap and do dishes in my underwear. I flit around in history—Vietnam, lost friends, love gone ugly, a little boy barricading himself in his bedroom out of fear of his father. I mumble in my head. I plot revenge. I rehearse bits of dialogue. I imagine the phone ringing with overdue apologies, the clever things I would say. Former drill sergeants receive scant mercy; Norman Mailer and his Vietnam-writer bullshit are sent packing. I talk to dead people. I revisit humiliations. At three in the morning, in my underwear, polishing the kitchen counters, I'm at an event in New York City, a literary event, and I'm surrounded by the famous and their many lieutenants—Vonnegut is there, Roth is there—and a cocktail party is in full swing, and I'm happy to be among the famous and their lieutenants here at the American Academy of Arts and Letters. I'm almost confident. I could be mistaken for one of them. But then to my lasting embarrassment I somehow cut my finger, which bleeds, and someone suggests I apply alcohol to the wound, and by terrible, terrible chance I'm standing within nine inches of an open bottle of Scotch, which I snatch up and into which I dip the bleeding finger—it was impulse, like this sentence—Christ, if that bottle of Scotch had been ten feet away, or two feet away, I would have surely had time to reconsider—but it was automatic, it was reflex, I wasn't a boor, I wasn't a moron—and at that moment, which has lasted forever, a fancy woman in a fancy dress, perhaps the wife of a famous composer, perhaps the grandmother of a Pulitzer Prize recipient, gasped. Dear Jesus. Dear Jesus for eternity. It's three in the morning. I *am* a moron. I watch helplessly as the bottle of Scotch is retired by a waiter—a young and handsome waiter—and twenty years later, at three in the morning, in my old-man underwear, I'm still trying to explain the impulse shit, the automatic shit, to a fancy lady in a fancy dress, who will hear none of it, not then, not now, not even after the passage of twenty excruciating years, no, the old biddy keeps gasping and glaring—she calls attention to my baseball cap as if it were part of the problem, the *cause* of the problem—she can't stop and won't stop proclaiming my hayseed sin to the handsome young waiter, who smiles his movie-star smile and keeps retiring that fucking bottle of Scotch, which never seems to retire, and this in the age of AIDS, this in the company of silver-haired *society*, this in the company of the accomplished and decorated and bejeweled and confident and beautifully mannered—Updike is there—and now at three in the morning, with the number seventy staring at me like Ted Bundy, I wonder if *this* is why I will never be at home in the presence of these unfailing exemplars of literary probity. Or is it just my crappy Vietnam stories? An old man is a nasty thing.

Seventy.

I will not see Tad's twenty-seventh birthday. I will not see Timmy's tears.

For me, as for my father, and as someday for Timmy and Tad and you, there is the burden of being human, which is the burden of consciousness, which is the burden of knowing that the lights will go out and that the café will close its doors.

27

The Language of Little Boys

Last week, Meredith asked Tad if he was prepared for an upcoming vocabulary test. "Sure," Tad said. "The words are already in my lexicon."

———

Why, I don't know, but Tad had been thinking about vocabulary from an early age.

"Why do cows go moo?" he asked as a four- or five-year-old.

"Because they have to," I said.

"But why do they have to?"

"Well, because it's the only word they know."

Tad thought this over.

"Did they learn that word in school?"

"Cows don't go to school."

"Well," Tad said, "they better try at least kindergarten."

———

As a vocabulary builder, back when Timmy and Tad were eleven and nine, we played a rhyming game as we lay in the dark at bed-time. I would toss out a word and the boys would take turns coming up with a word that rhymed. One night, the game went like this:

"Born," I said.

"Corn," said Tad.

"Torn," said Timmy.

"Worn," said Tad.

"Clown," said Timmy.

I hesitated and said, "Huh?"

"Clown," Timmy said. "You have to say it with an *r*, like you grew up in Canada."

"I don't think anybody in Canada says 'clorn,'" I told him.

"No," said Timmy, "but I bet they say 'porn.'"

———

Something had ignited my very, very short fuse one evening—maybe a newspaper piece, maybe a TV interview—and I was complaining to Meredith about how blithely and matter-of-factly people send other people off to war, and how nothing seems to stop it, and how useless my own books had been. "The only book that might do the trick," I said, "is one that shoots off your nose and lips and ears and tongue when you open it up."

Tad had been listening to this.

"I guess you shouldn't hold that book in your lap," he said.

———

Last summer, my longtime friend Richard Bausch, an accomplished novelist and short story writer, was scheduled to deliver a lecture to aspiring writers. The night before his talk, as our families dined together, Dick looked at my son Tad and said, "I don't know what to tell these people. I'm desperate, man. Give me some ideas."

"About what?" said Tad.

"You know—about how to write well."

"Sure," Tad said. "Let me think for a second."

The conversation went elsewhere for a while, and then Dick looked back at Tad.

"Learn grammar," said Tad.

"Excellent," said Dick. "Check."

"Be clear."

"Check."

"Be interesting."

"Check."

"Don't keep using the same word a million times."

"Absolutely. Check."

"Stop when you get to the end."

"Check," Dick said. "Hold on, I need to find a pencil."

———

Meredith was driving Tad to the dentist one afternoon. "All this traffic," Tad said. "Where exactly does it start?"

28

Home School

Back in the early 1990s, I received a letter from a twenty-six-year-old woman living in my home region of the American Midwest. I carried the letter with me for a long time, often reading passages aloud to audiences around the country. The letter was important to me. It made me feel things I had trouble feeling. But on a wintry night in Chicago, stepping out of a car, I stumbled. The letter was swept out of my hands and took flight down a dark and icy Michigan Avenue.

What a loss. Not just mine, but the world's.

The young woman's sentences had been so lucidly made, so carefully mortised, that the letter's final effect was as radiant and devastating as anything I had ever encountered. Even years later, although her letter is gone, I remember glittering bits and pieces with reasonable exactness, and the rest of it I remember the way I remember "Snow White," not the precise words, not every detail, but its modesty and its reflective tone and the flow of a very painful story.

In her opening pages, the young woman explained that as a little girl, around eight or nine, she had feared going to the dinner table. Night after night, her father would sit staring silently at his plate, the cords at his neck stiffening, his face reddening with a mix of sadness and inexplicable fury that to her was terrifying. The young woman's mother would make chitchat, trying to pretend, but then she too would fall silent. The tension—the danger—at that dinner table did not go away as the years passed. At one point, when the young woman was in middle school, she happened upon a small wooden box under a cot in the basement. In the box were relics of her father's history: a P-38 can opener, a pair of dog tags, a stripper's tasseled bra, a handful of military decorations, and a dented bullet casing. For the first time, the young woman realized that her father had once been a soldier and that she was living in a soldier's home. Later the same day, she dared to ask her father about the box in the basement. He shook his head. He made a joke. He shrugged and tried to say something but didn't. It was a house of few words; it was a house without emotional language. By the time she reached high school, the tensions between the young woman's mother and father had approached the intolerable. The girl felt more like a counselor than a daughter. And then one morning, not quite out of nowhere, her mother said to her, "You know, I've never really loved your father."

A moment passed. The girl said, "Why did you marry him?"

Her mother said, "I married him out of pity."

This is how it is, the young woman wrote to me, when your house burns down. This is how it is when the world ends. After a few seconds her mother explained that she had dated the girl's father for a very short time. He had then gone off to Vietnam. He had come home silent.

"How do you love someone," her mother said, "who won't talk to you?"

There was a bit more in the young woman's letter. The stresses multiplied, time went by, and then one day in her final year of high school, she was assigned a book called *The Things They Carried,* which she brought home and left lying on a coffee table. Her father picked it up and read a few pages, and at dinner that evening he said a few things, and the next evening he said more things, and then her mother said things and the girl herself said things, and in this way, very gradually, in fits and starts, a conversation began.

"What I wanted to tell you," the young woman wrote near the end of her letter, "is that this conversation hasn't ended—we're still talking ten years later. Of course, my mom and dad aren't perfect. They still have their problems. But they're *together.* And I don't think they would be if that book hadn't been lying on a coffee table so many years ago."

Essay Questions for Timmy and Tad

1. How do you feel about your own father's silences? (Ten points)

2. How can the narrator quote directly from a letter that was lost and never found? (Five points)
3. Can a book sometimes do things an author never intended? (Five points)
4. Will you ever go to war? (Eighty points)

29

Turkey Capital of the World

From the year of his birth in 1914 until the outbreak of war in 1941, my father lived in a mostly white, mostly working-class, mostly Irish Catholic neighborhood in Brooklyn, New York. He was an altar boy. He played stickball and freeze tag on safe, tree-lined streets. To hear my dad talk about it, one would've thought he had grown up in some long-lost Eden, an urban paradise that had vanished beneath the seas of history, and until his death a few years ago, he held fast to an impossibly idyllic, relentlessly romanticized Brooklyn of the 1920s and 1930s. No matter that his father died in 1925. No matter that my dad went to work as a twelve-year-old to help support a family of five. No matter the later hardships of the Great Depression. Despite such troubles, my dad's eyes would soften as he reminisced about weekend excursions to Coney Island, apartment buildings festooned with flower boxes, the aroma of hot bread at the corner bakery, Saturday afternoons at Ebbets Field, the noisy bustle along Flatbush

Avenue, pickup football games on the Parade Ground in Prospect Park, ice cream cones that could be had for a nickel and a polite thank-you.

Following Pearl Harbor, my father joined the US Navy, and soon afterward, without the dimmest inkling that he had stepped off a great cliff, he left behind both Brooklyn and his youth. He served on a destroyer at Iwo Jima and Okinawa, met my mother in Norfolk, Virginia, got married in 1945, and, for reasons unclear to me, set off with my mom to live amid the corn and soybeans of southern Minnesota. My mother had grown up in the area, but even so, why hadn't they chosen to settle down in a more exotic spot on the earth—the Cayman Islands, maybe, or along the coast of Maine, or virtually anyplace other than the repetitive prairies of southern Minnesota?

I showed up in October 1946, an early explosion in what would become a great nationwide baby boom. My sister, Kathy, was born a year later. In the summer of 1954, after several years in Austin, Minnesota, our family moved across the state to the small, rural town of Worthington, where my dad became regional manager for a life insurance company. To me, at age seven, Worthington seemed a splendid spot on the earth. There was ice skating in winter, organized baseball in summer, a fine old Carnegie library, a decent golf course, a Dairy Queen, an outdoor movie theater, and a lake clean enough for swimming. More impressively, the town styled itself Turkey Capital of the World, a title that struck me as both grand and peculiar. Among the earth's generous offerings, the turkey seemed a strange thing to boast about. Still, I was content for the first year or two. I was very close to happy.

My father, though, did not care for the place. It was too isolated, too dull, too pastoral, and too far removed from the big city of his youth.

He soon began drinking. He drank a lot, and he drank often, and with each passing year he drank more. Over the next decade he twice ended up in a state facility for the treatment of alcoholism. None of this, of course, was the fault of the town, any more than soybeans can be faulted for being soybeans. Rather, like a suit of clothes that may fit beautifully on one man but too snugly on another, I have come to believe that Worthington—or maybe the rural Midwest in general—made my dad feel somehow limited, squeezed into a life he hadn't planned for himself, marooned as a permanent stranger in a place he could not understand in his blood. An outgoing, extravagantly verbal man, he now lived among laconic Norwegians. A man accustomed to a certain vertical scale to things, he lived on prairies so flat and so unvaried that one spot could be mistaken for any other. A man who had dreamed of becoming a writer, my father found himself driving down lonely farm lanes with his insurance applications and a half-hearted sales pitch.

Then, as now, Worthington was a long way from Brooklyn, and not just in the geographical sense. Tucked into the southwestern corner of Minnesota—about twelve miles from Iowa, fifty-some miles from South Dakota—the town was home to roughly nine thousand people when our family arrived in 1954. For centuries, the surrounding plains had been the land of the Sisseton Dakota Sioux, but by the mid-fifties not much remained of that: a few burial mounds, an arrowhead here and there, and some borrowed nomenclature. To the south was Sioux City; to the west was Sioux Falls; to the northeast was Mankato, where, on December 26, 1862, thirty-eight Sioux were hanged in a single mass execution.

Founded in the 1870s as a railroad watering station, Worthington was an agricultural community almost from the start. Tidy farms sprang up. Sturdy Germans and Scandinavians began fencing in and squaring off the Sioux's stolen hunting grounds. Alongside the few surviving Indian names—Lake Okabena, Lake Okoboji—such solidly European names as Jackson and Fulda and Lismore and Worthington were soon transplanted upon the prairie. Throughout my youth, and still today, the town was at its core a support system for outlying farms. No coincidence that I played shortstop for the Rural Electric Association's Little League team. No coincidence that a meatpacking plant became, and remains, the town's primary employer.

For my father, still a relatively young man, it had to be bewildering and depressing to find himself in a landscape of grain elevators, silos, farm implement dealerships, feed stores, and livestock sales barns. I don't mean to be deterministic about this. Human suffering can rarely be reduced to a single cause, and my dad may have ended up with similar problems no matter where he lived. Yet, unlike Chicago or New York, small-town Minnesota did not permit a man's failings to go unnoticed. People talked. Secrets did not stay secret. My dad, whom I loved fiercely, was a town drunk. And for me, already full of shame and embarrassment, the humiliations of public scrutiny began eating away at my self-esteem. I overheard things in school. There was teasing and innuendo. I felt pitied at times. Other times I felt arraigned, tried, and convicted.

Some of this was imagined, no doubt, but some was as real as a toothache. One summer afternoon in the late fifties, I heard myself explaining to my Little League teammates that my dad would no longer be our coach, that he was in a state hospital, that he was sick, and that he might or might not be returning home that summer. I did not utter the word "alcohol"—nothing of the sort —but the mortification of that day still opens a trapdoor in my heart.

Decades later, my memories of Worthington are colored as much by what went on with my father—his increasing bitterness, the gossip, the midnight quarrels with my mother, the silent suppers, the vodka bottles hidden away in the garage and basement—as by anything having to do with the town itself. I began to hate the place. Not for what it was, but for what it was to *me*, and to my dad. After all, I loved my father. He was a good man. He was funny and intelligent and well read and conversant in history and a terrific storyteller and generous with his time and great with kids. Yet every object in town seemed to shimmer with an opposite judgment. The water tower overlooking Centennial Park seemed censorious and unforgiving. The Gobbler Café on Main Street, with its crowd of Sunday diners freshly invigorated by church bells, seemed to hum with rebuke.

Again, this was partly an echo of my own pain and fear. But pain and fear have a way of influencing our attitudes toward the most innocent, most inanimate objects in the world. Places on the earth are defined not just by their physicality, but also by all the joys and tragedies that transpire in those places. A tree is a tree until it is used for a hanging. A liquor store is a liquor store until your father almost owns the joint. (Years later, as a soldier in Vietnam, I would relearn this lesson. The paddies and mountains and red clay trails, all of it pulsed with the purest evil.) After departing for college in 1964, I never again lived in Worthington. My parents stayed on well into their old age, finally moving in 2002 to a retirement community in San Antonio. My dad died two years later.

———

A few months ago, when I paid a return visit to Worthington, a deep and familiar sadness settled inside me as I approached town on Highway 59. The flat, repetitive landscape carried the feel of eternity, a world without limit, the horizon bending away into foreverness just as our lives do. Maybe I was feeling old. Maybe, like my father, I was conscious of my lost youth.

I stayed in town only a short while, but long enough to discover that much had changed. In place of the almost entirely white community of fifty years ago, I found a town in which forty-two languages or dialects are spoken, a place teeming with immigrants from Laos, Peru, Ethiopia, Sudan, Thailand, Vietnam, Guatemala, and Mexico. More than forty percent of the town's citizens are Hispanic, many of them first-generation immigrants, and soccer is now played on the field where I once booted ground balls. On the premises of the old Coast to Coast hardware store is a thriving establishment called Top Asian Food; the Comunidad Cristiana de Worthington occupies the site of a restaurant where, long ago, I'd bribed high school dates with burgers and

French fries. In the town's phone book, alongside the Andersons and Jensens of my youth, I discovered such surnames as Ngamsang and Ngoc and Flores and Figuera.

All this startled me. What had once been true was no longer true. I had grown up inside a Sinclair Lewis story; I had returned to a story by Sandra Cisneros or Dagoberto Gilb.

The new, cosmopolitan Worthington, with a population of about thirteen thousand, did not arise without tensions, resentments, and serious assimilation troubles. During my chats with longtime residents, a number of them expressed nostalgia for the all-white Worthington of my youth. Their nostalgia was mostly bittersweet, but once or twice the sweetness disappeared. "You can't call it racism," said one old friend. "It's just that . . . like, you know, I can't understand a word my neighbor says to me; he can't understand me. It didn't use to be that way. I mean, how do you build understanding if you can't *understand* anybody?"

According to a county web page, the local jail hosts a hefty percentage of inmates bearing Spanish, Asian, and African names, and, as might be expected, non-Caucasians are rarely among Worthington's most prosperous citizens. Although the town's unemployment rate is low, wages are also low—substantially below the state average. At the local meatpacking plant, which employs about 2,400 wage earners, nearly a third of the workforce is Hispanic. The jobs there are grueling, monotonous, and often disgusting. (The blood-stink will suck mucus from your nose.) For many immigrants, I'm sure, any work is better than none, but no one is getting rich inside the plant where decades ago I stood trimming fat off pig jowls.

Altogether, in numerous ways, the town's transformation has mirrored that of America itself, sometimes smooth and uncontentious, other times bumpy and contentious in the extreme. Once or twice, race relations in Worthington have turned outright nasty.

In the summer of 2016, during a traffic stop, a young resident named Anthony Promvongsa, whose background is Laotian, was violently kicked and beaten by a local narcotics investigator while the young man was still strapped to his seat and putting up no resistance. A second officer stood watching. A police dashcam captured the incident on video, which later led to an ACLU lawsuit charging both officers with the use of excessive force. Also named in the lawsuit were the City of Worthington, the Worthington Police Department, and a regional narcotics agency called the Buffalo Ridge Drug Task Force. According to the ACLU, the 2016 assault—along with the town's subsequent failure to discipline the officers—was "part of a pattern and practice by the Worthington Police Department and the Buffalo Ridge Drug Task Force, who routinely fail to hold their officers accountable for their actions."

The senseless, animal brutality of the incident is shocking to behold on internet websites. But compounding the shock, at least for me, is that it occurred not in Los Angeles, not in the Bronx, but on the streets of *Ozzie and Harriet* country, in the Turkey Capital of the World, amid fields of corn and soybeans, in a landscape as bland as a slice of Wonder Bread, within striking distance of a dozen or so well-attended churches, and not far from the Benevolent and Protective Order of Elks.

I stayed that night in a motel on the outskirts of town. In the morning, after pancakes at a Perkins restaurant off I-90, I made the seven-minute drive to the first of two houses in which I'd lived during my years in Worthington.

I was alone in a rented car. I was feeling very lonely.

Except for the watchful presence of the kid I used to be, there was no one with whom to share my thoughts. Worthington had become a place populated by people as distant and unknown to me as the citizens of Pago Pago. Several old friends were now dead. Almost all others had fled for Minneapolis or wherever else soybeans did not grow.

I pulled over and parked in front of 1018 Elmwood Avenue. The house of my youth remained pretty much as I remembered it: tiny, low-slung, not quite ugly.

Oddly, or maybe not so oddly, I had trouble looking at the place; I'd steal quick glances, look elsewhere, then glance back again. Here, inside an undistinguished rectangle of nothingness, my dad's late-night drinking had made the shift from now-and-then to all-out-and-always. And it was also here, in the hours after midnight, that I had lain awake listening to my mother's weeping and my dad's bitter yelling. I was a third-grader then. I was terrified. None of it made sense to me, especially the angry words that did not carry meaning for a third-grader. The word "bitch" was one. The word "divorce" was another.

Now, in the car, I smoked a couple of cigarettes, composed myself, eventually opened the door, and got out and stood in the center of Elmwood Avenue. It was just after 9 a.m. There was no traffic at all. The morning was sunny and motionless. Across the street, behind a row of much nicer houses, lay the velvety seventeenth green of the Worthington Country Club, where, as a fourth-grader, I had sold glasses of lemonade to golfers worn down by hole after hole of frustration. My buddy Mike Bjerkesett and I worked the lemonade stand as a tag team, sharing the toil and the booty through hot summer afternoons back in the early fifties. Most evenings, after dusk had fallen, Mike and I strapped on our helmets and played soldier out among the sand traps and water hazards. Mike was now among the dead: a terrible car accident, decades of paralysis, then suicide. Though he never knew it, and though it won't help him now, my old lemonade pal had found his way into *The Things They Carried*, where I still hear his voice in the character of Norman Bowker.

A few blocks away, the model for another character once lived, a little girl named Lorna Lou Moeller, who, decades later, was transfigured into a very similar (though not identical) little girl named Linda. Linda and Lorna Lou are also dead. They died at age nine. Brain tumors. And so too with Mike Tracy, another early acquaintance who ended up in the same book under the name Nick Veenhof. This Mike—the second Mike—had been a mixture of bully and thug and occasional sweetness. After graduating from high school, Mike joined a motorcycle gang in the Twin Cities; a few years later, he was shot dead in a dispute with a rival gang. His funeral made big news in the Worthington *Daily Globe*. More than 150 motorcycles roared into town, filling the parking lot of a Presbyterian church, and, in an irony that would've tickled him, bad-boy Mike Tracy, troublemaker Mike Tracy, hopeless ne'er-do-well Mike Tracy, was dispatched into eternity with the celebrative renown of a war hero.

In a way, as I stood in front of 1018 Elmwood Avenue, these and other people from my youth seemed to be there with me. In fact, they *were* with me, just as your own dead father is with you during moments of remembrance. Not the body, but surely something. An absent presence, maybe, or a present absence.

———

For the remainder of my stay in Worthington, I visited a half-dozen other familiar places, each altered by time but each also twinkling with the afterglow of history. I stopped in front of the high school, at the band shell in Chautauqua Park, and near a field of soybeans that still stirred happy memories. I drove twice around Lake Okabena. At one point, as I sat with the engine running on the town's main street, I was struck by how stupid I had been not to bring Tad and Timmy on this return journey. I wanted them to see what I was seeing. More than that, I wanted them to feel at least a little of what I was feeling.

In part, probably like many people of my age, I was under the melancholic spell of a long-delayed and long-feared homecoming. For decades, I had borne a knotty, cancerous grudge against this place. I still did. The citizens of Worthington, Minnesota, had sent me to war, and I took it personally, and I took it personally because it was personal. Back then, in August of 1968, there was not yet a national draft lottery. Luck was not yet an issue. Mathematics did not yet govern. In those grim days just prior to the Democratic convention in Chicago, hometown draft boards did the dirty work. One father chose another father's son to go off to the other side of our planet and kill people and maybe die. Or it was *that* housewife and no other housewife—a housewife with a name, maybe Helen, maybe Dorothy—who circled the name of another housewife's fresh-faced little boy—or a man who had very recently been a little boy—and then, after the circling was done, it was that living, breathing circler of names who scurried off to Wednesday-night bingo or Friday-night church suppers or Saturday-night square dancing. How monstrous, I'd once thought. How monstrous, I still thought. Circle the name of your *own* darling son. Circle your *own* name. Circle the name of your precious daughter and your husband and the guy in the cowboy hat calling your Saturday-night square dances. And if you're so hot for war, what the fuck are you doing in Worthington, Minnesota? What the fuck are you doing choosing other people's kids to fight a war you're unwilling to go fight yourself? I used to yell these things, and many similar things, as I drove around Lake Okabena with a yellow draft notice in my billfold, and if Timmy and Tad were here, and if a Vietnam replay were in progress, I'd be yelling again and yelling louder and never shutting up—I'd be yelling at Tuesday-night country club socials and at Thursday-night meetings of the PTA—and if they don't like the word "fuck," they could get off their hypocritical asses and go do some killing and dying of their own, and if they don't get killed, if they just get wounded, they can lie in some filthy rice paddy and mutter to the Methodists, "Oh, darn, I shouldn't have drafted myself."

This fury may eventually go away. I hope not.

But as I sat looking out at a Worthington that was no longer Worthington, it became plain that my lifelong bitterness, though still present, had been noticeably softened—even a bit shrunken —by an emotional fuzziness that was brand new to me. I didn't —and don't—have a name for it. A creepy feeling, but creepy was not the word. A kind of dread, but dread too was not the word. In part, I guess, the buzzing fuzziness in my head had to do with a realization that what happened to my hometown was also happening to me. We were both old and getting older. Nothing had endured as it once was. Out on 10th Street, the town's main drag, the faces of passersby were mostly brown or black, a big change from forty years ago, and of course my own face had undergone some dramatic changes over those same forty years. And just as the names in the town's phone book had been replaced by new ones, so had my own name—I had been Timmy back then, and now I was not. Nor, beneath the old-man skin and the abbreviated new name, did I resemble the 1953 or 1968 version of myself, so confident in my moral rectitude, so certain of my courage, so naïve and ridiculously romantic about what the world would deliver to me. On the plus side, I suppose, I could no longer hate the way I used to hate. I had to work at it. But neither could I love the way I used to love—lemonade stands and playing soldier and Lorna Lou Moeller and my father and myself and the future. It wasn't that love was gone—it certainly was not gone—but love's urgency seemed diminished, and its immediacy now seemed vaporous and far less promising. "Getting old," my dad once told me, "is like sitting too long at a blackjack table. You hear the math chewing away at happy endings." Then, a second later, stone sober, he said, "But what can an old guy do? Cashing in is suicide. It's forever."

I'm pretty sure he thought about it. I'm pretty sure he thought about it for decades.

———

Around noon, as my final stop, I pulled up in front of 230 11th Avenue. Before me was the house in which my parents had lived from 1960 until they checked into a retirement home a quarter century later. Here I had spent my high school years. Here my father's alcoholism had gone from bad to horror. This was my hanging tree.

For a while I just sat in the car, half hoping for some closing benediction. The day was still sunny, still weirdly silent. I didn't know what I was doing there or what I was waiting for. Maybe a ghostly glimpse of my dad. Maybe the two of us playing catch on a summer afternoon. But of course he was gone now, and so was the town I grew up in.

30

Pride (III)

As I've discovered to my discredit, a father's pride involves the abandonment of reason, sometimes unconsciously, other times just shooing it away. A reasonable man, for instance, might acknowledge to himself and to others that his children have their weaknesses and their strengths, their successes and their failures. A reasonable man can certainly cheer as his son's three-pointer drops into the basket, but he might also leaven his joy by recalling the boy's six or seven previous bricks and air balls. Likewise, as a graduating daughter delivers her valedictory oration, a reasonable man might be expected to bear in mind that all across the country on that bright June day, thousands of other valedictorians are delivering their own earnest and mind-numbing orations.

I have reluctantly concluded that fatherly pride, my own included, requires a kind of temporary insanity. Not necessarily the raving, froth-at-the-mouth kind, but rather the sort we display on the Fourth of July as we celebrate our nation's virtues and eradicate its shortcomings. Few Fourth of July speeches touch on slavery. Few dwell on Jim Crow laws, lynchings, robber barons, McCarthyism, My Lai, the fate of the American Indian, the Mexican-American War, secret bombings, or the deaths of a few million Vietnamese.

These omissions, as with a father's omissions, are understandable. Who but an ingrate would sabotage his country's birthday party? Who but a lying liberal would insist on fidelity to fact? And who but a terrible father would catalog his child's vices as the birthday gifts are unwrapped and as the candles are blown out?

The pride we take in our country and in our children may well rank high among the seven deadly sins. But if pride is a sin, it is the hiccup of sins. It is not a committed sin. It commits itself. It is an unsought, unbidden, and frequently unwelcomed condition of being, and it is a crime only to the extent that mental illness is also a crime.

Still, we feel pity for the insane. We do not burst our prideful buttons inside a lunatic asylum.

It's the button-bursting that has me worried. As if propelled by rocket fuel, I'm launched into mindless delight at Tad's successful navigation of a third-grade spelling quiz. I cannot stop talking about it, not with friends, not with strangers: how a seven-year-old hula-hooper spelled "equilibrium" even while his father cannot seem to grasp the word's essential meaning. So what if Tad keeps inserting a *z* in the word "miserable"? So what if a million other seven-year-olds have correctly spelled "equilibrium"?

The unseemly thing about pride, I tell myself, is not its in-voluntary presence, not the reflexive hiccup or two, not the oc-casional burst of joy, but rather its unfiltered, unrestrained, and unqualified public expression. As Sophocles wrote in his great tragedy *Antigone,* "Zeus hates the noise of a bragging tongue." A modest half-smile may be forgiven; a top-of-the-lungs "Bravo, Tad!" may not be. Restraint of expression—the containment of madness—is in part what distinguishes the Gettysburg Address from the music of John Philip Sousa. It's not that I don't love a good tuba. It's not that I begrudge a country its fireworks. But a prideful, chattering, immodest father is no more tolerable than the forgotten piety of Edward Everett or the disagreeable harangues of any black-and-white, all-or-nothing, crown-thy-good patriot. "America the Beautiful" sounds great against purple mountains and fruited plains. It may sound not so great against a backdrop of dead children at Wounded Knee or Washita or My Lai. Again, no offense. But might not, and should not, a reasonable man seek ways of acknowledging virtue without ignoring vice?

If delusion is part of pride, and if the erasure of reality is part of delusion, the association of pride with madness is not as far-fetched as I had imagined before becoming the father of Timmy and Tad. A major tributary to pride is the love we feel for the sub-jects or objects of our pride—love of country, love of children—and I am not alone in believing that love too can have aspects of the deluded, the unreasonable, and the outright nuts. "Crazy," Patsy Cline crooned a few decades back. And a few centuries be-fore Patsy, another reputable songster noted in *Romeo and Juliet* that love "is a madness most discreet, / A choking gall and a preserving sweet." In the centuries between Cline and Shakespeare, plenty of other balladeers and poets and heartsick novelists have bewailed (and sometimes celebrated) the abandonment of reason in the name of love. It continues today with every quarter turn of the radio dial (Bono, U2). Only a few minutes ago, somewhere in the English-speaking world, Jack said to Jill, "Hey, I'm crazy about you."

My point is not that we should lock up fathers and patriots and Romeo and all the other madness-afflicted lovers of the world. Straitjackets are not the answer. Instead, what has been pestering me over the past several weeks is that I am in danger of becoming what I most despise: a shameless hypocrite, a zealot, a reality-obliterating Fourth of July tuba player, a man blinded by his own pride and love, a man who would fly an airplane into the Twin Towers for the sake of Timmy and Tad, just as others would do the same in behalf of Allah or Yahweh or the unconditional surrender of Japan. I would kill for love, and I would kill out of perverted pride. It's crazy, I realize, to think that my children are more sacred or more deserving of life than those I would kill to defend them. How could a reasonable man believe so? But then the answer screams at me down the ages—*because they are mine!*—which is the scream that has been screamed by children-loving madmen for three thousand children-slaughtering centuries.

I'm ashamed. I should be ashamed. Up to a point, fatherly pride is cute, something to chuckle about with other proud fathers, but when it intersects with religious and political and cultural pride, it can and often does become murderous.

Consider the poet Wendell Berry: "How many deaths of other

people's children by bombing or starvation are we willing to accept in order that we may be free, affluent, and (supposedly) at peace? To that question I answer: None. Please, no children. Don't kill any children for my benefit."

Consider Gandhi, who reputedly said: "There is no such thing as 'too insane' unless others turn up dead due to your actions."

Just a moment ago, I opened a desk drawer and pulled out a photograph taken in 1969 in a village along the coastline of Quang Ngai Province. A vanished version of me squats beside a Vietnamese girl of maybe seven or eight. I'm smiling a compassionate, beaming, children-loving smile. The girl is also smiling. All is peaceful. My weapon is slung over my left shoulder.

This photograph, with its Norman Rockwell innocence, could hang in the Pentagon as an advertisement for the benign, pure-hearted, rescue-the-world values of the American soldier and of America itself. Next to it, however, a second image appears. This is a memory photograph, and in it there is another Vietnamese girl, a bit older than the first, but the second girl lies dead in a rice paddy. The right side of her face is gone. Her mouth is open. One eye is half open. She had been caught in the middle of a two- or three-minute firefight. Moments earlier, during that short exchange of gunfire, I had fervently intended and hoped to kill, mostly because I was terrified, mostly to stop people from killing me, but as always there had been no visible enemy, only trees and bushes on the far side of a rice paddy, and so I had fired without aiming—without so much as the thought of aiming—just hosing down the whole green world before me. When the firefight ended, no one in my company had been injured. We found no enemy bodies and no blood trails. There was only the dead little girl. For a while I thought nothing. Then, after a second, I thought: Well, the world must be a better place. Because that's what wars are *for*, right? That's why we kill one another. To make the world a better place: "madness made of logic, principle turned frenzy" (Sophocles again). These thoughts were in no way cruel or callous. They were bitter thoughts. I hated myself. At that instant, as I looked down at the dead girl, the world did not seem any freer, any happier, any more democratic, any more just, any more tolerant, any more civilized, any more decent, any more loving, or any less endangered than it had seemed a few minutes earlier. The world felt evil. And I had made it more so. I had gone to the war and participated in the war out of the purest pride. To safeguard my reputation as a good son of America. To avoid small-town censure. To avoid ridicule. And so I had hosed down the green living world, and a little girl lay dead in the sunlight, and now my reputation-loving, ridicule-fearing pride was intact for some future Fourth of July. How can I, or we, celebrate such evil? How can the tubas keep playing? Madman pride—that's how.

31

Pacifism

Lately I've been worrying that Tad and Timmy might someday want to follow in my footsteps as a soldier, ending up dead or in a wheelchair. And so, at dinner one recent evening, I told them that I neither expected nor desired any such thing. "Just because I do something," I said, "doesn't mean you should do it."

"Like smoking?" Timmy said.

"Excellent example."

"Or like swearing?" said Tad.

"Right. Another good example. I mean, what if your father happened to be a bully? Would you start beating up teachers?"

"Not too badly," Tad said. "Not like you."

A couple of years back, out of the blue, Timmy asked if I considered myself a pacifist.

"Yes," I said. "Unless some terrorist or burglar broke down the door and threatened to hurt you."

"What would you do?"

"Anything," I said.

"Even kill the guy?"

"Well, first I'd try to talk to him."

"But what if the guy's totally crazy and really mean?" said Timmy. "What if he has a gun or something? Would you try to kill him?"

"I guess so," I said.

Timmy looked at me for a second. "What kind of pacifist is *that*?"

"The father kind," I told him.

32

Timmy and Tad and Papa and I (II)

It is June 20, 2016, and today Timmy becomes a teenager. What I've feared for thirteen years has occurred: my son knows he will not have a father one day. Sometimes he forgets what he knows, but he does know.

Back in 2003, when the first frail lines of these love letters were written, I had wanted simply to tell my infant son that he was adored by his father and that I yearned to be with him forever, always present, despite knowing that it cannot and will not happen. Biology is implacable. Hearts go still. And now Timmy's thoughts are where mine had been in 2003. He has noticed that the fathers of his friends are a generation younger than I am. He has noticed my deafness and gray hair, my Swiss-cheese memory, my difficulties on the basketball court.

Twice over the past several months the boy has come to me crying. He can't sleep. He goes over the horror in his head. He knows exactly what time knows. Timmy, too, will be a cat in the rain.

I don't know what to say to him, but I say, "Yes, I know."

June 28, 2016, just after 6 a.m., and Tad turned eleven a few hours ago.

I've been at my desk since just before 3 a.m. I sat down with the intent of writing a few lines to present to him as a little gift, not just for this birthday but also for birthdays to come, when he turns seventeen or twenty-one or twenty-seven.

But what a struggle. Stop. Start over. Stop. The sentences are filled with goo and I'm ready to cash out. Permanently, I mean. Toss this bitch computer out the window and move to the Arctic and buy an igloo and enjoy the freeze. Hemingway had it right: "There is nothing to writing. All you do is sit down at a typewriter and bleed."

So, Tad, here's my beautiful and profound literary gift. It's the best I could do. Happy birthday.

My father was born in Brooklyn, New York, on February 28, 1914; he died in San Antonio, Texas, on August 10, 2004. His name was Bill O'Brien. (In his youth he was called Willie.) Children loved him. He loved children. He was fun and he was funny.

He spent hours throwing baseballs to me. He spent numerous Christmas Eves assembling model trains and Erector sets and Tinkertoys I would never play with. He presented me with large stacks of books from the public library. He sang beautifully. He read constantly. His eyes, unlike mine, were blue and backlit. He was a good man. I loved him and idolized him, but I was sometimes afraid he was going to kill me, and during my grade school years I crept into the kitchen late at night and removed the sharpest knives from a drawer and hid the knives beneath my mattress. I barricaded my bedroom door. I invented an alarm system with string and two little bells. But then the police came to get him. In the Turkey Capital of the World, surrounded by Lutherans, he sat in his favorite reading chair and swore at the police while my mother cried. I was eleven or twelve. This was the summer of 1957 or 1958, the summer during which my father had carried that fat book into my bedroom, the summer when the police came, two of them, to protect my mother and my sister and my brother and me, to protect us from my father, my unrequited love, who swore in embarrassment and in terrible fury in his favorite reading chair in our tiny living room as the police coaxed and said sir and as my mother cried—it was she who had summoned the police, it was she who had committed my father to an institution for the treatment of alcoholism, and it was she, too, who was afraid of my father—and so the police took him away and he vanished again for many more weeks that summer. He was treated for alcoholism. The treatment didn't take. He came home, he tried, except it was chemistry, and things went on in our tiny house as they had gone on before and as they would go on for decades afterward, until he became an old man.

If you have read "The Doctor and the Doctor's Wife" by Ernest Hemingway, or if you have read "My Old Man," you have felt something—not enough, but a little—of what I felt when the police came to get my father and when my little-boy life caught fire.

On the day my father died, having lived to the age of ninety-one, I was awakened near dawn by Meredith, who gently delivered the news. I said something like—although this is not precisely what I said—"Okay, thanks," and then I went back to sleep. I had been imagining that news since I was a kid, just as my own son Timmy is now imagining the news for himself. I had imagined going insane. I had imagined crawling into my father's coffin. But I went to sleep. It was not denial. It was not a means of escape. I was sleepy.

A writer of stories does not only write about the world as it is, but also about the world as it almost is or as it could be or as it should be. In the days just before my father's death, I could've and I should've driven the lousy seventy miles to a hospital in San Antonio. I could've and I should've taken my father in my arms. I could've and I should've said, "Dad, I love you so much." I did not. But in a story, miracles can happen. In a story, my father can sit up from the dead and take me in *his* arms. In a story, he can say, "That's okay, I *know* you love me."

Sentimentalism, I guess, but the alternative is silence.

———

The critics don't care, Hemingway once noted, if you're a good father. Readers don't care either. Not at midnight, not as a last page is turned. Good fathers and good fishermen and good citizens and good anything—the reader doesn't care, and can't care, not as that last page is turned, because the reader is inside the story, exhausted by too much drink and too many dead bulls and too much longing for what will never be, which is partly the story Timmy and Tad will find inside *The Sun Also Rises*, but which is also the story they will find inside their own lives, not exactly, but inexactly, because they will absorb the story and then carry it with them into their own love affairs and their own longings for what will never be. That is why I want to talk to them now about Ernest Hemingway and some pretty abstract things about telling stories. I care about these things. I want my sons to understand what their dad cared about, and what he worried about, as he tried to write his own stories. The ordinary reader, who may not be interested, is invited to skip the next several pages. My children, however, are required to keep going.

What if I were to say there is no Timmy and there is no Tad? And what if I were to say I had no father? I would be lying, of course. There is a Timmy, there is a Tad, and I did have a father. Lying, yes, but telling the truth. The Bill O'Brien and the Timmy and the Tad in these pages are not people. They are not living creatures.

To the best of my knowledge, the only way to put people in a book is to make a very large book and stock it with food and drink.

Here, as the reader encounters them, Timmy and Tad and my father are type on a page. I have tried to portray them fairly and accurately, but in doing so I have omitted virtually everything. I have included only that which is necessary. And so it always is for a writer: almost everything is subtracted. Although I am attempting at the moment what is called "nonfiction," and although everything I have written in these pages is pretty true —true in the sense of "happening truth," true in the sense that these things were actually said and were actually done—despite that, despite actuality, I am nonetheless at the mercy of memory. Yes, Timmy *did* utter the word "shenanigans." Yes, my father *did* enter my bedroom bearing a fat, heavy-looking book on a hot summer afternoon in the late 1950s. But faulty memory, or the passage of time, or both, or something else, has erased the detail. What had I been thinking or doing in the instant before my bedroom door swung open? I have no idea. It's purely gone. It's so purely gone, it never was. All of us, writers more than most, are left with the cruel and taunting illusion of memory. What we call memory is failed memory. What we call memory is forgetfulness. And if memory has failed—failed so colossally, failed so apocalyptically—how can we pretend to be faithful to it? How can we pretend to tell the truth? Is one small fraction of the truth the truth? Memory speaks, yes. But it stutters. It speaks in ellipses.

Again, how much of yesterday do you really remember?

And further, how much do you remember of March 23, 1998? Do you remember your worries that day, your daydreams, your meals, your conversations—all of them, *any* of them?—and do you remember if you cried, and do you remember picking out a head of lettuce at the Safeway, and do you remember that knock-out cashier to whom, in rapt fantasy, you devoted a precious portion of your life?

We lose our lives as we live them. Memory is a problem. Even more of a problem, much more, is that I am also at the mercy of my abilities as a writer, and at the mercy of recalcitrant, never-quite-right nouns and verbs. I am at the mercy of the bullying word "nonfiction," which prohibits make-believe. I am at the mercy of my endurance, and at the mercy of my estimation of your endurance, and at the mercy of the demagogic rhythm of a sentence, and at the mercy of a spectacular image just off the tip of my imagination.

What is important to me in all this, and what makes me seem to digress, although I'm not, is the problem of moving from actuality to art and from art to actuality. If it's so treacherous to seek "real" people in the pages of nonfiction, then how much more treacherous must it be to seek "real" people in the pages of fiction?

"Cat in the Rain" is an example. (Read it, Timmy. Read it, Tad.) The story can be—and often has been—interpreted through the lens of history. Hemingway's wife Hadley becomes the "American wife" of the story. Hemingway becomes the story's husband, George. In the world of real people and real events, which is the world in which the story was conceived, Hadley had been responsible for the loss of Hemingway's sacred manuscripts; there was tension over that loss; there was Hadley's guilt and there was Hemingway's despair and emptiness. On top of that, still in the world of actuality, we know that Hadley discovered she was pregnant around the time Hemingway first took notes for the story, in February of 1923, and we know that Hemingway later bemoaned the pregnancy to his mentors Ezra Pound and Gertrude Stein. He believed he was too young for parenthood; he believed his career and his art and his time to make art were in jeopardy. We know that Hadley very much wanted a child. We know that Hemingway very much wanted publication. There were other marital strains, too, among them financial worries, the age difference between wife and husband, and Hadley's well-documented generosity of spirit in collision with Hemingway's frankly declared ambition.

Given these facts of the actual, real-world world, who could be surprised that "Cat in the Rain" has been received by critics through the lens of history? The facts tell their own spellbinding story. If "Cat in the Rain" is lifted from, and explained by, the actual, lived-in world, is not the story incidental to the history? Is not the story a pathetic substitute for the real deal? Who needs "Cat in the Rain"?

Ernest Hemingway famously denied that his story was about Hadley. "'Cat in the Rain' wasn't about Hadley," he wrote to F. Scott Fitzgerald. "I knew you and Zelda always thought it was." Maybe Hemingway was being disingenuous in his letter to Fitzgerald. Maybe he was writing in haste. Maybe he had been drinking. But there is also the possibility that he was telling his friend the precise truth as he knew and understood it: "Cat in the Rain" was not about Hadley, nor about Rapallo, Italy, nor about lost manuscripts, nor about anything else of the actual, lived-in world.

In Hemingway's defense, but also in defense of anyone who has toiled over a short story or a novel, I wonder if a piece of fiction had partially replaced reality—or created an additional reality—in the author's memory. As words go onto paper, including the proper noun "George," images appear in a writer's head, and those images are as vividly real to the writer as anything in the so-called real world. Hemingway could *see* the imagined George. He could *hear* George's thoughts. The proper noun itself—the mere naming—instantly distances a writer from his own being. The proper noun creates *otherness*. Type the word "George," and Hemingway isn't quite Hemingway, and you, the author, aren't quite you. Type the words "the American wife," and Hadley is a mile away. Add an adjective, add an adverb, and she's half a continent away. Add a made-up detail, maybe a bit of dialogue, maybe a wart on her nose, maybe a nervous laugh, maybe a trip outside to pick up a wet cat, and Hadley is no longer on or of planet Earth. She has vanished completely, and the author is now in the company of a new and separate living creature, and the creature is not Hadley.

In this sense, the storyteller's imaginative labor can be described as the willful obliteration of self and as the willful replacement of self with a piece of art. Knocking on Faulkner's door: "It is my ambition to be, as a private individual, abolished and voided from history, leaving it markless, no refuse save the printed books . . . He made the books and he died." And it was Faulkner, too, who described his life's work as an effort "to create out of the materials of the human spirit something which did not exist before."

For a writer of novels and stories, the real and remembered world combines with imagination, and that combination combines with language, and that combination combines with the inner eye and the inner ear and the inner heart to produce wholly new, wholly individual, and wholly unique spirits in the head: an American wife who is not Hadley and a husband named George who is not Hemingway and a story called "Cat in the Rain," which is completely and only about itself. And although the story may well have been launched out of real-world pain, and probably was, it is still the case that lost manuscripts and unwanted babies were transmuted into a new dream reality titled "Cat in the Rain."

————

As a personal matter, I want Timmy and Tad to know what was happening in their father's head during those hours when I sat writing in my study all evening. I left one kind of reality behind. Including you, Timmy. And you, Tad. It was a kind of betrayal, I suppose, but both of you disappeared for a while, and your mom disappeared, too, and so did I. Fact blurred into fiction and fiction blurred into fact. For all of us, but especially for a writer of stories, memory fades, and reality fades with it, and the imagined people and events in my stories became, over time, as real as reality, just as my dreams are real, and just as your dreams are real, because they *are* real, for who in the history of our planet has ever dreamed an unreal dream?—the dreamed dream, *your* dream, is a *real* dream, is it not? For my part, as I travel at light speed toward the grave, I realize that my collision with Vietnam occurred half a century ago. It's almost all forgotten. It's not even a dream. The names, the faces, the shaggy little villages, the endless sweeps of obscenity and monotony and humidity and greenery, the endless terror, the endless uncertainties—will I die here, will I die there, will I die with the next step or the next step or the next?—the land mines, the scary firefights—those long and numbing marches up into the mountains and down into the paddies and then up again into the mountains, the pranks, the horseplay, the ghosts, the nights, the mumblings of the freshly dead, the things I thought, the things I said—it's almost entirely gone—all those unoccupied ticking seconds of my life that had once been so intensely occupied—gone and gone forever—as gone as a soap bubble winking out at the bottom of a sink—as gone as my father is gone and as gone as I will be gone—and now, especially at night, my made-up stories are what I have instead of memory.

This, as nearly as I can express it, represents my experience— and, I suspect, Hemingway's experience—on the contested frontier between actuality and story. For the writer of fiction, there is enormous fear of biographical determinism. Determinism of any sort, but particularly biographical determinism, seems in the writer's view to demean and sometimes to deny the faculty of imagination, which for the writer is where stories get made. Artistic playfulness cuts against determinism. As does whimsy. As does a sentence's insistent call for musicality. As does a character named Jack, let's say, who, completely unbidden, suddenly blurts out a marriage proposal to a baffled duck. What do we do with miracles? What do we do with the inexplicable? Do we comb through history in search of love-sick ducks?

Even these early-morning sentences, including this one, represent the limitations of biographical determinism. The literary historian and the writer see differently. The historian cries, "There is your father!" and the writer cries, "There is *your* father!"

And so, Timmy and Tad, if a man is defined at least in part by the things he thinks about, these are among the thoughts I've been thinking in those hours when I should have been thinking of you.

33

Home School

Our lesson for today is titled "Outrage." The bullet points for discussion are these:

1. If you support a war, go to it.
2. Unless, of course, you support a war only to the extent that other people — but not you — should die and kill.
3. If you speak out in behalf of a war, put your blood where your belligerence is.
4. Unless, of course, you don't mind the word "hypocrite."
5. Dead bodies are heavy and awkward to carry. Also, the smell of death can be unpleasant. This is the case even if the dead are very freshly dead.
6. The death-smell will one day be pumped into the nostrils of those who support wars. It's only fair. It's the Golden Rule. Therefore, inhaling the death-smell will become a popular fad among Christian war apologists.

7. Unless, of course, Christian war apologists support war only insofar as they will neither go to it nor smell it.

8. One day, also, television networks and internet providers will offer photographs and video clips of war casualties, twenty-four hours a day, nothing else, just the dead and the mutilated, and this programming will become an overnight sensation among those who cry out for war.

9. Unless, of course, they cry out for wars that they will neither visit nor smell nor look at.

10. A bullet can kill the enemy.

11. A bullet can manufacture an enemy.

12. If your bullet strikes a father's child in the head, you have manufactured an enemy.

13. The ratio of dead children to manufactured enemies, however, is never one-to-one. Each child also has a mother. Maybe an uncle, too, and a brother, and a doting grandmother, and a few cousins and sisters and playmates. The Pentagon will one day generously agree to provide a daily ratio of enemies killed to enemies manufactured.

14. Blowing up houses also manufactures enemies, especially if the blown-up house is yours. The Pentagon will be factoring this statistic into its future daily summary.

15. Is violence practical? It's obvious, isn't it? Behold the tranquility and democracy and neighborliness and justice and religious tolerance and civility and concord and quiet streets of the Middle East. Impressive, yes? All this was accomplished after only a decade and a half of people

killing people. Fifty years ago, this was called "light at the end of the tunnel."

16. If you become a father one day, Timmy and Tad, and if you support a war, encourage your son and daughter to shoulder a weapon and take their chances in battle. Better yet, insist. Don't tuck them away at Iowa State.

17. If you support a war, Tad, stop bitching about your tax bill. You asked for it. You begged for it. Last night at the Rotary Club, your rhetoric got expensive.

18. And Timmy: if you support a war in the present day and age, it would not hurt to know the actual differences between Shia and Sunni Muslims. It would not hurt to locate Iraq on a map.

19. If you despise those who publicly object to wars, you despise Abraham Lincoln, who publicly and firmly objected to the Mexican-American War.

20. Think this over, Timmy, and then give me your best answer: If it is morally okay for your country to torture its prisoners of war, is it therefore morally okay for your country's enemies to do the same to our captured troops?

21. And you, Tad: If it is morally okay to target and assassinate leaders of al-Qaeda and ISIS, is it therefore morally okay for al-Qaeda and ISIS to target and assassinate our own leaders?

22. Also, if it is morally okay to put on public display the corpses of Saddam Hussein's sons, is it therefore morally okay for our enemies to put on public display the corpses of America's sons and daughters?

23. Is not war the large-scale equivalent of one man saying to another man: "I am so civilized, and you are so barbaric —I am so virtuous, and you are so evil—I am so God-loving, and you are so devilish—I am so rational, and you are so irrational—I am so right, and you are so wrong— that I am going to kill you"?

24. In the case of Vietnam, 3 million people died, and last month at a ritzy private high school, I was asked by a per-plexed young student, soberly and earnestly, "Who won?"

25. Three million dead people, and I have been quizzed, over and over and over, in colleges, in big-city auditoriums: "What was it all about?"

26. Three million dead people, and how many of us think about Vietnam at all?

27. And who wakes up each day and thinks, "Thank God for the Vietnam War"? Does anyone? And if we don't wake up thanking God for the Vietnam War, why all the dead people?

28. And who really cares about the war dead other than those who loved them?

29. Who wails over the 20,000 dead in the Ragamuffin War?

30. Who grieves for—or who celebrates—the estimated 30 million dead during the Mongol conquests?

31. Who gives a passing thought to the 25 million dead dur-ing the Qing conquest of the Ming Empire?

32. Who has even heard of the Taiping Rebellion and its esti-mated 20 million dead?

33. For that matter, who knows a single objective fact about

the Dungan Revolt (around 8 million dead), the Reconquista (5 million dead), the An Lushan Rebellion (13 million to 36 million dead), the Huguenot Wars (about 2.8 million dead), the Moorish Wars (about 3 million dead), the Yellow Turban Rebellion (about 4.5 million dead), the Indian Rebellion of 1857 (800,000 dead), the Second Sudanese Civil War (1 million to 2 million dead), the Panthay Rebellion (890,000 to 1 million dead), the Paraguayan War (300,000 to 1.2 million dead), the Cimbrian War (410,000 to 850,000 dead), or the Kitos War (440,000 dead)?

34. If we know nothing about these and other wars, how *can* we care? And if we, the inheritors, cannot care, what is the lasting moral outcome of an estimated 488 million wartime deaths over the recorded history of our planet?

35. Outrage, Timmy and Tad, is ferocious caring. But caring comes hard for all of us. We go icy inside. We accept the murderous daily headlines. Out of fatigue, perhaps, we abandon our own humanity. We offer a quick "Thank you for your service" and then hustle back to the Packers game or to Grand Theft Auto.

36. My hope for you, Timmy and Tad, is a life of outrage.

37. We will resume our lesson tomorrow, perhaps discussing a single episode from a single war—maybe the Bataan Death March, maybe the battles of Lexington and Concord. Afterward, we will continue to contemplate the topic of outrage for what remains of my life with you.

34

Home School

Today, Tad and Timmy, we will consider a tiny slice of your country's history, a single night followed by a single long day. We will do so in considerable detail. I do not apologize for this, because history *is* detail, not swift synopsis, and because when it comes to people killing other people, the devil lives within and feasts upon the dirty details. Also, when the Fourth of July rolls around, I want you to know a little something about what it is you are celebrating and at what cost your celebration was made possible. People died so you could watch the parades go by, so you could run through the dark with your sparklers sparkling, and so you could ooh and aah at the night sky opening up with color. Finally, history is not only a record of other human lives, but it is also a record of your own lives, Timmy and Tad, because you were conceived in history and dwell in history and will one day return to history. Please focus.

It's a good story. And there will be a bit of homework once we have concluded.

Here we go—

———

Around nine o'clock on the cool, starry night of April 18, 1775, some 700 British grenadiers and light-infantry troops were roused from their encampments on Boston Common, Boston Neck, and the warehouse barracks near Long Wharf. Groggy and half asleep, many of the men with no sleep at all, twenty-one companies of redcoats found themselves tramping through the town's narrow streets to an assembly point on a small beach at the foot of the common.

Mutterings and complaints filled the chilly dark. Why so much secrecy? Why the late hour? Why couldn't the king's army ever do things in a plain, straightforward way?

At about ten o'clock, under a nearly full moon, the men began boarding twenty longboats that had been brought to shore from war vessels anchored nearby. A detachment of British sailors lashed the boats together and began rowing the troops across the Charles River basin to a swampy landing area at Lechmere Point in East Cambridge. The crossing was a bungle from the start. Insufficient boats were on hand, which required a tedious shuttle operation, each boat making the mile-long passage and then returning to the Boston shore to pick up more troops.

Among the soldiers, as always, there was surely grumbling. The military's centuries-old clusterfuck had taken hold. Units that had been separated during the landings now had to be located and re-assembled. Provisions had to be loaded aboard longboats, ferried to the Cambridge shore, and handed out to the men.

Altogether, the crossing ate up nearly three hours. By one o'clock in the morning, after all their troubles, the British regulars had traveled barely a cannon shot's distance from their encampments back in Boston.

And then, typically enough, things went from bad to miserable. Moving out into the dark, the column followed a dirt road that occasionally dipped down into marshes and tidal inlets. Already cold and weary, the troops found themselves wading through icy, thigh-deep waters, struggling under sixty pounds of gear—muskets and ammunition and haversacks and bayonets and woolen coats and cooking utensils and water bottles and rations.

It was approaching two in the morning. The twenty-mile march to Concord had just started.

———

Some things never change.

Close my eyes and I'm there again: an evening in early May of 1969.

The foxholes had been dug, the trip flares and claymores were out, and we were watching the last sparks of twilight do magic over the mountains to the west. It had been a difficult day. The usual bullshit—rice paddies and sullen villages—and all we wanted now was a decent night's sleep.

Except this was a funhouse called Vietnam.

At full dark, around 2100 hours, Alpha Company received orders to saddle up for a search-and-destroy operation in a string of villages along the South China Sea, about nine or ten kilometers from our night encampment. We were already zeroed out on sleep. Now we would be getting less than none at all.

Quietly, in the spongy dark, we went through the familiar rituals. Checking weapons. Strapping on the rucksacks and ammo and canteens and flares and grenades and helmets and mess kits and radios and numerous other odds and ends.

The weight was enormous. And, of course, there was the war, too, which had its own mass and density. I had been in-country only a couple of months, but Vietnam was already a stone in my stomach. I hated the place. I hated myself for being there. Beyond that, as a purely practical problem, we were caught up in a confusing and deadly civil struggle. No front, no rear, no clear battle lines, no clear military purpose, no way to distinguish friend from foe. The enemy was everywhere and nowhere, vanishing into tunnels and popping up behind us and then sliding away again. We didn't know the language. We didn't know the culture. We didn't know where we were at any given time or why we were there.

Now, saddled up for a night march, Alpha Company began plodding east into the Vietnam dark, at times following a narrow clay trail, other times sloshing through thick, knee-deep rice paddies. Nearly three hours passed. I remember sticky wet heat, mosquitoes everywhere, a leaden numbness in my feet and thighs. Humping, we called it, which meant the endless march, soldiering with our legs. This was the infantry, now and always, the legions of Caesar and the columns of Napoleon, one step and then another and then another.

At one point, on the far side of midnight, we skirted a small sleeping village. Orders were passed down to keep quiet—the place was bad news, the VC owned it. I remember one of my buddies glancing over his shoulder at me, making a funny face, as if to say, "What's *not* bad news?"

It took a half hour or more to maneuver around the tiny ville. I remember a dog barking, a gauzy yellow moon, and how oppressive the night was.

For a long, empty time, we kept slogging on. I was terrified, of course, but in another sense, nothing felt real. Fatigue dulled the senses. A strange fogginess seemed to swirl through my thoughts, except my thoughts were not really thoughts, just scraps of thought. Moving slowly, trying for silence, we trudged on toward the South China Sea, a company of donkeys, stiff and mechanical and dumb.

———

The expedition of 700 British troops passed quietly through parts of what is now Somerville, waded across Willis Creek toward Union Square, and then turned almost straight north toward Cambridge. At Massachusetts Avenue the column swiveled right and followed the road in a northwesterly direction into present-day Arlington. The town (then called Menotomy) had long been asleep. Here and there a few candles burned in houses along the road.

It was now close to three-thirty in the morning. Counting the river passage and several long waits, the weary troops had been on the move for more than six hours. Most had been without sleep for nearly a full day. Still, they kept grinding forward, loaded down with drums and flags and leather boots and ammunition pouches and ten-pound firelocks.

By now rumors of their destination had trickled from man to man: a prosperous little farming town called Concord. The unit's commanding officer, Lieutenant Colonel Francis Smith, had been issued orders to proceed "with the utmost expedition and secrecy to Concord, where you will seize and destroy all artillery, ammunition, provisions, tents, small arms, and all military stores whatever." Oddly, though, Smith's orders did not include stipulations regarding the possibility of armed resistance, despite signs that hostilities might break out at any moment. Earlier sorties into the countryside had led to confrontations with angry colonists, each side posturing and baiting the other, and for weeks there had been compelling evidence that the Provincial Congress was preparing for outright war.

Almost certainly, then, Colonel Smith had at least discussed the possibility of resistance with his superior in Boston, General Thomas Gage, the man responsible for conceiving the plan of action for April 19. Gage himself had predicted the details of an armed rebel response. "Should hostilities unhappily commence," he wrote, "the first opposition would be irregular, impetuous, and incessant from the numerous Bodys that would swarm to the place of action, and all actuated by an enthusiasm wild and ungovernable."

The 700 British regulars had to be wound tight as they tramped through the dark toward Concord. Up ahead, a few warning shots rang out. Later, outside Menotomy, a British patrol trotted up on horseback to report that some 500 armed colonists had assembled on the green at Lexington. A dispatch rider named Paul Revere had been captured. Prudently, Colonel Smith sent back a message to Boston requesting reinforcements from General Gage—a message that would later save his force from annihilation.

In fact, only seventy-five to eighty colonists were waiting at Lexington, but the exaggerated report did not reassure the oncoming British troops. For months, they had been garrisoned in Boston under conditions of growing unrest and hostility. The port had been shut down to commerce; rebel leaders Samuel Adams and John Hancock had gone into hiding; the self-declared Provincial Congress had formed a Committee of Safety with the power to "alarm" and "muster" local militia. More ominous yet, the rebel Congress had recently authorized the creation of a regular army, organized into formal regiments and battalions.

The ordinary soldier is not stupid. He may be illiterate, but he knows danger when he sees it.

Foot-weary and back-weary, the twenty-one companies of British regulars had every reason to feel edgy as the first ripples of sunrise spilled out to the east. The men were largely untested in battle. Some had been on the North American continent only three months, others six or seven months. They did not know the terrain, or the back roads, or the stone walls, or the paths across pastureland, or the likely sites of ambush. They had no artillery support and no means of resupply. They carried only thirty-six rounds of ammunition apiece. Worse yet, the 700-man column was composed of units that had never operated together. Companies had been drawn willy-nilly from various regiments, a patchwork led by officers with unfamiliar habits and routines.

Around five in the morning, with dawn spreading out fast, the column approached the outskirts of Lexington. Six light-infantry companies were sent ahead under the command of Major John Pitcairn.

On the town's green some seventy-five or eighty colonial militiamen waited.

At that point, as the British advanced, a kind of gravity took command—exhaustion and frayed nerves. As always, time collapsed and history squeezed itself into an instant.

———

In 1970, six months after returning from Vietnam, I arrived in Cambridge to begin graduate studies at Harvard University. In many ways, the war was still with me. Any sudden noise would fill my belly with acid. Other times, without much reason, I'd feel the need for a nice deep foxhole, a place where I could curl up and close my eyes and wait for forgetfulness.

Talking about the war just wasn't possible. I could speak, yes, but I couldn't say anything. I did not know where to start or where to stop or which story to tell. And who wanted to hear about it anyway?

At some point during those first weeks in Cambridge, I happened upon a map tracing the British route from Boston to Concord almost two hundred years earlier. The sheer distance startled me: some forty miles there and back. I remember showing the map to a friend, trying to explain how dreadful that long march must have been, just the labor alone, and how mere mileage did not take into account all the detours and countermarches and flanking movements, nor the cold swamps at Lechmere Point, nor the fear, nor the feel of a ten-pound firelock in your hands, nor the weight on your back and shoulders and spine, nor the spiritual burdens, nor the drudgery, nor the spookiness of a march through Indian country, nor the inarticulate drone of your mortality.

My friend gave me a pleasant nod, but he didn't seem to feel what I was feeling. It was asking too much.

In a backdoor way, no doubt, I was trying to say something about my own war, and about the ordeal of foot soldiers in any war. Even without much detailed knowledge, I identified with those British troops. The parallels seemed obvious. A civil war. Faulty intelligence. An enemy without uniforms. A distrustful, often hostile rural population. A powerful world-class army blundering through unfamiliar terrain. A myth of invincibility. Immense resources of wealth and firepower that somehow never added up to a happy ending. A sense of bewilderment and dislocation. Cultural haughtiness. Overconfidence gone sour. Smugness replaced by terror. A tough, homespun, ragtag enemy that for years had been grossly underestimated. Growing frustration and rage at guerrilla tactics —the constant sniping, the deadly little ambushes.

Down inside, in some deeply human way, I had more in common with those long-dead redcoats than with the living men and women all around me. I felt like a member of a mysterious old brotherhood—all that shared knowledge and shared terror. I could hear British boots on the road. I could hear my own boots. The circumstances were not identical, of course, but identical was not the point. The point was how much I had in common with 700 men tramping through the dark two hundred years ago. We were walking targets. We were conspicuous in our fine uniforms. We kept humping. We endured it all. And so somewhere in my stomach, or in my dreams, Vietnam and Battle Road intersected and began to merge into a single ghostly blur across history.

———

At Lexington that morning, eight colonists lay dead or dying. No one knows, or will ever know, who fired the first shot. What seems certain is that Major John Pitcairn called on the rebels to lay down their arms, that at least some of the militia began dispersing, that the British infantry continued to press forward, and that a single shot rang out. In quick succession, without orders, British troops fired two sharp volleys. One colonist was bayoneted to death. Others were killed or wounded as they sought cover. At that point, although Pitcairn signaled for a cease-fire, the dawn was full of gunfire. According to one eyewitness, the British regulars "were so wild they cou'd hear no orders."

Altogether, it lasted only a few minutes, but a terrible inertia had taken hold. One volley led to the next. Ordinary field discipline collapsed. In various measures, the first bloodshed that day can be traced to the rawness of the troops, to the hodgepodge composition of their units, and to the unfamiliar leadership of

Major Pitcairn. Ultimately, though, the causes were pedestrian. History is made not only by plan or policy, but also by fear and fatigue and adrenaline.

The fight at Lexington was lopsided. The colonists suffered a 23 percent casualty rate: eight dead, nine or ten wounded. Only a single British soldier had been injured.

When it was over, at roughly five-thirty in the morning, the British formed up and resumed their march toward the small town of Concord off to the west. An exuberant, almost heady confidence filled their ranks. They had received only the lightest resistance at Lexington, none of it lethal, and they had swiftly routed an assemblage of farmers and merchants. For weeks, they had openly ridiculed the rebels, using language of contempt. One British officer sneered at the colonists' deficiencies of "patience, coolness, and bravery." Another officer, commenting on an incident only a month earlier, had expressed amusement at the rebels' lax discipline: "They got 2 pieces of Cannon to the Bridge and loaded 'em but nobody wou'd stay to fire them."

For the moment, the redcoats' scorn for the colonists seemed justified. There were hurrahs and thumping drums. There was singing.

But the 19,000-man Massachusetts militia was no pushover. Drilled and trained by competent officers, organized into 47 formal regiments, the colonial force far outnumbered the British troops stationed in Boston. In addition, the Provincial Congress had recently developed a new rapid-deployment system called "the minute men," by which a full quarter of the militia had been assigned to units capable of responding "at a minute's warning" to any emergency. The towns and villages of Massachusetts had been directed to provide each minuteman "with an effective fire arm, bayonet, pouch, knapsack, thirty rounds of cartridges and balls, and that they be disciplined three times a week, and oftener, as opportunity may offer." Moreover, on the early morning of April 19, 1775, the rebels had the formidable advantages of nearby reinforcements, an intimate knowledge of the region's roads and woods and fields, and a smoldering—now boiling—indignation at years of perceived British tyranny, corruption, and arrogance. Most powerfully, however, the colonists were now stirred by outrage at the one-sided casualty count in Lexington. Politics aside, men will kill for revenge.

For five more miles, the twenty-one companies of redcoats toiled through the early-morning hours, and it was close to eight in the morning when the column finally marched into Concord. The men had been roused from their Boston encampments eleven hours earlier. They had come twenty hard miles. Now, the most difficult moments of their lives lay ahead.

———

I remember crossing the Diem Diem River late in the night, turning north for a time, then back to the east. We did not know where we were, exactly, or the names of the villages we passed, or where the enemy might be, or which trails were mined and which were not, or how the night would end. The moon was still up there, still gauzy yellow, but now it seemed to cast no light at all, and for short bursts of time I lost touch with myself, as if another guy had suddenly occupied my boots, some dumb dipstick who let himself get drafted and ended up here in this tropical killer-dreamscape. I tried counting my steps. I tried pretending I was elsewhere.

A chunk of eternity swept by, then another chunk, and then I smelled salt. Somewhere ahead was the South China Sea—maybe a mile, maybe a step or two.

Not much later, in a silvery gray predawn light, we stopped along a paddy dike outside a hamlet that lay hidden behind trees and thick brush.

We waited for a time. Officers conferred. We waited a little longer, then two platoons circled around to the far side of the village, and a few minutes later, after another wait, the rest of us formed into a rank and moved across the paddy and into brush surrounding the village.

Off to my left, as we pushed forward, I heard a muted, almost gentle-sounding thud. There was an instant of silence. Automatic gunfire then picked me up, or seemed to pick me up, and threw me, or seemed to throw me, headfirst into the dark. I remember spinning sideways. I remember men yelling. A great noise exploded between my eyes, which was the sound of my own weapon, and then everything else became crawling and squealing and hoping to stay alive.

I'm not sure how long it lasted. Not long.

Later, we found two dead VC. One was a boy, maybe fifteen, but maybe not a VC, maybe just fifteen. The other's age was impossible to guess.

We spent another half hour in the ville, searching for weapons, then we straggled off toward the next village of the day.

———

In Concord that morning, Lieutenant Colonel Francis Smith divided his expedition into three parts. Six companies were dispatched to seize the North Bridge outside town and then to proceed to a nearby farm where the provincials were suspected of storing military supplies. The second unit marched west to capture and hold another bridge. The bulk of Smith's command remained in Concord itself, where troops began searching for hidden weapons, gunpowder, and other provisions.

It was just after nine in the morning.

North of town, on a ridge overlooking the Concord River, about 300 militiamen had already gathered under the command of Colonel James Barrett, a local farmer. Warned of the British approach, the colonists had already relocated most of their supplies, and now they stood glaring down at the detachment of six redcoat companies holding the bridge below. After a short while, three of those companies continued across the bridge and headed up a narrow road toward the Barrett farm. The remaining three British companies—between 90 and 100 men—took up positions on and around North Bridge. For the first time that day, raw numbers swung in favor of the colonists. Armed militiamen were still streaming in from Acton, Lincoln, Westford, Littleton, Groton, Stow, Chelmsford, Bedford, and Carlisle. The 300 angry colonists soon became 400, then closer to 500. For the British troops waiting below, there was the pinch of unpleasant arithmetic. Captain Walter Laurie, in command of the British detachment at North Bridge, estimated the total provincial force to be about 1,300—an exaggeration not unknown among officers in my own war. As the rebel force strengthened, Laurie rushed a request for reinforcements back to Colonel Smith in Concord. But requests are only requests: a rider had to be dispatched, Smith had to be located, the request had to be approved, orders had to be issued, reinforcing units had to be scrabbled together, officers had to arrange and straighten the ranks, and tired men had to move by foot from Concord to North Bridge.

Meanwhile, north of town, Captain Laurie's 100 or so redcoats eyed a growing force of rebels only a few hundred yards away. Neither Laurie nor the militia commander, James Barrett, seemed willing to initiate hostilities, and except for an accident of history, things may well have ended there—a standoff. But around nine-thirty, rebel gun carriages and heavy cannon were discovered in Concord. Hastily, Smith's redcoats put the carriages and other supplies to the torch, and plumes of black smoke were soon rising high over the town. Among the militiamen about a mile away, there were rumblings that Concord itself might be razed and burned. (In fact, British troops were trying to extinguish fires that had spread to the town's meetinghouse.) Colonel Barrett, a Concord native, met with his officers and instructed a regiment to advance down to the bridge. According to one colonist, "We were all ordered to load, and had strict orders not to fire till they fired first, but then to fire as fast as we could."

Hostilities were now nearly inevitable. On both sides, retreat was out of the question.

Quickly, as the militia pressed forward, Captain Laurie brought his three redcoat companies to the Concord side of the bridge. He had little room to maneuver. A few planks were torn up; flanking units were sent out along the riverbank. "By this time," Laurie wrote, "they were very close upon us." With battle imminent, it is doubtful that the British responded with amused or disdainful comments about an enemy refusing to stand and fight. "They halted for a considerable time, looking at us," Laurie wrote, "and then moved down upon me in a seeming regular manner." Another British officer described the rebel force as "very military" in its bearing and comportment.

If discipline broke down at all, it was among Laurie's own men.

Badly outnumbered, tense and weary, the British troops watched the colonists approach to within fifty yards. A moment passed, and then, almost at the same instant, several redcoats fired without orders. Two militiamen fell dead; two or three others were wounded. Slowly at first, then rapidly, the colonists returned fire at almost point-blank range.

Within seconds, more than a tenth of the British force at North Bridge went down under intense musketry. Half the officers were hit—four out of eight. Three privates lay dead or dying. Five others were wounded.

The much-celebrated professionalism of the British army evaporated. Orders went unheeded or unheard. Standard infantry tactics were abandoned.

According to Lieutenant William Sutherland, himself among the wounded, "Captain Laurie desired the men to form a line to the right and left of the bridge, and the soldiers to keep up their fire. I jumped over the hedge into a meadow just opposite to the enemy as they were advancing to the bridge and beg'd they [his own men] would follow me . . . which only 3 or 4 did."

The redcoat resistance was feeble at best. Captain Laurie exhorted his troops to stay steady, but the men soon broke and ran "in spite of all that could be done to prevent them."

It was the beginning of a bloody, headlong retreat that would last another twenty miles, another nine or ten excruciating hours.

For the British, their opponents were "demons," or "devils," or "savages."

For us, in Vietnam, they were "dinks," or "slopes," or "gooks."

Today, they are "ragheads," or "camel jockeys," or worse.

The enemy is never wholly human. Never civilized, never virtuous, never honorable or righteous.

The enemy is barbarous, and we are not.

The enemy is fanatical, and we are not.

The enemy is godless, and we are not.

"What do you get," went the joke in Alpha Company, "if you breed VC with rats?"

Midget rats.

"Sneaky little critters," a tired old master sergeant once said. He was going home; he'd had enough. "I mean, hell, they don't even got the nuts to duke it out, they don't never barely stand up. Like snakes or something. Slither around and stick their fangs up your ass and then slither away."

Snakes. Rats. Devils. Demons.

The enemy isn't human, and we are.

Easier to kill a rat than a man. And afterward, easier to sleep at night.

In Vietnam, much as the British had two hundred years earlier, we viewed the enemy with a bizarre mixture of contempt and awe. Ridicule suddenly became terror. A rat suddenly became a demon. Moreover, again like the British in 1775, we hailed our army as the most powerful and proficient on the planet. We were the inheritors of Patton and Eisenhower and MacArthur. No vitamin deficiencies. Good bones, good teeth, good all-American genes. And if genes didn't do the trick, there was always the glorious fruit of American industry, the choppers and jets and napalm and five-hundred-pound bombs and scrambler radios and starlight scopes and endless crates of ammunition, C rations, and whatever else the doctor ordered.

The typical VC carried a rifle, two or three magazines of ammunition, maybe a pouch of rice.

We chuckled at this, and then later we didn't.

Contempt and awe, ridicule and astonishment—these dizygotic twins have coexisted in armies down through the ages, and the same double-sided image of the enemy lived on in Alpha Company during the month of May 1969 as we made our way from one hostile village to the next along the South China Sea. Roy Arnold was shot dead. Chip Merricks and Tom Marcunas were killed by a rigged artillery round. Several others, whose names I didn't know, were badly wounded by gunfire. A kid named Clauson, whose first name long ago escaped me, was wounded by a homemade VC grenade. There were others, too. It was a terrible time. In a way, all these years afterward, it's as if none of it ever happened, but in another way, it's still happening and will never stop. I remember the dust-off choppers settling down, and how we carried our casualties aboard and then stood back and watched the helicopters lift off and dip their noses and bank out over the South China Sea. In those moments I'd imagine grabbing a skid, hanging on tight, and taking a long, high ride out of the horror. Maybe others in Alpha Company found comfort in the same fantasy. I don't know.

Either way, we saddled up and plodded on—more villages, more dead, more wounded. The sniper fire never seemed to stop. We took fire from tree lines, from bamboo hedges, from the banks of the Tra Bong River, from paddy dikes, from pitiful little hooches out on the Batangan Peninsula, and yet through all that, we had very little to shoot back at. The VC were ghosts. It was their land, and they knew it well, and they disappeared without ever appearing.

Partly we were terrified, but we were also full of tight, hot payback fury, especially as the dead and wounded were choppered away.

At one point in mid-May, diving into a ditch, I somehow lost my glasses, and instantly, as if a gas burner had been turned on, a searing rage bubbled up inside me—my goddamn *glasses*—and it was those lost glasses, or my own incompetence, not just the endless gunfire, that made me truly and dearly want to kill and keep killing. I remember crabbing around in the ditch, full of fury, yelling at God and the war because I couldn't find my goddamned glasses.

In different ways, we all felt it. Sometimes there were jokes, which was one way of feeling it. Mostly, though, we felt it in less pleasant ways. Shooting dogs and water buffalo, for instance. Calling in the Cobras and jets and artillery, for instance, and watching things burn.

———

About noon on April 19, 1775, the British expedition began its long march back to Boston. With flankers off to each side of the road, the column retraced its route back toward Lexington, now shadowed by militia units along a ridge just to the north. A mile or so outside Concord, at a road junction called Merriam's Corner, the militia took up positions behind stone walls and farm buildings, waiting for the British to cross a narrow bridge to their front. According to a militiaman, "As soon as the British had gained the main road and passed a small bridge near the corner, they faced about suddenly and fired a volley of musketry upon us. They overshot, and no one to my knowledge was injured by the fire. The fire was immediately returned by the Americans, and two British soldiers fell dead at a little distance from each other in the road near the brook."

In total, eight redcoats lay dead or dying. Not a single colonist had been hurt.

Heartened by ineffective British fire, the militiamen ran ahead to establish new positions along the road to Lexington. At a place called Hardy's Hill, five full companies of provincial soldiers opened up on the redcoat column, killing two, wounding several others, while at the same time, to the rear, snipers and small groups of colonists kept up a steady harassing fire.

The pressure of superior numbers had begun to tell. In the woods and fields, everywhere, fresh militiamen from surrounding towns were arriving to swell the American forces. At a spot that would later be known as Bloody Angle, two hundred provincials triggered a savage ambush that killed eight British soldiers and wounded about twenty more. Confusion and terror filled the British ranks. They had been trained to maneuver in formal alignment, standing upright in tidy rows, and now they were both horrified and enraged at the colonists' Indian-style tactics.

"They did not fight us like a regular army," wrote an anonymous redcoat, "only like savages, behind trees and stone walls, and out of the woods and houses."

The same soldier complained that the provincials were "as bad as the Indians for scalping and cutting the dead men's ears and noses off."

Reports—and rumors—of atrocity were not unfounded. Earlier in the day, at North Bridge, a young colonist had used his hatchet to finish off a wounded redcoat, badly maiming the man. Accounts of the incident, perhaps embellished a bit, had circulated among the British rank and file. "The rebels fought like the savages of the country," wrote a British officer, "and treated some, that had the misfortune to fall, like savages, for they scalped and cut off their ears with the most unmanly barbarity. This has irritated the troops to a very high degree."

It was more than irritation. It was revulsion.

Later in the day, as British casualties mounted, the "scalping" episode became a justification for revenge—what we called payback in Vietnam.

Stumbling along, carrying their wounded, terrified and half dizzy with fatigue, the once-elegant British column seemed to disintegrate under ceaseless rebel musketry. Two more regulars died in a field of boulders along the road. Minutes later, members of the Lexington militia triggered an ambush that killed four British soldiers and wounded several others—among them the expedition's commanding officer, Colonel Francis Smith.

At a spot called Fiske Hill, still another rebel ambush ended with eight more British dead.

Low on ammunition, virtually surrounded by a mostly invisible enemy, the expedition was now in danger of annihilation. Discipline had collapsed. Troops began to break and run. A British ensign, John DeBerniere, would later write: "We at first kept our order and returned their fire as hot as we received it, but when we arrived within a mile of Lexington, our ammunition began to fail, and the light companies were so fatigued with flanking that they were scarce able to act, and a great number of wounded scarce able to get forward . . . A number of officers were also wounded, so that we began to run rather than retreat in order. We attempted to stop the men and form them two deep, but to no purpose, the confusion increased rather than lessened."

Eventually, DeBerniere wrote, British officers were forced to threaten their own troops. "The officers got to the front and presented their bayonets, and told the men if they advanced they should die."

By then, 25 British soldiers had died, dozens more were

wounded, and organized resistance had almost entirely ceased. Worse, if worse can be imagined, 2,000 militiamen had converged on Lexington, with other fresh provincial units waiting along the road ahead. The unthinkable seemed minutes away—perhaps surrender, perhaps slaughter.

———

It's odd how the mind subdues and sometimes erases horror. Now, after almost fifty years, not much remains of those terrible days in May 1969. My company commander bending over a dead soldier (or was he wounded?), wiping the man's face with a towel. A lieutenant with a bundled corpse over his shoulder like a great sack of birdfeed. My own hands. A patch of rice paddy bubbling with machine-gun fire. The rest is a smudge of trails and tangled foliage and trees and red clay soil and land mines and snipers and death. I know what happened in a factual sort of way—the way other people know they attended kindergarten and learned to ride a bicycle —but it's intellectual knowing, abstract knowing, not memory knowing. I do recall, though not vividly, that Alpha Company moved like sleepwalkers through chains of sullen, near-deserted villages, always shadowed by an invisible enemy. I know we took turns running across a bridge while under fire, but I don't remember *doing* it, just the relief of making it across the finish line. I remember calling in numerous dust-offs, probably a dozen or more, but I don't remember my voice or my words or where I was or who needed each dust-off or how I was able to speak at all. I can't see much. I can't feel much. Maybe erasure is necessary. Maybe the human spirit defends itself as the body does, attacking infection, poisoning those malignancies that would otherwise destroy us.

Still, it's odd.

My own war doesn't quite belong to me.

In a peculiar way, at this very instant, the ordeal of those British troops more than two centuries ago has an animate, living clarity that seems more authentic than my own experience. Maybe that's what history is for. Maybe that's why people started writing things down two thousand years ago. To remind us. To give us back our lives.

––––––

In Hollywood, a troop of cavalry would have galloped to the rescue. In Lexington, it was the appearance of almost a thousand fresh British troops under the command of Brigadier General Lord Hugh Percy.

Accompanied by two cannon, Percy's brigade had marched out of Boston after receipt of Colonel Smith's plea for reinforcements. It was a coincidence of history, almost a miracle, that Percy's command arrived very near—or precisely at—the moment of collapse. An officer with Smith's expedition would later write that without reinforcements "not one of us would have got into Boston again."

Under Percy's skilled direction, using cannon fire to keep the rebels at bay, the combined British force regrouped and began moving out of Lexington at about three in the afternoon. At that point, members of Smith's expedition had been without sleep and on the move for eighteen hours, and as a consequence, even with fresh troops, the retreat was slow, laborious, and lethal. British lieutenant Frederick Mackenzie reported afterward that large numbers of armed colonists "were continually coming from all parts guided by the [gun]fire, and before the column had advanced a mile on the road, we were fired at from all quarters, but particularly from the houses on the roadside, and the adjacent stone walls. Several of the troops were killed and wounded in this way."

In fact, Mackenzie understated things. The fighting soon became some of the most vicious of the day, with flanking companies racing through fields and backyards to dislodge rebel sharpshooters. Over the next four miles, the British suffered another sixteen casualties.

Everywhere, in the fields and woods and all along the road, provincial resistance remained disciplined and deadly. These were more than "embattled farmers," and Lord Percy later went out of his way to debunk the condescending stereotype:

> Whoever looks upon them as an irregular mob,
> will find himself much mistaken. They have men
> amongst them who know very well what they are
> about, having been employed as Rangers [against]
> the Indians & Canadians . . . Nor are several of their
> men void of a spirit of enthusiasm, as we experienced
> yesterday, for many of them concealed themselves
> in houses, & advanced within 10 yards to fire at me
> & other officers, tho' they were morally certain of
> being put to death themselves in an instant . . . For

my part, I never believed, I confess, that they would have attacked the King's troops, or have had the perseverance I found in them yesterday.

Respect for the enemy, however, was rare that afternoon. The militia's tactics infuriated British officers and enlisted men. Colonel Francis Smith, whose command had faced annihilation, seemed almost petulant in his anger: "Notwithstanding the enemy's numbers, they did not make one gallant attempt during so long an action, though our men were so very much fatigued, but kept under cover."

The exhausted redcoats began taking revenge. One British witness called it "a fury of madness."

Lieutenant Mackenzie would later write that many "houses were plundered by the soldiers, notwithstanding the efforts of the officers to prevent it." And plunder was the least of it. Outrage exploded into murder. Mackenzie wrote that his men "were so enraged at suffering from an unseen enemy that they forced open many of the houses . . . and put to death all those found in them." Another British account declared that redcoat units "committed every wanton wickedness that a brutal revenge could stimulate." Four days after the battle, an officer issued a blistering indictment of his own troops: "On the road, in our route home, we found every house full of people, and the fences lined as before. Every house from which they fired was immediately forced, and EVERY SOUL IN THEM PUT TO DEATH. Horrible carnage! O Englishmen, to what depth of brutal degeneracy are ye fallen!"

Late in the afternoon of April 19, in the small village of Menotomy, the day's savagery reached a point of almost incredible wildness. Thirty-five new rebel companies lay waiting for the British column, with armed militiamen arriving from Watertown, Malden, Norfolk, Dedham, Roxbury, Brookline, Weston, Danvers, Lynn, Beverly, Needham, Medford, and Menotomy itself. Altogether, some 4,000 provincial troops had taken up positions in the village and along the road ahead. Lieutenant John Barker, a member of Smith's original expedition, reported that the redcoats were "obliged to force almost every house in the road . . . All that were found in the houses were put to death." In one case, at the home of Jason Russell in Menotomy, British flanking units attacked a group of militiamen from the rear, trapping them inside, eventually killing eleven men—seven from Danvers alone. Jason Russell lay dead in his doorway, mutilated with almost a dozen bayonet wounds. Worse yet, colonists would later charge that British troops had begun executing prisoners of war. One captured militiaman named Dennison Wallis reported that, although he had escaped, three or four others "were butchered with savage barbarity."

Plainly, war crimes were committed. A few days after the battle, General Thomas Gage acknowledged gross misconduct, issuing orders that the troops under his command immediately cease such behavior "upon pain of death."

To an extent, at least, British atrocities were born of astonishment that mere farmers and shopkeepers had the temerity to pick up their weapons and fight back. Professional hubris, mixed with a generous dose of cultural hubris, lay like a hard, deep foundation beneath the terrible events of that afternoon. Also, convenient forgetfulness was in play. After all, it was the British, not the colonists, who had done the first killing at Lexington. And it was the British, not the colonists, who had first marched, 700-strong, on Concord.

Clearly, though, the causes went deeper. It is easy to underestimate, and easy to ignore, the effects of raw fatigue: How exhaustion impairs intellectual and moral judgment. How eighteen hours of sleeplessness can erode the barrier between decency and brutality. How physical exertion can dull the conscience just as it does the body—eighteen hours of marching and running and jumping and bayoneting and humping sixty-pound packs and firing ten-pound weapons and carrying the wounded and then running again and jumping again and marching again. A man's legs, if pressed hard enough, will tremble and fail, and so too, eventually, will the mechanisms that govern restraint. British witnesses, including Colonel Smith and Ensign DeBerniere, called explicit attention to fatigue as an ingredient in the day's concoction of criminal butchery, and I will add my own testimony to theirs: exhaustion can turn the conscience to stone.

April 1775 slides into May 1969.

Time puts on a new uniform, revs up the firepower, and calls itself progress.

We were angry.

We were scared.

We threw cartons of milk at old men. We pistol-whipped prisoners and detainees. We tied people to saplings and beat on their
shins with sticks. We shot chickens and pigs and water buffalo.
We peed in village wells. We called in gunships and artillery, took
cover, and watched villages fry. We—or too many of us—cut off
noses and ears. We—or too many of us—called the enemy animals, and worse, and more or less believed it. Although to my
knowledge Alpha Company never intentionally slaughtered the
innocent, not face to face, we certainly and repetitively caused
the innocent to die with our radios and code books, calling in jets
loaded with napalm and bombs of many types and sizes. We certainly and repetitively sprayed automatic fire into hedgerows and
villages without thought of the innocent who might receive our
wrath. For us—or for too many of us—there *were* no innocent.
"If it squawks and walks," a friend said to me, "it's a gook."

Now, among the memories I bear is that of a village elder—a
monk, I believe—carrying the body of a shot-dead little girl into
Alpha's night perimeter. She had been killed by H&I fire, which
was a nightly ritual, all of us firing out into the dark at nothing
and at everything, firing blindly, hoping to "harass and interdict"
an unseen phantom enemy.

A year before I arrived in Quang Ngai Province, in a village
that Alpha Company knew well, a village called My Lai 4, our
American predecessors had gunned down and otherwise put to
death hundreds of unarmed civilians, including babies, including
teenagers, including old and middle-aged and young women,
including grandfathers and aunts and uncles. The soldiers who
committed these crimes justified their actions very much as the

British had done in 1775, often with precisely the same language — "hidden enemy," "devils," "savages" — and any historian who would claim that history is purely singular, that human behavior cannot be repetitive over the centuries, that the present cannot inform us of the past, or the past of the present, is an idiot or a demagogue. The events of 1775 and 1969 are not identical. But those events are similar in important causative, experiential, historical, and moral ways. A zoologist might cry out that a giraffe is not a zebra, but, cry out as he might, both are mammals, and both have flesh, and both can be eaten in a pinch. A zoologist who claims otherwise is not a starving zoologist.

So, yes, 1775 isn't 1969, and Battle Road isn't Vietnam. But for me, and for others who have seen war, the din of Bedlam and moral nullity echoes across the centuries.

———

Through the late afternoon, with darkness approaching, the British column made its way across the Menotomy River and down the long road toward Cambridge. Even with Percy's reinforcements, ammunition was running low, and here and there bloody skirmishes broke out along the flanks. At a road junction outside Cambridge, with fresh militia units to his front, Percy ordered his beleaguered troops to turn left toward Charlestown. To Percy's rear, a force of 3,000 militiamen kept up steady pressure, which slowed the retreat, while at the same time, to the east, other provincial units were arriving from as far north as Essex County. It was not until nearly seven in the evening that the column finally rounded Prospect Hill. Despite orders from Percy, and despite approaching nightfall and the threat of entrapment, British soldiers continued to force houses along the road, stopping to loot and plunder. Lieutenant John Barker wrote that his men "were so wild and irregular that there was no keeping them in any order . . . the plundering was shameful."

Around eight in the evening, in deep twilight, the column straggled across the neck of land that connected the mainland to Charlestown. Defensive positions were established on Bunker Hill.

Moving slowly through the dark, British officers began the grim task of tallying up their casualties. Ensign Jeremy Lister, himself wounded in the arm, described a scene of almost hellish desolation: "A sergeant of the company came to me and informed me he had but 11 men and could not find any other officer of the company." The final British casualty count, which was not complete until days later, came to an astonishing 16 percent: 73 dead, 174 wounded, and 26 missing. The great bulk of those casualties were suffered by Smith's original 700-man expeditionary force, whose casualty rate probably exceeded 30 percent.

———

As one measure of the terrible violence on April 19, 1775, the butcher's bill that day was similar to that inflicted on US forces in May 1969 at a place called Hamburger Hill in Vietnam, where 72 GIs died and 372 were wounded. However, the casualties at Hamburger Hill were incurred over ten days; the British absorbed their losses in under twenty-four hours. Moreover, British casualties fell one shot at a time, with muzzle-loaded musketry fire, while at Hamburger Hill the killing was done with modern automatic weapons, modern grenades, and modern mortars.

For the dead, of course, none of this matters.

And even for the living, both Vietnam and Battle Road have largely faded from collective memory, dissolving into a few sterile facts to be trotted out on Patriots' Day and the Fourth of July. The horrors go unfelt. The death gurgles go unheard. Often, instead of sorrow, and instead of outrage at what one human being will do to another, the events of April 19, 1775, are now celebrated with a strange blend of cheery delight and solemn reverence, which in my recollection are not the emotions of terrified and dying men.

Names of the Alpha Company dead are preserved in marble.

Names of the British dead are not so well preserved.

Either way, a name in stone is not a man, and even if it were, stone finally crumbles and slides to the sea. In the end, what soldiers must share with all others is the anonymous oblivion of Black Hawk's warriors, Kitchener's brigades, the defenders of Troy, and the aging men of Alpha Company.

Homework

1. Tonight, Timmy and Tad, beginning at 9 p.m. sharp, you will embark with your mother on an eight-mile march from our front door to the outskirts of Manchaca, Texas, and then home again.

2. On account of your youth, your mother will not be issuing weapons or ammunition.

3. She will not ask you to kill anyone or otherwise behave inappropriately.

4. Your mother will insist, however, that each of you carry thirty pounds of sugar in your backpacks, plus plenty of water and canned fruit.

5. Along the way, you will do some running and jumping and rigorous calisthenics. Wear comfortable shoes, both of you, and be sure to pack rubber boots in case of creek crossings.

6. No dawdling, Tad.

7. No griping, Timmy.

8. I will be waiting to greet you and your mom at the conclusion of the hike.

9. The idea, obviously, is to absorb a little history by living it, not just by reading about it. Your eight-mile march will amount to only a fifth of the distance covered by British troops on the night of April 18 and the following day of April 19, 1775, and of course you will not be fighting for your life most of the way home. But perhaps you will gain a modest appreciation for what soldiers must endure, not only the physical hardships but also the tyranny of unwelcome orders like these I am giving you now.

10. After a good night's sleep, you will begin composing a short (say, five-page) essay based on your evening's march. Grammar will count. Spelling will count. Address the following question: Is war glamorous?

35

Easier Homework

About two years ago, I asked Timmy to read "A Very Short Story" by Ernest Hemingway. A half hour later, Timmy came into my office and said, "Okay, I finished. What do you want me to tell you?"

"Just your opinion," I said.

Timmy was young then, easily embarrassed, and for a while he squirmed. "Well, the story was pretty blunt," he said.

"Blunt how?"

"You know. At the end. When the guy gets gonorrhea in a taxi-cab."

"Is blunt bad?"

"Not usually," said Timmy. "Except when your dad tells you to read about sex diseases."

36

Timmy's Bedroom Door

In a couple of months, Timmy will turn fifteen. Other parents have been warning me for years that big changes accompany adolescence, but until a few months ago I had arrogantly concluded that those warnings were false alarms. Not so. My snuggly little "Row, Row" boy is closing doors on me. Lots of doors—literally. Bathroom doors, bedroom doors, closet doors. The word "door" has become the equivalent of the words "buzz off." In particular, the door to his bedroom now gives me the willies, and I'll sometimes look at it as if seeing it for the first time, the very door I had so carefully painted more than a decade ago, a huge and handsome door with metallic gold trim and a sparkly champagne glaze that makes it shimmer as light strikes it from shifting angles. I had once been ridiculously and insanely proud of that gorgeous door —so proud of my handiwork, so proud of how the door's surface rippled like a coat of cat fur as it opened and closed—but now, standing before it, listening, wondering, partly curious and partly terrified and partly lonely, that fortified bedroom door makes me want to buy a keg of dynamite and blow it forever off its hinges.

I am afraid to open it. I am afraid not to open it. There is nothing symbolic about this. I am truly afraid. Nor is there anything at all symbolic about the door itself, that monstrous and glittery bedroom door—it is a thick, heavy, high, imposing, physical door. It once belonged to a bank in England. Two strong men had trouble hanging it.

Maybe dynamite isn't the answer. Maybe artillery.

———

"How was school today?"

"Good."

"Any fun?"

"Sure."

"Well, like what?"

"Art."

"Okay, that's great. Tell me what you learned."

"Huh?"

———

The hormones are kicking in, bubbling from scalp to soul, fizzling and stewing and eating away at youth, turning my son Timmy secretive and silent and evasive and cryptic and sullen and withdrawn, a zealous guardian of all that is happening in his handsome head.

Growth hormones: Timmy is three inches taller than I am. Each week, he gets taller. My neck hurts.

Hair hormones: shave his armpits, gather up the clippings, stuff a mattress.

Acne hormones: nothing terrible, but worth watching.

Door-closing hormones: terrible, but what's the answer?

Ear hormones: "Timmy," I said to him yesterday, "I don't want to lose you." He was wearing headphones. He didn't hear me.

———

"Any homework, Timmy?"

"Yeah."

"Like what?"

"Math."

"So what happened in school? Anything interesting?"

"Nope."

"Well, did you talk to anybody?"

"Sean."

"How's Sean doing?

"Fine."

"Is there a God up in heaven? Does e still equal mc squared? Will you become a sculptor someday? Do you dream about girls? Do you dream about me? Is there something on your mind? Do you want to talk about it? Have you murdered your best friend?"

"Huh?"

37

Lip Kissing

It has become perfunctory, obligatory, and abashed. It once lingered, but no more. A clock whirs in Timmy's head, one calibrated to milliseconds. A buzzer sounds. *Basium interruptus* with an almost fifteen-year-old. "Bye," he says.

Sometimes I will be as cool and dismissive as my son, as if I'm uncrushed, as if my heart isn't broken, as if this is how it is meant to be and therefore should be, as if we must all grow up and accept a law out of John Wayne's textbook on male-to-male, father-to-son propriety. No lips. No moisture.

"Bye," I'll say, but I'll be thinking, "Row, Row."

38

The King of Slippery

"Hey, kiddo," I'll say, "is your homework finished?"

Timmy will say, "Yes."

I'll say, "Completely?"

He'll say, "Almost."

I'll say, "Then it's *not* finished?"

He'll say, "I just told you it's almost finished."

I'll say, "I know, but at first you told me it *was* finished. Didn't you say the word 'yes'?"

He'll say, "Yes meant almost."

I'll say, "Almost does not mean yes."

He'll say, "Well, I worked on it for a whole hour. It *felt* finished."

I'll say, "In other words, yes means no?"

He'll say, "Not exactly."

I'll say, "Yes means yes. Finished means finished. Almost means almost."

He'll roll his eyes. What he wants to say, but doesn't dare, is that his dad is a hairsplitting pedant.

"Go finish your damned homework," I'll say.

He'll say, "Okay, in just a minute."

———

On weekends and over Christmas break, Timmy stays up late. He's testing the boundaries of my indulgence. I issue precise orders—"Be in bed, lights out, at 11:15 and not a second later"—and then, at 11:15 sharp, I go check on him. He'll be in bed, lights out, except he's playing Angry Birds on his iPhone.

I raise hell. He pushes back.

"I'm in bed," he says, as if he doesn't know better, as if he's not splitting his own regulatory hairs. "The lights are out. What more do you want?"

"I want you asleep. At least trying to sleep."

"You didn't actually *say* that."

And off we go.

———

All right, granted, Meredith and I should have banned electronic games of any sort from day one. We did not. We regret it. We had no idea.

And so, at the moment, we are living under a set of emergency decrees put in place after a long, sometimes tearful, sometimes bitter discussion about my intention to permanently and absolutely and without exception outlaw video gaming within the brick walls of our house. Zero tolerance. Harsh penalties. Although I'm tempted to recount our three-hour discussion in all its convoluted and emotional detail, I will merely list a few of the topics we covered: sleep deprivation, addiction, obsession, immobility, anxiety, disobedience, pallid skin, optic dysfunction, crankiness, willful deception, and (according to Timmy and Tad) the stunning educative virtues of Minecraft. "You wrote a whole chapter about how terrible absolutism is," Timmy said at one point, "and now you want to take away all our video games. Like a complete dictator. You should just erase that chapter."

He then used the word "hypocrisy."

He did not use the words "police state," but he bracketed the concept.

In the heat of argument, I was unable to summon a reasonable reply, and we soon came to an uncomfortable compromise: x number of hours on weekends, y number of hours on school days, z number of hours on holidays and in the summer months.

But now, after nine days, our agreement is in ruins. Amid the hurricane of daily life, Meredith and I have been unable to track the actual hours Tad and Timmy spend staring cross-eyed into video screens. And how could we? Do we burst into their bedrooms like a SWAT team? Do we set alarm clocks? Do we take away their iPhones at certain hours of the day, and if so, which hours, and which days? And what about their schoolwork, much of which requires a good deal of computer time? How do we know—actually *know*—if Timmy is peering intently at Google

Classroom or at Clash Royale? How do we know if he's composing an essay or gunning down pixel villains? Do we spy? Do we deploy parental guile and stealth and subterfuge? Do we purchase computer surveillance software? Do we install cameras? Do we organize a do-it-yourself FBI? Do we want to live that way?

For the past nine days, Meredith and I have been beating ourselves up, losing sleep, trying desperately to hold on to some trust in our kids. Timmy and Tad are under orders to keep written records of every minute devoted to electronic screens of any type —iPads, iPhones, TVs, and computers. But they forget. Or they fudge. Or we think they fudge. Or we aren't sure if they're fudging. Or we suspect they're fudging. Or—and this is terrible—we suspect much worse. We suspect subterfuge. We suspect cunning.

Last night, I knocked on Timmy's bedroom door, waited a moment, walked in, and saw his computer screen instantly flash from one website to another.

I said nothing. I didn't dare.

To mention it to him, even now, would be received by my son as the next closest thing to outright accusation. Timmy was supposed to be doing homework. And perhaps he was—perhaps I had stepped into his room just as he switched from Spanish to algebra—but regardless of that, something sour and sickening wobbled in my stomach.

This was no longer about video games.

Only a few months ago, suspicion did not exist. Doubt did not exist. Somehow, stupidly, I had conceived of my sons as unblemished innocents, immune to the corruptions of adolescence, beyond petty betrayals, beyond deception, and what had been so utterly unthinkable—so unthinkable I didn't think about it—has now become all I can think about. Is the fault my own? Probably so. Maybe even certainly so. The corrosion of trust, in any case, is more than the corrosion of trust, because I fear I've lost Timmy's absolute and untainted love, the confidence of absolute love, the bond of oneness, the shared valences, the unbreakable and eternal unity between father and son. I had *believed* in all that. I had believed there would be no secrets. I had believed, ludicrously but faithfully, that there would be no differences at all between us, ever. I had believed he would not grow up.

"Dad," Timmy says, his voice deeper than my own, "I just want things you don't want."

"I know," I tell him.

"I like video games. I like YouTube. I learn things."

"I know."

"I'm not you," he says. "I'm me."

And I say, "I know," though the knowing hurts and won't ever stop hurting.

39

Timmy and Tad and Papa and I (III)

Even at this moment, as I try again to speak to my kids about Ernest Hemingway, I'm doing what I can to give Timmy and Tad the father they deserve. I want their lives to be rich with stories—not just those by Hemingway—and I want them to feel the moral push and pull that is the heartbeat of good stories. Hemingway is a place to start. Also, I want my sons to begin thinking about what they read; I want them to quarrel with Nobel Prize winners, to challenge Homer, and to feud with Aristotle; I want them to receive the pleasures I have received. More than that, years from now, the boys may be curious about their dad's interior life, the things I had once thought about, and through the work of Ernest Hemingway, I can approach my own childhood, my father, my time at war, and my struggle to tell stories about those things.

I will begin not with Hemingway but with a relevant real-world incident.

A couple of years back, Meredith and Tad watched a movie called *The Impossible,* which involves a vacationing family caught up in a real-world tsunami that struck Thailand in 2004. Much of the film's story line is devoted to the anguish of separation: a father frantically searches for his missing wife and missing son; the missing son searches for his missing brothers and missing father; a missing mother lies badly injured in a Thai hospital. Near the film's conclusion, two of the young boys are seated in an open-air shuttle bus parked in a crowded area outside the very hospital in which their mother now recuperates. One of the boys needs to urinate. He jumps out of the bus and elbows his way through a throng of survivors. Miraculously—in that precise instant in time—the boy finishes peeing and looks up to see his long-missing older brother. A moment later he sees his long-missing father. In this happy and poignant way, the family is finally reunited—impossibly reunited, as the movie's title alerts us.

Meredith turned off the TV set. She asked Tad what he thought.

"Well," the boy said, "I liked it, but I know what the moral is."

"What?" said Meredith.

"Take your time peeing," said Tad.

He was deadly serious. He was also being clever. And he was being serious and clever in a certain way, in the way irony is serious and clever, poking serious fun at a film designed to elicit tears of poignancy and joy. My son was aware, if only in his nine-year-old way, that what works very happily in the real world may work not so happily in the mediated world of storytelling. Coincidence can be read as contrivance, and contrivance can be read as pothole. The reader is jolted awake.

"I know it really happened," Tad said, "but that doesn't mean I believe it."

———

With Ernest Hemingway's story "The Killers," I react in a similar though not quite identical way. The story's potholes, at least for me, involve coincidence that seems to teeter on the edge of contrivance. Nick Adams, the story's point-of-view character, appears in exactly the right place at exactly the right hour to encounter a pair of mathematically unlikely human beings. How often have you encountered even a single homicidal thug? How often have you, or has anyone, been tied up by a homicidal thug? It's not that such coincidences *can't* happen. It's not that such coincidences *don't* happen or *haven't* happened. Rather, as a reader, I find myself straying off into thoughts about coincidence itself. I'm thinking about the author, and about convenience, and about what strikes me as a strained arrangement of improbabilities. I react to "The Killers" just as I would react to a stranger relating these events at a dinner party. I'd be thinking, Yeah, right—tied up? Belief would come hard. At least for me, this story falls off what Vladimir Nabokov's biographer Andrea Pitzer calls "the narrow ledge between coherence and coincidence."

At one point, Hemingway himself seems unsure of his story:

"I was up at Henry's," Nick said, "and two fellows came in

and tied up me and the cook, and they said they were going to kill you."

The next sentence is: "It sounded silly when he said it."

"Hills Like White Elephants" does not sound silly in summary. Nor does "Fifty Grand," another story involving boxers. Nor does "The End of Something" or "A Clean, Well-Lighted Place" or "Soldier's Home" or "The Doctor and the Doctor's Wife" or "Out of Season" or "A Very Short Story" or the haunting and oddly neglected "A Simple Enquiry." I see little coincidence and even less contrivance in these and most other Hemingway stories.

Coincidence alone, however, is not what stops me as I read "The Killers." Any number of well-known and convincing stories depend on improbable intersections in time and space, among them O'Connor's "A Good Man Is Hard to Find." For me—and maybe only for me—the story-dream of "The Killers" is dispelled by an unpleasant convergence of coincidence with melodrama, cliché, and stereotype. The potholes multiply. The two thugs in Hemingway's story seem to me uniformly and relentlessly thuggish, often in familiar ways. There is little contradiction between fact and fact, and as a consequence—again, maybe only for me—the whole reads less than human and exact. The thugs dress identically, like a pair of B-movie hoodlums, in "overcoats too tight for them"; their dialogue rarely strays from the glibly villainous: "Another bright boy," Al said. "Ain't he a bright boy, Max?" To which Max replies: "The town's full of bright boys." The repetitive "bright boy" stuff, which continues off and on for some time, begins to sound cartoonish, inhuman, and at times almost humorous. I hear typicality, not individuality. While it may be true that Hemingway knew such characters in his early Chicago days, and while it may also be true that all such mobsters once spoke in identical tones and with identical tough-guy lingo, I am nonetheless snagged up in ungracious thoughts involving George Raft and Edward G. Robinson and gangland homogeneity. By contrast, O'Connor's Misfit goes about his business with good Southern manners, more like a Milledgeville bank teller than a criminal, and this, for me, creates the impression not of a caricature but of a twisted and disfigured fellow creature —a murderer, to be sure, but still an ill-fitting member of our own species.

————

My unenthusiastic response to "The Killers" is of course personal, and I do not expect Timmy or Tad to share my opinions. What I do expect is that they will think about what I have to say. I hope they will reread the story, maybe on my birthday in the year 2037, partly to recall how much I loved them, partly to engage in a conversation with the dead.

"The Killers" is a popular story. Many readers find it wonderful. Each of us, Timmy and Tad included, has his own Hemingway, and, beyond that, we should bear in mind that there is not and never was a single Ernest Hemingway, but rather many, many Hemingways, and that with each of his stories there was made, or born, a new and revised Hemingway—recognizable, yes, but still altered in the ways that each passing day alters all of us. Also, I hope Timmy and Tad realize that admiration for a writer does not require hero worship. As with any reader, I have often simultaneously adored and despised the same piece of writing. I adored and despised *For Whom the Bell Tolls*. I adored Pilar. I adored the moving earth. (I was sixteen then.) I despised the resigned, tough-guy stoicism of Robert Jordan at the novel's conclusion, which seemed to me an ideological echo of the resigned, tough-guy stoicism of Ole Andreson at the conclusion of "The Killers." Robert Jordan I was not, except when sharing a level patch of ground with Maria.

Additionally, with both "The Killers" and *For Whom the Bells Tolls,* I had the uncomfortable sense that the author was imposing on me a pretty dubious moral code. Even as a kid—and now much more so—I found it difficult to swallow without complaint a questionable notion of the heroic. Ole Andreson and Robert Jordan choose to respond to similar dangers with what amounts to passive suicide; they reject the obvious and wholly honorable alternatives—flight in Andreson's case, surrender in Jordan's case. (Did the survivors of Bataan behave dishonorably for having surrendered in hopeless circumstances? Was Robert E. Lee—or Kurt Vonnegut, for that matter—morally culpable for calling it quits?) "Couldn't you get out of town?" Nick asks Ole, to which the boxer replies, "No. I'm through with all that running around."

Similarly, at the conclusion of *For Whom the Bell Tolls,* in what strikes me as a convoluted bit of nitpicking, Robert Jordan decides against killing himself in favor of allowing the approaching enemy to do the dirty work for him. Moreover, as the fascist troops close in on Jordan, and as the novel reaches its deadly climax, coincidence once again yanks me out of the story. I'm thinking not about the pending extinction of Robert Jordan but rather about the improbable contrivance of the novel's final paragraphs. How unlikely, I think, that Lieutenant Paco Berrendo—the one and only enemy soldier we've come to know over hundreds of pages —suddenly dashes into the story to become the one and only human being whom Jordan will slay as his final earthly act. How tidy. How symmetrical. How heart-tuggingly convenient. Berrendo appears on the battlefield at exactly the right melodramatic instant; he has "ridden hard" so as to show up for his own death. Hemingway orchestrates this baffling development by abruptly veering away from Jordan's point of view, inserting an "explanation" for Berrendo's rendezvous with eternity, and then just as abruptly the author veers back to Jordan's perspective.

The scene is not just contrived. It's heavy-handed. It's a Gary Cooper movie.

On top of that, the novel's concluding scene seems to me weirdly Victorian in its celebration of self-sacrificial military values (honor, duty, discipline)—more like "The Charge of the Light Brigade" than "Dulce et Decorum Est." My Vietnam-infected blood begins to boil. I yell at my iPad. As Jordan prepares to die, and as his last worldly act is to take aim at a fellow human being, I get the feeling that I am supposed to applaud, that I am supposed to draw down on the enemy and then take my time peeing.

———

September 15, 2016, 5:10 a.m. Big trouble. I've been at work for more than two hours, trying to express a thought that does not wish to be expressed. My nerves and the delete key are worn to stubs. Part of the problem involves the folly of writing itself, the lunatic illusion that a writer is somehow the master of what appears on the page. Language won't take me where I want to go; it takes me where *it* wants to go. Stupidly, I've been forcing things, struggling to make words march to the command of intention, which for decades has been my chief failing as a writer. Intention may guide a writer, but it must not insist.

A couple of hours ago, when I embarked on what seemed a simple little passage, I had hoped to explore a recurring sensation that almost always comes over me in the early-morning hours: the pitiless voice of my own mortality bubbling up from somewhere in my belly, jabbering away as I wash dishes and polish the kitchen counters. It's as if my internal organs have foreknowledge of what is soon coming down the pike, as if my heart and bowels are taking advantage of the wee-hour silence to remind me of what is so easily ignored in the clatter of daylight: everybody dies.

"Why do old men wake so early?" Hemingway asks. "Is it to have one longer day?"

Maybe so.

Or maybe old men wake early to practice dying.

Day before yesterday I was informed by email that a "moderate amount of calcium" had been detected in my hard artery, suggesting "moderate heart disease." The same briskly worded message noted a 4 mm "ground-glass nodule" in the right upper lobe of my lungs. No surprise, really. I smoke. I take Lipitor. I'm fucking old. The odd thing about it—the only odd thing, I suppose—was that the news had been delivered many, many months earlier by way of those three-in-the-morning belly whisperings, by some chemical communiqué between the hard artery—whatever that is—and the coils of the brain. The body is one organism, is it not? Therefore, why should not our morning reveries be influenced by gall bladders and kidneys and hardened arteries? I see nothing mystical about this. I would be shocked if it were otherwise.

In any event, the bad news was not all that bad. I had expected worse. I had deserved worse. I mention this medical development not to solicit pity, and not out of (much) self-pity, but rather because of a peculiar incident that occurred only minutes after the unpleasant diagnosis popped up on my computer screen. I had stopped writing for the day. I had fixed myself a drink, settled into a chair, and opened up a novel I'd been reading over the past couple of days. The novel was *Arch of Triumph* by Erich Maria Remarque. I had turned to page 850 of my iTunes edition and within seconds slammed into this scrap of language: "From there he disappeared through a ground-glass door . . ."

My uncharitable comments about coincidence returned to me with vindictive, eat-your-own-words retribution.

Papa cackled.

It's possible, I suppose, that at some point in my life I had encountered the adjective "ground-glass" in another work of fiction, or in another context entirely, but I cannot cite an example.

Only minutes earlier I'd been searching Google for "ground-glass nodule," a term that was new to me, wondering how bits of glass had ended up in my lungs. How many books on this planet contain the adjective "ground-glass"? How many times have I or you or anyone else uttered that adjective in conversation? Additionally, there is the coincidence of coincidence itself. A few pages back, in my consideration of "The Killers," I might easily have ignored the entire notion of coincidence, or I might at least have sought more compassion. Call it retribution, call it distributive justice, but we get what we give.

Justice or otherwise, retribution or otherwise, it remains the case that my early-morning thoughts have taken on a distinct summing-up quality. As in *The Tempest*, "And every third thought shall be my grave," I worry about Timmy and Tad without a father. I worry about the futile, helpless pain they will endure. In the stillness and quiet of 3 a.m., I perform a sloppy, hit-and-miss review of my own aspirations and failures. The successes have been few. The failures have been numerous and decisive. Almost always, individual human beings are involved in these predawn appraisals—people I have loved, for the most part. Faces come and go. Time scrambles itself. Scenes from fifty years ago are replayed and then altered in imagination and then altered again. I say no instead of yes. I become an electrician, something sensible, and leave the writing to stouter hearts. I burn my draft notice and head for Winnipeg. I cross uncrossed bridges. I jump off cliffs where I once stood paralyzed. Alone in my underwear, hosting a bizarre daybreak cocktail party attended by the beloved and the dead, I repair things with my father, ask forgiveness of the betrayed, renew lapsed friendships, revisit Quang Ngai, rewrite failed sentences, find courage where there was none, request clarification as to what exactly transpired on July 7, 1969, reinvent chronologies, attend to finalities, attend to now or never, attend to loose ends and split ends and ends that never end, attend to all that old men attend to when they wake early—rehearsal of act three, preparation for game day.

———

It's 3:12 a.m., October 1, 2016. I have turned seventy. Daylight will bring slices of cake and cheerful goodwill. It will be like celebrating a hernia.

40

Timmy's Gamble

On one other long-gone day, back when Timmy was a fifth-grader, I sat at his desk for half an hour, trying to help him improve his writing skills, and somehow we came to an impasse involving the arcane topic of italics. Timmy seemed to be overusing them. I objected. I told him italics could seem gimmicky. I suggested that he choose words that would do the italicizing for him. I went on and on about how italics instruct the reader to notice certain words more than others, or in a different way than others. In the end, I recommended moderation, italicizing words sparsely and only when other possibilities failed.

"All right," Timmy said, "I get it, but you were using italics just now. When you were talking to me."

"Yes," I said, "but I wouldn't write it that way."

"I bet you *would*," Timmy said.

41

Dulce et Decorum Est

In the small rural town of Ors, France, our family is visiting the battlefield upon which the poet Wilfred Owen died, precisely one week before the armistice ending World War One. It is a hot day in July. There is no traffic. There are no tourists. There are no people at all. Nothing stirs, nothing moves. The waters of the Sambre Canal look like a sheet of tar winding past old houses and meadows and a few sluggish cattle.

For what seems a very long time, we walk along a narrow tractor path flanked by barbed wire on both sides, eventually coming upon a small, fenced-in cemetery. The place is deserted. Timmy and Tad are quiet. They know this is important to me.

For twenty minutes, I study the names and regiments etched into one hundred or so headstones that mark the graves of British soldiers who, along with Wilfred Owen, died on November 4, 1918. Owen himself is buried elsewhere in Ors, in a larger and less secluded cemetery, but somehow the pastoral silence and languor and isolation of this place seem to thunder with the wastage that fills the lines of Owen's poetry. Here, with cattle as company, in a few tidy rows, in the heat of July, are the men and boys who perished in the last terrible week of a terrible war that would soon breed another terrible war.

I ask Timmy to read aloud from Owen's "Dulce et Decorum Est."

He does so, flatly and without flourish.

He is four years younger than the youngest of the dead beneath us. He reads like a man.

42

Pride (IV)

MY 15TH STREET FRIEND

by Timmy O'Brien

Sixth Grade

I saw you on 15th Street,
Holding out your hat, asking for a treat,
Because you needed something to eat.

I told my mom to stop the car.
She was too stressed and pushed too far,
But I still wanted to give you my granola bar.

You had served the nation by fighting a war,
I could tell by the cap you wore,
It said "Vietnam Veteran" (written in white)
I prayed that your future would someday be bright.

I felt really sad and mad,
As we drove away,
Because no one was helping you
Find your way.

Hadn't you obeyed your orders,
And gone across the ocean to fight,
And tried to do what they said was right?

If that's how veterans get treated,
Then I don't know what our nation is doing,
I bet you wished that you could be suing,
The people who drafted you far from home,
And tore your life apart, bone by bone.
I saw you crying as you watched us drive by,
And it made me feel like I could also cry.
I wasn't ready to say goodbye.

Next day before school I packed you a sack.
Inside were a yo-yo, a book, and a nice, healthy snack.

It's sad that I never saw you again,
But I search the streets every day.

"You're a hero," I would say,
"And I know that you saved at least one life,
And now it's terrible that you're so full of strife."

Then I wrote you a letter because I cared
That you were crying and seemed so scared.
I wrote that you were my 15th Street friend
And that I wanted your long, sad war to end.

43

War Buddies

Except for my family and a couple of close friends, I am most at home and most wholly happy in the company of former members of my unit in Vietnam. I see these men only rarely; I don't know them well and never did; many are like ghosts, or like ghosts of ghosts, whose faces are familiar but weirdly indefinite. I recall only a few complete names. A good number of them I remember only by nicknames. Many, perhaps most, are entirely nameless.

Still, on those rare occasions when I bump into my former comrades, I feel a sense of belonging that otherwise escapes me in life. There is nothing we must prove. Abstraction and generalization vanish. What we have, when we are together, is *that* particular paddy dike, *that* firefight, *that* corpse, *that* tree line, *that* deserted village, *that* one and only killer afternoon in July of 1969. We refresh one another's memories with scraps of detail; we laugh at things most people don't laugh at; we occasionally debate matters of sequence and chronology—who died first, who died next.

There is no boasting. No one uses the word "glory." If anything, the tone of conversation has a rueful, excessively modest, almost puzzled quality, as though none of us can truly believe that what happened happened, or that what happened actually happened to *us*. There is a shocking gentleness to these guys, something close to shyness, and it seems improbable that nearly a half century ago they were the fist of American power in Vietnam. My buddies were grunts, 11-Bravo, and they did the daily, nasty, grinding, lethal work of war. They slept in the rain; they fought the firefights; they spent their nights lying in ambush and their days trudging through minefields out on the Batangan Peninsula; they were not cooks or clerks or mechanics or supply specialists; they were infantry; they lived in the war, and the war lived in them, and fifty years ago they did your killing and your dying for you. These quiet old coots, these war buddies of mine, seem generally untroubled by all they had once witnessed and endured. As far as I can tell, they entertain few second thoughts about the righteousness of their war and few doubts about whether all the dead people should be dead. Now and then, mostly through the back door, politics will slide into the give-and-take of reminiscence — "that lefty *New York Times* rag" — and in those instances, for a moment or two, I'll feel the solid world buckling beneath me, but then somebody else will say, "Hey, this ain't the John friggin' Birch Society," and another guy will say, "Yeah, and you're pissing off O'Brien," and then the first guy will shrug and grin at me and say, "Sorry, man, I forgot you was a communist."

With only a couple of exceptions, my buddies avoid mention of my books. Privately, I'm almost certain, they disapprove of my outrage at the war, and I'm even more certain that they take vigorous exception to my literary portrayal of the American soldier as less than purely virtuous. (One member of my platoon named his son after a lieutenant whose behavior I considered plainly criminal.) In an unspoken, matter-of-fact way, the former members of Alpha Company view themselves as the good guys, the angels of liberty and decency. They display scarce sympathy for their old enemy. Over the years, in fact, I've heard only one or two of them express a word of distress, much less remorse, about an estimated three million dead Vietnamese. Reflexively, but without real enmity, they still speak of their former enemy as gooks and dinks and slants and slopes, and yet most of my buddies would claim—indignantly and forcefully—that no racist intent lurks behind such language: it's grunt talk, pure shorthand, just another way of distinguishing the cowboys from the Indians.

I have serious trouble with this, and yet, for all our differences, there remains the paradoxical fact that I do love these men. I dream about them. I feel their presence when they are not present. Cop and Willy and Reno and Kid and Howard and Vince and Wayne and Red and Joe and Greg and Roger and Chip and Tom and Squirrel and Ben and Buddy Barney and Buddy Wolf and Myron and Everett and Doc and Art and Frenchie—these are the names that endure in my moth-eaten memory, and right now, as I try to complete this sentence, their faces are once again youthful, and together we're again humping through the Vietnam dark, heading for some murderous destiny, the moon overhead, a dog barking, our boots making sucking sounds in the foul paddy slush.

The closeness I feel toward the men of Alpha Company can be represented only dimly with language. The feel of blood-fraternity requires a kind of willful dreaming, a summoning of the actual here-and-now shuffle of troops on the move; the long nights of pulling guard along the shoreline of the South China Sea; the smells of poverty and mold and smoke and tropical decay as you enter a bad-ass village at dawn, and how those smells combine into a single brain-deep tapeworm that stays with you forever, even in your sleep, but how, when you try to talk about it, all the adjectives in the dictionary can't make you *smell* anything and can't do anything to your pulse or blood pressure or bowels. When I'm with my buddies, no one struggles to explain these things. We know soldiering the way a lover knows love. Without ever saying so, we understand that the word "Pinkville" does not mean "pink village" or anything remotely rosy or cheerful. It means we might die today. It means, man, this is one nasty piece of a nasty war.

———

Back in 1968 and 1969, when Vietnam collided with my life, I yearned for revenge against the cheerleaders and celebrators of war. Somehow, I imagined, I would strike back with sentences, make the monsters squirm in shame. This was a ludicrous and naïve fantasy. Sentences don't do shit. We just keep killing and killing, always for godly reasons—just as the enemy kills for its own godly reasons—and then we all stagger up Main Street with our walkers and war stories and watery old-man nostalgia. Three million dead. What if it were seventy million? Four hundred million? Every human on earth? There is no known limit to what we will tolerate. There is precious little shame. And so now, on this Thanksgiving Day in 2016, I remain torn between my affection for the men of Alpha Company and my dismay at their mostly self-congratulatory, mostly uncritical, mostly America-right-or-wrong values. It's like being married to Oliver North. True, plenty of Vietnam veterans opposed the war, and plenty spoke out against it, and yet studies show that the social and political attitudes of Vietnam veterans generally mirror those of nonveterans of the same age—traditionalist, conservative, pro-military, and hawkish. These findings are predictable. Even back when they were young, the men in Alpha Company seemed more or less to fit the standard profile, and now, decades later, it's no surprise that their opinions have hardened along the lines of the aging male population as a whole. The real surprise, at least for me, is that the historical judgments of my old war buddies are served up without the linguistic spices of Vietnam, without a touch of the weird, without sarcasm or astonishment, without rock 'n' roll dissonance, without wit, without ginger, and without the old FTA skepticism that was once scribbled on helmets and jeeps and M-16s from Danang to the Delta. The tone of their voices—the music beneath their politics—sounds to me more like Sinatra than the Animals, more like "My Kind of Town" than "We Gotta Get Out of This Place."

———

Recently a member of my old unit emailed me a 1968 Thanksgiving message to the troops from General Creighton Abrams, once the commander of American forces in Vietnam. "We should never forget," wrote Abrams all those years ago, "that in Vietnam our actions are defending free men everywhere. We pray that peace will come to all the world and that all of us can return to our loved ones in the not too distant future."

Forget the Mad Hatter weirdness of praying for peace while spending every waking second hell-bent on slaughtering people.

Forget the Orwellian doublethink and the "smelly little ortho-doxies."

Forget that "free men everywhere" were freely standing in peace vigils.

Forget that free men were freely burning draft cards.

Forget that nearly three-quarters of the dwellings in Quang Ngai Province had been obliterated by Thanksgiving Day of 1968 and that at least some free men were having trouble digesting this.

Forget, as the general did, the untidy complications of French colonialism, Vietnamese nationalism, the Geneva Accords, Buddhist monks aflame in the streets of Saigon. Forget that only months earlier, outside the Chicago Hilton, free men had been using clubs to beat on the heads of other free men. Forget that all across America, in the halls of Congress and at family dinner tables, free men everywhere were disputing the general's felicitous proposition that in Vietnam our actions were "defending free men everywhere."

What unnerved me was not the pass-the-napalm Thanksgiving Day piety of Creighton Abrams. Any grunt takes such crap for granted; it's what a general *is*. Rather, I was startled that my old war buddies, nearly all kind and decent guys, seemed to receive this platitudinous nonsense without any trace of the bitter, hooting irony they had shown as grunts back during the war itself. Was it amnesia? Had some gigantic eraser wiped away the daily, second-by-second realities of our war? When a guy died, for instance, did any of us shake our heads and say, "Well, he's dead, for sure, but he defended free men everywhere"? Did any of us talk that way? Did any of us think that way? Am I wrong in remembering that instead we said things like, "There it is, man—don't mean nothin'—the poor guy's wasted."

———

In various ways, to various degrees, virtually everything I've written over the past several pages will seriously irritate a large number of Vietnam veterans. A substantial majority, I'd guess. And beyond any doubt it will irritate one particular Vietnam veteran, a man who declared in a 2016 letter to the *Austin American-Statesman:* "For me, the war was never about right or wrong but duty and honoring my uniform."

Three million dead people.

Never about right or wrong.

Granted, it's dangerous to generalize, but over the decades I've encountered thousands of Vietnam veterans with strikingly similar attitudes. The bulk of my fellow veterans, like the author of that letter, seems to believe that in the last analysis it doesn't matter much whether their war was a righteous one. Their country told them to fight. They did. Inflated body counts and free-fire zones and secret bombings and dead children and burning villages and

Ngo Dinh Diem and Bao Dai and the Pentagon Papers and the recorded Oval Office lies of Nixon and Johnson—all this is irrelevant. It's not a question of disagreement. It's a question of *relevance*. What seems to matter to my former war buddies is not politics or history—certainly not disputes over what occurred on that dark night in the Gulf of Tonkin in 1964—but rather something almost wholly personal: personal sacrifice, personal honor, personal duty, personal suffering, personal patriotism, personal courage, and personal pride. Most Vietnam veterans, I think, will concede that their war was far from morally ideal or clear-cut. It wasn't World War Two. But even so—in fact, especially so—they saluted and sucked it up and endured the nightmare. Good war or bad war, they did their best. And now many of them are bitter. As they move into old age, most of my former buddies see themselves as unappreciated scapegoats, victims of an unpopular war, and as a consequence they have retreated from discursive politics, shying away from contested judgments about the war's rectitude, taking refuge in personal (and therefore incontestable) values of honor, duty, sacrifice, pride, and service to country.

In a way this is understandable. I feel the bitterness myself. I feel the resentment. I yell at my TV set when I hear World War Two veterans described as "the greatest generation," as if the blood spilled on Okinawa was of higher quality per pint than the blood spilled in Vietnam. "The greatest generation"—it doesn't merely sound like an insult. It *is* an insult. No wonder so many of my buddies have retreated into a private interior space, a space insulated from challenges to the war's rectitude, a space in which they can hold fast to their beleaguered sense of virtue.

Still, although I sympathize with this insularity, I fear that a dangerous egocentrism—a kind of selfishness, a kind of narcissism—has blinded many Vietnam veterans to what the war did to *other* people. They don't seem to care much. They don't seem to think about it much. Among my fellow veterans I almost never hear expressions of pity for the orphans and widows and grieving mothers of Vietnam; in fact, I rarely hear the word "Vietnamese" at all. It's as if the country had never been populated by the very people we had come to rescue from the legions of evil. What about the sacrifices of the Vietnamese? What about *their* honor? What about *their* victimization? What about *their* three million dead? What about *their* burned-to-the-ground houses? What about *their* PTSD problems? What about *their* missing legs? What about *their* Gold Star Mothers? What about *their* 300,000 husbands and sons and brothers who have been listed as missing in action for almost half a century?

I'm appalled.

It is one thing to take personal pride in military service. It is another thing to do so without somehow acknowledging the consequences your service had on others—including millions of noncombatants. One man's pride is another man's sorrow. One man's service to country is another man's dead son. Rectitude is not a one-way street.

———

For all the differences between us, I can't help but feel the instantaneous urge to sob when I encounter my old war buddies. An email will do it to me. I'll choke up at old photographs. On several occasions—maybe a dozen or so times over the years—former members of Alpha Company have shown up when I speak at colleges around the country, and when I see their timeworn faces in the audience, the urge to cry stops being just an urge and becomes a fast heartbeat and stinging eyes and a voice that cracks and won't behave itself. This is love, I guess. And love forgives a great deal.

More than that, I admire so much about these men.

Half a century ago, amid the horror, their courage and comportment had seemed to me close to miraculous. They stood up under fire. They made their legs move. They did what they believed to be necessary and even virtuous. They searched tunnels, walked point, gave aid to one another, and obeyed even the silliest and most lethal commands. No one faked illness; no one refused to advance under fire. Also, what made them special, at least to me, was how relentlessly ordinary they were—so matter-of-fact, so impassive, so young, so stolidly unexceptional as they endured things that seemed beyond enduring. In a way, my war buddies are like a mirrored reflection of all the anonymous grunts populating the age-old record of man killing man, including a reflection of the enemy we had once faced, an enemy who also made their legs move, who also did what they believed to be necessary and virtuous, who also obeyed the silliest and most lethal orders, and who also endured the unendurable.

After my buddies and I shake hands and say goodbye, returning to our decaying lives, there is always a melancholy that stays with me for a day or two.

The melancholy reaches into history.

I'll think about Willy and Cop and Kid and Buddy Wolf and Buddy Barney, and then I'll think about Shakespeare's band of brothers, we happy few. I'll find myself deleting the word "happy." I'll wonder how happy the dead were to become the dead, or how happy the legless were to become the legless, and although Shakespeare's music stirs the brotherhood inside me, it is also true that the toneless dead must be included among my war buddies. To them, as much as to the living, I am allegiant.

44

A Maybe Book (II)

I'm an old man now, and when I put the period on this sentence I will be a minute or two older. How many more sentences can there be?

Though this can be taken as self-pitying, it is not. True, I feel desperate this morning, and I feel sad, but the desperation and sadness are not for me but for Timmy and Tad. I want them to have a living father and not a dead one. For a couple of hours I've been repeatedly bending over to get blood to my brain and to stop my heart from racing. If I don't bend, I will pass out. Something is wrong, obviously, and whatever is wrong has been wrong for several weeks. Tests have been inconclusive. Tomorrow I'll be tested again. For now, I will just keep making sentences for my sons, none of which will replace an actual living father, but perhaps, with some luck, they might one day know that their father was thinking of them on a scary, subfreezing January morning.

Three times in the past twenty minutes, I've had to lay my head on my desk, hoping to make my heart behave.

When I look over the very few words I've written this morning, I think of how much more I have to say to Timmy and Tad, and I think about the urgency of saying it, and how, in that urgency, I have written things that only the most generous reader would not at times find sentimental. But what can I do? Delete what I care about? Delete the squeeze inside me? Ernest Hemingway once suggested writing the truest sentence you know, which is excellent advice, but what if your truest sentence is a sentimental one? Do you fancy it up? Do you sober it up? Do you chill it with literary ice? Do you insert distance where there is none? Do you lie? Do you write an untrue sentence and hope no one notices?

I think about Faulkner's Nobel speech: "I believe that man will not merely endure: he will prevail." There is the sound of comfort in this sentence, and yet I cannot make myself believe what Faulkner believes. Prevailing is out of the question. It's ridiculous.

I do believe Faulkner when he declares, in *The Sound and the Fury*, that "victory is an illusion of philosophers and fools."

The café will close its doors.

And yet we live otherwise, don't we?

Faulkner deployed the word "illusion" a few sentences ago, and by and large, despite my bleak thoughts this morning, I dawdle here in the wee-hour café for a last drink or two, toasting my sleeping sons, wishing to leave a mark of love with these nouns and verbs. It's illusion, I know. The nouns, too, will burn with the flaring of the sun. The verbs will twinkle out. And yet—precious illusion—when daylight comes, when my boys awaken, I will fill their bowls with Frosted Flakes, make sure their teeth get brushed, wash and dry the breakfast dishes, chuckle at ditzy politicians getting in their licks on NPR, and then, perhaps later, before I nap, I will try to push this maybe book forward another paragraph or two.

If it is not an ailing heart, it will be ailing lungs, and if it is not ailing lungs, it will someday be an ailing something, as it will be for all of us, and what has been bothering me over the past few weeks, and what brings on the clock-ticking urgency, is the hundred or so little notes piled up on my desk, things I want to tell Timmy and Tad, things I want them to know.

I write so slowly—how can I tell my kids all I want to tell them? Each of the scraps of paper on my desk seems to whisper, "Tell me, put me in, don't forget me," and yet this is only a maybe book, and I am only a maybe-writer, just as every writer was once a maybe-writer and just as every book was once a maybe book. Things intervene between maybe and is. Words fail, energy flags, imagination runs dry, influenza rages, lungs collapse, insanity intrudes, the second hand jerks to a stop, and what had been a maybe book sails off into the oblivion of a never book. So now, as a safeguard, I want to scribble down a few details about how this maybe book came to maybe be. Much earlier in these pages, I mentioned that the idea was Tad's, who several years ago asked how my book was going. I told him I wasn't sure it would ever be a book. I loathed writing. I was struggling. I'm always struggling.

"Well," Tad said, "then I guess you should call it your maybe book. Why not call it what it really is?"

I thought this over and then jotted down the idea and added it to my pile of notes.

Tad turned, began to walk away, but stopped and looked back at me. "You get paid for these books, don't you?"

"Only if they're good," I told him.

"What does that mean?"

"It means sometimes everything ends up in a trash can. It's one of the maybe-problems."

"But what if you get lucky?" Tad said. "What if the book's okay? *Then* do they pay you?"

"Usually," I said.

"Do they pay extra for the title?"

Tad, who will one day own the Western Hemisphere, went off to prepare an IOU for my signature.

Title or no title, I've been calling these pages my maybe book over the years since that short conversation, as has everyone else in our family, because embedded in Tad's effortlessly minted ne-ologism is both hopefulness and fatalism. Who knows? If I don't lose heart, if I keep whacking away, maybe I will reach the end of this maybe book before the end reaches me. And of course I'm not alone. We are all writing our maybe books full of maybe-tomorrows, and each maybe-tomorrow brings another maybe-tomorrow, and then another, until the last line of the last page receives its period.

45

The Magic Show (II)

Magicians, like storytellers, have been burned at the stake, nailed to the cross, beheaded, and otherwise eliminated for their blasphemous violations of prevailing orthodoxy. John the Baptist and Jesus are two miracle-working storytellers who reportedly paid the dearest price. More recently, in 2011, a Saudi Arabian performer of "black" magic was publicly and very bloodily beheaded. In the centuries between the time of Christ and 2011, storytellers and magicians, poets and witches, artists and fortunetellers, scientists and dabblers in the occult, have time and again collided with deadly orthodoxy, sometimes of a religious variety, sometimes political, and very often a flammable mix of the two. Heresy has a long and distinguished list of victims, among them Dietrich Bonhoeffer, and also among them Isaac Babel and Thomas More and the good mothers of Salem, Massachusetts.

These days, magicians have little reason to fear the death penalty. (But stay away from Saudi Arabia and parts of rural Texas.)

The writer, however, still risks a great deal, including life itself, in the pursuit of an interesting story, mainly because "interesting" and "orthodoxy" do not always travel in the same company. Even in the United States, with the protections of the First Amendment, a writer's work may be banned by school boards, forbidden from the pulpit, and denounced in the halls of Congress. For the writer, this is death more obliterating than death.

Speaking for myself, I have observed that book banners do not seem to be crying "Wow" as they read my stories.

They take little delight in my magic shows.

Cannily, they have figured out that a soldier's desperate "Oh fuck" is corruptive of virgins; they have also figured out that exposure to wartime profanity undermines the mental health of wrestling fans. While they do not wish to ban the obscenity of war itself, and while they do not forbid their children from marching off to kill people (where they will learn some exceptionally inventive, fresh-off-the-press dirty words), they have concluded that the filthy truth is filthier than the filthy lie. The denouncers and forbidders want a mangled, gurgling, dying man to get a grip on his dignity, to bear in mind his Christian values, to stuff his intestines tidily out of sight, and to murmur to his grieving buddy, "Oh poop, I've been shot."

How this connects to magic may seem tenuous. But it connects.

Like the mangled soldier, like the betrayed housewife, like the abandoned child, like the lonely piano teacher, like the bereft widower, like the forsaken bride, like the humiliated accountant, like the forgotten saint, like the unappreciated mother, like the alcoholic father, like the fallen angel, like the toe-tapping politician in his toilet stall, like the paraplegic in his wheelchair, like the sinner on his hands and knees, like you and me — all of us, even those who despise magic, even book banners, even those who repair machine guns and deconstruct art, will almost certainly, at one terrible time or another, peer into the dark and yearn for a miracle.

46

Practical Magic

After one of our living room magic shows, as I tucked Tad into bed, he said to me, "You should do something useful with your magic."

"Like what?"

"Like make spinach disappear. And bedtime."

47

An Immodest and
Altogether Earnest Proposal

In furtherance of transparency, to which a great many politicians have lately pledged their allegiance if not always their behavior, I propose we eliminate the word "war" from our vocabulary and substitute the words "killing people, including children."

Wordy, to be sure, and maybe a trifle difficult to push off the tongue. But imagine the frank, openhearted transparency that will ensue if we dispense with declarations of war—already quaintly outdated—in favor of more refreshing congressional resolves to kill people, including children. When we revisit Cervantes, imagine how poetic it will be to read: "All's fair in love and killing people, including children." Monuments will be renamed, statues will be rededicated. Instead of Sergeant York the war hero, we will honor Sergeant York the killing-people hero. Instead of Woodrow Wilson's war to end all wars, we will have Woodrow Wilson's killing people (including children) to end all killing people. It is true, of course, that we may have to resign ourselves to some unfortunate linguistic constructions, as when we retranslate the title of Tolstoy's masterpiece to *Killing People, Including Children, and Not Killing People, Including Children*. Musicality may suffer with the redesigned jacket cover of H. G. Wells's *The Killing People, Including Children, of the Worlds*. Occasionally, as a means of avoiding the most painful tongue twisters, we may find it helpful to reverse a word order here and there: "people-killing" instead of "killing people." Thereby, in classrooms across our great republic, children will study the People-Killing of the Roses and the First World People-Killing and the Second World People-Killing and the Korean People-Killing and the Vietnam People-Killing and the People-Killing on Terror. With practice, taking care to lubricate our tongues, we shall surely conquer the oxymoronic mouthful of the American Civil People-Killing.

Yes, a certain klutziness of expression may be our fate, yet who but an effete fuddy-duddy will not celebrate the salutary effects of my proposal?

Forthrightness as never before.

Straight shooting as never before.

Since we are plainly without shame in our people-killing, including children, why not square our shoulders and also without shame call people-killing people-killing? What is there to fear? A few extra syllables? A few startled English teachers? Instantly, and with invigorating transparency, a hurricane of fresh sea air will blow through our musty old dictionaries—war brides becoming people-killing brides, war horses becoming people-killing horses, war crimes becoming (perhaps a tad redundantly) people-killing crimes. Moreover, as a purely personal matter, I will no longer be compelled to complain about being called a war writer. Henceforth I will be known as a people-killing writer, or, at the very least, as an ordinary writer-writer writing about people-killing and people-killers. My war buddies will be people-killing buddies; my war medals will be people-killing medals; my war stories will be (suspiciously embittered) people-killing stories.

For our admirals and generals, who understand the importance of blunt, no-nonsense language, it will undoubtedly come as a welcome relief to call a spade a spade and a war a people-killing. Theaters of war will become theaters of people-killing, including children; the US Army War College will gratefully and with soldierly pride rename its flagship course The Theory of People-Killing, Including Children, and Strategies for Doing So. "The Marines' Hymn," a title missing from most Baptist hymnals, will henceforth go for the jugular, just as Marines have been trained to do over the centuries. Hymn, be damned. It may only be a song, but it's a Semper Fi song, and the Corps will jubilantly dispense with the song's gooey, bloodless words "fight" and "fought" and "serve" and "guard," replacing them with a reverent "Hoo-rah! Kill people! Children, too!" (Marines are groomed to kill people, not gazelles and ladybugs.) In the same spirit of transparent clarity, the collected correspondence of Grant, Sherman, Patton, Pershing, MacArthur, Rommel, Bradley, and LeMay will require exhaustive vetting. "War is hell" may be fine for ostriches, but "People-killing is hell" zooms up the food chain to embrace our own advanced species, which includes both people-killers and those clumsy enough to get themselves people-killed. Also, after some precision sandblasting, the amended words of General

Robert E. Lee will blaze for eons on monuments from Atlanta to Richmond: "It is well that people-killing is so terrible, otherwise we should grow too fond of it." (Fondness, in this instance, may be partly a function of a good pair of binoculars and a distance of just over half a mile. But fun is still fun.)

As a corollary to my proposal, the Defense Department—soon to be rechristened the People-Killing Department—will assign new and completely transparent military ranks to its personnel. A lowly private, for example, will become an apprentice people-killer. A first lieutenant will enjoy the rank, pay grade, and perks of a midlevel people-killer, and, in the role of head people-killing honcho, a general of the army will from this point onward be known as a super-duper-expert people-killer. Or something equally deserved.

————

And let us not ignore the venerable ancients—the Joshuas and Mark Antonys and Charlemagnes of our people-killing history. They too will be among the beneficiaries of my proposal. Pericles's Funeral Oration will vibrate with greater chutzpah, greater brilliance, as he declaims, "Our city is equally admirable in peace and in people-killing," for what else could resound through the ages with more evident virtue than killing people? Likewise, the wisdom of Plato suffers not a whit from some immodest substitutive updating. "Only the dead have seen the end of people-killing" loses nothing of the original and gains a nice lurid zing of modernity. Same with

Aquinas. Same with Aristotle. Same with Sophocles. Why keep the slaughter secret? After all, we are not killing Muppets. We are killing people, are we not? And therefore let us heed the bipartisan call of Paul Ryan and Hillary Clinton—transparency!

Imagine how much more forcefully the DEA will wage the People-Killing on Drugs.

Imagine, too, a People-Killing on Poverty that solves the problem of lazy idleness once and for all.

And—admit it—the heart gladdens to envision Carl von Clausewitz's ponderous prose suddenly selling in the millions after it is juiced up with the title *On Killing People, Including Children*. Fill the book with grisly photographs, lose the Teutonic lingo, and behold a coffee table masterpiece.

Granted, a few ivory-tower purists may rebel at my proposed overhaul of William Shakespeare's collected works. The Bard's spineless and tragically euphemistic cop-outs are too numerous to mention, but here, for the purposes of illustration, are a few revamped outtakes: \"the dogs of people-killing," "the fire-eyed maid of smoky people-killing," "once more unto the people-killing (including children) breach, dear people-killers, once more."

What we lose in Shakespearian beats-per-line we salvage in dying-beats-per-human-heart. If we do not mean what we say, why say it? And conversely, if we must cloak our people-killing in the guise of prettifying simile, and if we must bury people-killing in a grave of weak-willed lyricism, why bother to kill people at all? There is no reason to be bashful. Let each of us, the blushing Bard included, strip away pretense and stand naked before those who would subvert meat-and-potatoes people-killing.

In addition to refurbishing the discredited plays of Shakespeare, my proposal would require that other canonized works of drama, history, philosophy, religion, fiction, poetry, and film be transported immediately to the offices of a competent linguistic surgeon. Without dwelling on details, the obvious list includes, but is not limited to, the following:

> *The Story of Civilization* (all eleven volumes)
> *Encyclopædia Britannica*
> *Webster's Third New International Dictionary*
> The *Bhagavad Gita*
> The *Iliad* and parts of the *Odyssey*
> *Beowulf*
> *The Decline and Fall of the Roman Empire* (unabridged, but thoroughly expurgated)
> The Old Testament and much of the New
> *Saving Private Ryan*
> *The Collected Speeches of Joseph Goebbels*
> *Artillery of the Napoleonic Wars: A Concise Dictionary*
> *A Tale of Two Cities*
> *On the Town*
> *Anchors Aweigh*
> and so on.

Once these cultural mainstays have undergone a good attic-to-basement scrubbing, my proposal will pay dividends of the most forthright, uninhibited, and brilliantly transparent sort. From sea to sea, pastors and priests, rabbis and imams, will find it a relief to be rid of the bland, abstract, and colorless euphemism "war." Now, liberated by my proposal, the clergy will declaim from the pulpit our stirring retranslation of Ecclesiastes: "a time to love and a time to hate, a time for killing people, including children, and a time for not killing people, including children." Why pull divine punches? Why kowtow to squeamish congregations? Did not the Lord himself command Saul to attack the Amalekites, to "put to death men and women, children and infants"? If God Almighty can go children-killing berserk, why not accept His example as a helpful guide to Presbyterians and Lutherans and, of course, to be fair, discontented Sunni Muslims? Would not Numbers 31:3 ring with considerably more poetic charm if it were to read: "from all the tribes of Israel you shall send to people-killing, including children"? If my proposal takes its anticipated course—and why should it not?—a modern-day People's Crusade might soon be led by the evangelical inheritors of Peter the Hermit, a determined flock of people-killers, people-killing their way through the holy lands and then well beyond, people-killing their way north to Kabul, south to Sudan, east to the ill-named Pacific, and west to the thatched cottages of Stratford-upon-Avon, where all the wishy-washy euphemisms rose to their pathetic zenith.

And—delight of delights—how can we overlook the hallelujahs of those fire-eyed literalists among us?

Who more than they will raise their voices in praise of the strict, word-for-word literalism of "killing people, including children"? No metaphors here! No figurative evasions! If literal means literal, and if literalism is more than a selective convenience, Liberty University will soon break ground for its $8.3 million Center for the Study and Advancement of Killing People, Including Children.

Immodestly, perhaps, yet with the confidence of blazing, people-killing rectitude, I expect to be on hand for the center's inaugural dispersal of honorary doctorates.

To be sure, certain minor but essential linguistic revisions will be needed to fine-tune my proposal. For instance, "battlefield" must be banished in favor of "people-killing field." A "battle cry" will become a "people-killing cry." On July Fourth we will gather on the town square to sing that celebrative tearjerker "The People-Killing Hymn of the Republic." Most such repairs can be completed in an instant. A few will require the exercise of a censor's bluest blue pencil. A case in point is the Gettysburg Address, a piece of prose that, despite its economical genius, could profit from some extended and uneconomical tinkering. After all, brevity is not everything—not when the stakes are high. With some judicious editing, our nation's collective pulse will still quicken at the phrase "Now we are engaged in a great civil people-killing," and at the words "We are met on a great people-killing field of that people-killing," and at the rhetorically soul-thumping crescendo: "The brave people-killers, living and dead, who people-killed here, have consecrated it, far above our poor power to add or detract."

The author's marble statuary, like our hearts, will melt in appreciation. Abraham Lincoln was nothing if he was not Honest Abe.

Similarly, the word "service" demands our attention. Rather than receiving still another heartfelt "Thank you for your service," veterans will now pridefully blush at the phrase "Thank you for killing people." Or at the very minimum, "Thank you for *trying* to kill people." Furthermore, in the spirit of linguistic consistency, it goes without saying that the term "serviceman" must be replaced by the more precise "people-killing man" (or woman). And why not? Are we so terrified of the dentist as to call his (or her) office a "tooth spa"? Of course not. Therefore, why shoot our vocabulary full of Novocain when it comes to age-old, time-tested people-killing? Are we afraid we may not visit the office quite as often? Are we afraid of the explicit? Are we ashamed? Exactly the reverse. We people-kill for freedom, we people-kill for honor, we people-kill for democracy, we people-kill for our way of life and for a better and richer and happier and more prosperous tomorrow. Let us summon a backbone! Why stoop to the nitpicking, hairsplitting language of diplomats and negotiators and other such enfeebled and cowardly non-people-killers?

Along almost identical lines, the term "soldier" cries out for lexical refreshment. Already, the US armed forces and the Veterans Administration are well on the road to that end, substituting the word "warriors" for "soldiers," as in the recent adoption of the sobriquet "wounded warriors." However, on the patriotic downside, this glowing honorific may cause problems in the long run, since our famed American fairness might compel us to dignify the injured troops of ISIS and al-Qaida with the same rhetorical sympathy. That would never do. Only a terrorist-traitor would feel at home calling a bearded jihadist a wounded warrior. May I therefore suggest the more descriptively accurate use of "people-killers" when referring to troops of any variety. Thus, back in church again, we will lustily sing "Onward, Christian People-Killers." Peter, Paul and Mary will sing "Gone for people-killers every one." (Again, the purpose of people-killing is to kill *people*, not goldfish.) Along the same lines, my proposal would incorporate slight improvements to the word "fight," with the inspiring and emboldening result that Winston Churchill's famous speech will now read: "We shall kill people on the beaches, we shall kill people on the landing grounds, we shall kill people in the fields and in the streets, we shall kill people, including children, in the hills; we shall never surrender." How could even the dullest, most apathetic citizen fail to take up arms?

Arms—still another sanitizing term in desperate need of modernization.

Also: *force, struggle, contest, combat, incursion, intervention, hostilities, military means, conflict,* and *police action.*

With the speedy adoption of my proposal, the Spokane Police Department, among others, will be much indebted to me for having removed its burdensome and expensive worldwide policing obligations. Newscasters will no longer fritter away precious hours in search of heartwarming euphemisms for other heartwarming euphemisms. Down at the American Legion hall, old fogies will no longer swap war stories, or hostilities stories, or intervention stories, or incursion stories. They will spin people-killing yarns. The roll will be called, the flag will be raised, and eyes will moisten as ex-people-killers salute their fallen comrades-in-people-killing. In the nation's capital, steely-eyed Presidents will lay wreathes at the Tomb of the Unknown People-Killer. In the Cayman Islands, seersucker-suited arms dealers—now people-killing dealers—will do people-killing business with a fresh new slate. In boardrooms from California to Delaware, Fortune 500 arms manufacturers—now people-killing manufacturers—will pop the cork in celebration of steady, upward-trending people-killing revenues. Granted, with all its variants, the term "arms" will take time to eradicate —armed forces, armies, armor, armory, armament—but who except a contentiously ungrateful Norman Mailer could object to a reissue of *The People-Killers of the Night*? Who but the Hemingway Society would dare deny that *A Farewell to People-Killing, Including Children* comes melodiously—even bitingly—off the tongue? Can anyone of sound mind doubt that the United States People-Killing Academy will attract a more stalwart pool of applicants after its grand people-killing reopening? Hats will soar skyward; parents will beam; a golden age of people-killing candor will swiftly and surely dawn.

All in all, despite pockets of resistance, only the embattled (uh-oh) few will fail to recognize the value of linguistic transparency in a world of head-in-the-sand, avoid-the-obvious opacity. A few tipsy members of the Veterans of Foreign Wars will probably call into question the motives that underlie my proposal, yet even they will soon grow fond of their paper napkins imprinted with a brand-new and attractively symmetrical logo: Ex-People-Killers of Foreign People-Killings. In any event, for now, I look forward to delivering the keynote at the EPKFPK's annual convention in Tuscaloosa. My people-killing attire—formerly called a Class A uniform—has been dry-cleaned, pressed, and encased in plastic. The standing ovation, I immodestly anticipate, will be thunderous.

48

The Golden Viking

It is March 12, 2017, and I have awakened from lunacy. Almost a month ago, I was diagnosed with influenza, which evolved into undiagnosed pneumonia, which soon carried me away into a hallucinatory dreamscape that even now seems as real as last night's pot roast. I had been instructed to take fluids and to sleep. I did so for many days, sleeping virtually nonstop, and on a Saturday afternoon in mid-February I seemed to slither into half-wakefulness when I heard Meredith and Timmy and Tad return home from a middle school basketball game.

As Timmy passed by my sick-couch in the living room, I asked if the food had arrived.

"What food?" Timmy asked.

"The food you ordered."

"But I didn't order any food. I just got home from my game."

"No, I heard you order food," I said sternly. "I saw you do it."

Timmy looked at me with bewilderment, then fear. "Dad," he said, "I didn't order anything. I haven't even *been* here."

This upset me. I told him not to lie.

At that point things tumbled.

Timmy asked who was delivering the food. I told him it was coming from a body shop, on a conveyor belt.

For a second or two, I fell asleep again.

And then, distantly, as if from another room, I heard Timmy explaining that body shops don't deliver food, that conveyor belts can't carry hamburgers and French fries to every house in town. Again, I drifted off. And later—maybe a split second later—Meredith was there, trying to reason with me, and Timmy was crying, and for an instant there was a flash of clarity—I was sick, I knew that—but then I heard myself, a different self, getting angry, really angry, telling them I wasn't crazy, that I'd heard Timmy ordering food, that I'd watched him place the phone call, that this particular body shop delivered food, and that I'd seen the actual conveyor belt running up to our front door. I fell asleep again. I woke up again. Timmy was still crying. Meredith was bending over me with a bottle of water. To me, it was the flu, but to Meredith, and especially to Timmy, it was (I learned much later) indescribable helplessness and fear.

"You dreamed it all," Meredith kept saying, which infuriated me.

My whole family, I thought, had lost its marbles.

Later in the day, probably around nightfall, I awakened once more to find Timmy staring at me from what seemed a million miles away. I asked how his basketball game had turned out. I asked if the Golden Viking had been there.

My son's eyes shifted.

"What's a Golden Viking?" he asked.

"You didn't see him?"

"See who?"

Now, a month afterward, it's a complete jumble in my head, but at the time the Golden Viking was an actual human being, as real as the words I'm now typing: I had found his photo online. He was a Scandinavian graduate student. He played center on the opposing school's eighth-grade basketball team. He stood six feet five inches. His hair was golden blond. His name was Lars. He wore heavy chain armor and a helmet topped with a pair of Viking horns. At game time, he descended to the basketball floor by way of wires attached to the ceiling. He was a basketball magician. He was unstoppable. You couldn't miss him.

"There wasn't any Viking," Timmy said.

"What about the Vikingettes?"

"Who?"

"The cheerleaders. The ones wearing Viking helmets."

"I didn't see that," said Timmy, "and I don't think—"

"What about the Viking ship?"

Timmy moistened his lips. He wasn't looking at me now. "A ship at a basketball game?"

"Up in the bleachers," I said.

It did not end there. I quizzed Timmy about several other such Vikingesque details, each of which had—for me and for me alone

—the blistering clarity of the here and now. For Timmy, though, there was the fearful and delicate problem of dealing with a father who had plainly gone insane.

That night, Timmy slept with his mother. He was afraid of me.

Around noon on the following day, after the intervention of a physician friend, I was transported to an emergency room and within minutes found myself hospitalized with pneumonia. My white blood cell count was off the charts; I was dehydrated; I was anemic; I had trouble answering yes-or-no questions; my brain felt like lard; my kidneys and liver and pancreas and digestive system were shutting down. Though I remember very little from that time, I have the distinct recollection of a thick, slushy infection rolling around in my chest cavity, sloshing from organ to organ, and in retrospect I am pretty sure that this cement-mixer sensation was not fictitious. I'm pretty sure I was dying.

I remember no fear. I was too sick to know how sick I was. In fact, if there was any emotion at all, it amounted to a kind of spellbound curiosity, an awestruck, almost reverent fascination with the bizarre goings-on inside me and all around me. During my first several nights in the hospital, a pair of identical Asian nurses paid frequent visits to my bedside, speaking not a word, hovering in the pitch dark as they took turns stabbing at my forearms until one of them found a vein. They were inept. They were silent as stone. They were pitiless. They were incapable of pity. These mute, nearsighted twins may have been a product of my imagination, or a product of raging disease, but in the hospital dark they seemed to me as real as Tad and Timmy, as real as the Golden Viking, and as real as a body-shop burger riding its conveyor belt to my front door.

A month has passed.

I'm still weak, still sleeping a great deal, but the worst is over. For the present.

In the days since my discharge from the hospital, I've learned that hallucinations can be a consequence of high fever, dehydration, extreme fatigue, and kidney failure, all of which accompanied my encounter with pneumonia. I've also discovered that hallucinations often precede, and may even predict, the onset of death. It's comforting, I suppose, to know that our bodies seem to shield us, at least in part, from the terrors of approaching extinction, replacing reality with an alternate reality, sending Golden Vikings and body-shop burgers to the rescue. Hallucination eases the way. (Again, I remember no fear at all.) Maybe it's a crackpot theory, but in the aftermath of my sickness, I've often wondered if what we call insanity might be a biological response to mankind's consciousness of its own mortality, a way of unknowing what we know, a defense against the specter of nothingness and foreverness and intolerable finality.

Even more than this, I now have the peculiar feeling that I've spent the past month hitting buckets of balls in preparation for a final round of golf. I needed the practice. I hope it helps. Like any prudent seventy-one-year-old father, I've engaged in other such preparations—signing a will, doing some estate planning—and my brush with delusion has left me with a similar sense of preparatory peace. It is the peace of which John Dryden speaks in *The Spanish Friar:* "There is pleasure sure, / In being mad, which none but madmen know." Likewise, in the face of cruel and incomprehensible extinction, it is also the peace of which William Blake speaks in *The Marriage of Heaven and Hell:* "I was walking among the fires of Hell, delighted with the enjoyments of Genius; which to Angels look like torment and insanity."

As nearly as I will ever know, this is how the end will be. A benevolent fog will precede the dark. Reality will vanish before reality claims me.

And so, now, though still dazed by recent events, I am convinced it was all for the better. If nothing else, the ordeal amounted to a Vietnam refresher course—an intimate, dreamlike, hello-again reacquaintance with the beasts of oblivion howling at the doorstep. The whole war was hallucination—every evil tick of the clock—the air in my lungs, the whispering rice paddies, the dripping sounds in the grass and trees, the sunlight striking the faces of the dead. Also, at the conclusion of any battle, there was always a shocking slap of aliveness—the miracle of aliveness, the surprise of aliveness, the undeserved gift of aliveness—a sensation that has again come over me in these quiet days after my discharge from the hospital. I am alive, yes, and the world is alive, and yet, in an upside-down way, the aliveness is as bizarre and unsettling as body-shop burgers riding a conveyor belt. After living for two weeks in a world of lunacy, I'm having trouble shifting back into the everyday world of so-called reality. It is surreal and alien. Fatherhood seems implausible. Gravity seems implausible. Breakfast seems implausible. My face in a mirror seems implausible—how can I still be here? And where is *here*? Is it a place? Or is hereness in my head? And who is this bruised and sunken-eyed creature staring back at me? Although it's hard to admit, even Timmy and Tad and Meredith sometimes seem to have stepped out of a feverish pneumonia dream, as if from another universe, or as if Lars the Golden Viking had suddenly rung the doorbell and joined us for a dinner of meatballs and red wine and Scandinavian chitchat.

Still, I'm improving.

Lars did not visit last night. Perhaps we bore him. Perhaps he has other engagements.

And Tad and Timmy and Meredith seem more real with each passing hour. As I gradually rejoin the waking world, I realize with some sadness that I'm exchanging one illusion for another. The Golden Viking is being replaced by the familiar old hallucination of immortality, the hallucination that keeps us moving through our lives, the hallucination that keeps us sane, the hallucination that sends us off to cocktail parties and bridge tournaments, the hallucination that protects us from the astonishing reality that what now exists will one day not exist. In any event, there is comfort in having completed a two-week dress rehearsal, shedding some stage fright, learning my lines, getting my act together for opening night.

49

Timmy and Tad and Papa and I (IV)

Half a century ago, after returning from Vietnam, I took a do-nothing job in the Twin Cities, quit the job after a few weeks, loafed, pretended I was okay, discovered I was not, and then eventually drove north and spent time on Madeline Island in Lake Superior. I slept on a beach, without company, which was unpleasant, but which seemed necessary. I rarely spoke with anyone. At night I drank beer and sat listening to the radio in my car. Nothing in particular was bothering me—no panic attacks, no bad dreams—and the war seemed impossibly distant, almost unreal, as if for the past year I'd been soundly asleep on this pretty beach in Lake Superior. Very occasionally, and only at night, a disagreeable image might come to mind, but the image seemed to be the property of another human being, or the property of history. I'd picture a corpse, for instance, and then a short film would unwind in my head, a few seconds of horror and disbelief, except both the horror and the disbelief belonged to the man in the moon.

By and large, despite this, I was content on Madeline Island. I ate fresh fish in a small and mostly deserted café. I lay in the sun and thought about girls. I worried about the coming months and what I might realistically do with myself, whether to attend graduate school in Massachusetts or husk corn in South Dakota. Vietnam was absent. It was not that I *could* not remember; it was not that I *tried* not to remember; remembering simply did not *happen*. When night came, I scooped out a shallow trench on the beach along Lake Superior and climbed into my sleeping bag and swiftly and deeply slept.

Now, at age seventy-one, I'm still scooping out a trench each night. The trench is how I get by. It's how I've gotten by for decades. In imagination, after the lights go out, I transform my bed into a shallow hole in the earth. I string barbed wire, emplace machine guns, put out the claymores and trip flares, establish listening posts, load my weapon, walk the perimeter for a time, check to be sure my helmet and flak jacket are nearby, and then ease into the make-believe sleeping trench and eventually sleep. Some people lock their doors at night. I lock the doors in my head.

In Ernest Hemingway's "Big Two-Hearted River: Part I," Nick Adams, another war veteran, goes through a similar ritual as he prepares for the approaching dark:

> Already there was something mysterious and home-like. Nick was happy as he crawled inside the tent.

He had not been unhappy all day. This was different
though. Now things were done. There had been
this to do. Now it was done. It had been a hard trip.
He was very tired. That was done. He had made his
camp. He was settled. Nothing could touch him.

Like Hemingway's Nick Adams, I am not unhappy. I don't
think much about Vietnam. And yet there is always the pressure
of the past, an unspecified and disembodied pressure, a kind of absent weight, a toneless, droning, unrecollected recollection. The
absence of specific references to war in Hemingway's fine story
is typically treated as a literary device—an example of the power
of omission. I certainly don't quarrel with that. But in this case
omission is not entirely a literary strategy; it is also a meticulous
and powerful representation of how war's evil and war's jeopardy
remain present even when they are unsummoned by memory,
even when they are unattached to a particular incident or image.
The evil is faceless. The jeopardy is everywhere. For me and for
Nick Adams, sleep requires the surrender of vigilance, that nothing-can-touch-you sensation. In reality, of course, neither a sheet
of canvas nor an imagined trench offers much in the way of genuine security. But the security that a former soldier seeks is not of
the realistic or genuine sort. What a soldier seeks is a necessary
fantasy, a "mysterious and homelike" illusion of safety, just as we
all seek such illusion as we build our houses and install our security systems and take our vitamins and go to church and erect our
nighttime fortifications against the laws of nature. Birth is a death
sentence. We know this, but we don't want to know.

In his novel *The Night in Lisbon,* Erich Maria Remarque writes: "why is death forever tugging us by the hand, making us move on, even when we are tired, even when we are trying, for one short hour, to keep up the illusion of eternity?"

Once disillusioned, a person gets careful. The cave, the foxhole, the fortress, the fire escape, the seat belt, the nothing-can-touch-you tent—each of these is effaced by time and by the assaults of mortality. For those who have seen combat, as for those who have spent time in a cancer ward or sat at the bedside of a dying child, the illusion of eternity demands assiduous late-hour maintenance, and now, forty-six years after my return from Vietnam, I'm still at it each night, still mending the barbed wire and then repairing my pitiful little sleeping trench.

———

Yesterday morning, Timmy asked what I was writing about. I told him I was writing about coming home from war. My son laughed and said, "Except you *never* came home."

The boy has a point. Some essential part of me remains in Quang Ngai Province, still young and scared, still astonished by my own moral diminishment. Getting old hasn't helped.

Among the strange and bitter ironies that have visited me over these seven decades is the certainty that I will be remembered, if I am remembered at all, as a war writer, despite my hatred for war, despite my ineptitude at war, despite my abiding shame at having participated in war, and despite the fact that I am in no way a spokesman or a "voice" for the 2.6 million American military personnel who served in Vietnam from August 1964 to May 1975. In the eyes of many Vietnam veterans—probably a majority—I'm an outlier. I don't fit in and never did. As far as I can tell, the bulk of those who fought in Vietnam are proud of their service. I am not. They generally believe their cause was just. I do not. Many profess nostalgia about their days in uniform. I do not. Many would do it all again. I would not. A sizable number see themselves as victims—betrayed by politicians, by Hollywood, by *Ramparts* magazine, by an indecisive and weak-willed citizenry, by ivory-tower idiots who blamed them for a failed war. I don't feel that way. I never did. Numerous Vietnam veterans, including a few of my own war buddies, claim to have been spat on when they returned from the war. I make no such claim. (And I was *not* spat on.) Many wanted ticker-tape parades. I did not. I wanted to go home. A good number of the men with whom I served—probably most—view antiwar activity, past and present, as unpatriotic to the point of treasonous. I do not. Many believe the American war in Vietnam was lost not by the United States but rather by leftist news organizations, by ungrateful protesters, by Jane Fonda and Jerry Rubin and Daniel Ellsberg, by intellectuals, by hippies, by Eugene McCarthy, by the South Vietnamese army, by spineless bureaucrats, by Quakers and college professors and the NAACP and draft-card burners and the Chicago Seven and flower children and more or less the entire population of San Francisco back in the year 1969. In fact, as far as I can tell, a substantial number of my fellow veterans believe the United States did not lose the war at all, at least not in a military sense. Many are convinced that the war could have been won, and should have been won, if only vastly superior American firepower had been brought to bear without restraint. I believe none of this. Granted, Vietnam veterans are a mixed bag, as diverse in their opinions as any large population, but for many of them I'm off in left field, a black sheep, a nonplayer, a prodigal son who by some peculiar fluke happened to hump the paddies alongside the real soldiers, the intrepid believers. I'm a softie. I'm a fucking peace writer.

––––––––

We're in the Bahamas, it's Thanksgiving Day, and a few minutes ago Tad wandered out onto the hotel balcony where I sat wrestling with these sentences.

Tad squinted down at my computer screen.

"You shouldn't write the f word," he said sternly.

"Okay. I'll delete it."

"Do it now, before you forget," Tad said. "You'll be in huge trouble if somebody actually *reads* that."

I told him I was already in trouble. It had been a difficult morning at the computer, I explained, and the f word was the least of my problems.

"So what's wrong?" Tad asked.

"The usual. Finding a way to say something."

"About what?"

"About being called a war writer."

"What's so terrible about that?"

"I'm sick of it. I hate war. They don't call Updike a suburb writer. They don't call Conrad an ocean writer."

"Who's Conrad?"

"Joseph Conrad," I said, "was a famous ocean writer specializing in sea turtles. Forget it."

"Well, okay, I will," Tad said quietly, "but I think you should forget it, too. At least they call you *something*."

"You're right," I told him. "Who cares?"

The boy seemed concerned, even agitated. After a moment he wagged his head.

"Obviously *you* care," he said. He opened the balcony's sliding glass door, went into the hotel room, and then poked out his head and said, "Why not tell them to go f themselves?"

———

A war writer, and more narrowly a Vietnam writer, and so it will always be. It's my own fault. I could have said no; I should have said no. There is a sting, though, to the knowledge that the worst thing that ever happened to me will determine almost the entire content of my obituary.

For the record, and for my sons Timmy and Tad, I'll point out that only a minuscule fraction of my interior or exterior life is in any way associated with Vietnam. Although I do daydream about the war occasionally, and although I sometimes night-dream about it, nonetheless, minute by minute, I make my way through the world as a contented civilian. I play Scrabble with my sons. I root for the Minnesota Vikings. I enjoy clam chowder on Christmas Eve, camp out comfortably at the blackjack table when I'm in Vegas, laugh at a good joke, practice sleight of hand in front of the bathroom mirror, try to hit a golf ball, oversee homework, travel too much, attend the boys' basketball games, and generally take surprised pleasure at having made my way out of the blackness of 1969. I'm lucky. My name is not emblazoned on a wall in Washington, D.C. I have both legs and both arms. My mom did not open the door to an army chaplain.

Over the years, both Vietnam-the-war and Vietnam-the-memory have gone from solid to ineffable, from way too real to way too surreal, from up-to-your-eyeballs horror to a kind of hazy uncertainty as to whether any of it had ever occurred. Impossible, it seems. How did I keep my legs moving? How did I, or anyone, not go insane in the midst of all that terror and death? Or *did* I go insane? Or did everybody *else* go insane? Or do we *all* go insane at the very instant of birth, out of necessity, as our only means of continuing to move through a world that cannot be survived?

Lately, in my old age, I've been asking such questions not only about Vietnam but about pretty much everything. All seems vaporous. What has happened over the course of my life, it now appears, could not have happened.

———

Four months before he died, my father and I were seated in matching rocking chairs on a porch attached to his retirement home, sneaking cigarettes, pretty much at peace with each other, and at one point I asked him about his medals from World War

Two: why had they vanished from his dresser drawer? My dad looked up at me and said, "*What* medals?"

"The medals under your socks," I said. "They're gone now."

"Medals," he murmured. "Was I in a war?"

I assured him he had been—Iwo Jima, Okinawa.

It took a while. My father was suffering from in-and-out senility, some days better than others, but after a minute or two he chuckled and said, "Oh, yeah. The navy, you mean. But that was Willie O'Brien. Now I'm Bill O'Brien."

"Good point," I said.

Ten or fifteen minutes later, after we had moved on to other topics, my father suddenly snorted and said, "The navy, those goddamn kamikazes. You sail off to war young and stupid, and then you sail home the oldest man on earth."

A bit later he said, "Not that getting old is all that terrible. You don't worry about the future when there isn't any."

———

Now, years after my father's death, it occurs to me that the most searing events of our lives are those to which we have the least immediate access. "Was I in a war?" said my father, and that question, in various shapes and formulations, swirls in my own head right now, at 4:23 a.m. on January 31, 2017. The very reality of reality makes reality feel tight-skinned and unreal. For instance, a hand grenade sails out of the dense brush of fifty years ago—it's real, it's a real grenade—and I dive behind a paddy dike and squeeze my eyes shut and then open them again to catch a glimpse of that very real fizzling grenade from fifty years ago—a homemade grenade, a red cylindrical can a little bigger than the smallest can of Hunt's tomato paste, and I spin sideways and turn my back to the grenade and squeal Dear Jesus—not aloud, I'm pretty sure (though now, an instant later, I'm not pretty sure, just sort of sure), and then there is blank time that was once filled with who knows what—squirrel talk, caught-fish talk, the terrified mind-chatter of a young boy from the Turkey Capital of the World—and then, after a lapse of ten or twenty centuries, the grenade detonates—not loud, I'm pretty sure (though not pretty sure, just sort of sure)—a popping sound, I'm pretty sure—and yet everything that is happening isn't happening because it absolutely and positively *can't* be happening—the bee-sting sensation in my left hand—a kid named Clauson holding his stomach —somebody shouting, but not shouting words, shouting lizard shouts—another bee sting—and all around me and above me there are the unzipping sounds of eternity passing by—these are bullets, I'm pretty sure—and then nearly fifty years later, at 5:08 a.m. on January 31, 2017, I light a cigarette and take a breath and stare at this paragraph and think, Christ, was I in a war?

In a recent email, one of my old war buddies, Bob Wolf, helped me realize that I'm not alone in this dreamscape of endless seemingness, endless uncertainty, and endless maybes.

"I lost my own history," Buddy Wolf wrote. "I spent a year in the Republic of South Viet Nam, and I came away with a chest full of medals, but no memories. Oh, I remember names and faces and home towns of my friends, but I have no recollection of events. Perhaps this is why I am asking so many questions. I'm sending e-mails pleading for memories."

———

In *A Farewell to Arms*, Ernest Hemingway's protagonist, Frederic Henry, has similar difficulty disentangling the fragile threads of reality. For all the detailed, precise, and firmly convincing realism with which Hemingway gives us the Italian retreat from Caporetto in 1917—a piece of sustained prose that has been justly praised over the decades—what most moves me in this celebrated passage is the dreamlike delicacy of disbelief and uncertainty that questions and challenges and ultimately subverts all that famous rock-hard realism. In the course of recounting his story, Frederic Henry performs a kind of division of the self, the pronoun "I" blurring into the pronoun "you" and then blurring back again into "I," much as my father had moved from Willie O'Brien to Bill O'Brien as he sought a handhold on his own life. At one point during the chaotic retreat, Frederic Henry remarks, "You saw emptily," which reminds me of the emptiness of my own vision as a homemade grenade sails out of the brush at 5:16 a.m. and as the lizard squeals Dear Jesus. Am I actually *seeing* what I am seeing? If not, then what exactly *am* I seeing? And without some central solidity of vision, aren't we doomed to doubt the very reality of our own lives?

A little later in *A Farewell to Arms*, Henry's sense of reality is further warped by, and further diminished by, the feeling that he has become "a masquerader," a man now suddenly dressed in civilian clothes, a wartime absentee who sits in a Milan bar eating almonds and sipping a martini. Nearly five decades ago, having just returned from my own war, I too felt a shaky, counterfeit sensation as I put on a suit and tie for my do-nothing job in the Twin Cities. It was as if I were in disguise, partly a physical one, partly emotional. Nothing seemed real. Not the suit, not the tie, not me. Also, it's worth noting that even during the war I often had the sensation of performing as an actor in a long and very realistic war movie. I put on the rubber mask of fatalism. I copped cool bits of dialogue from old movies and old comic strips—wistful lines, macho lines, funny lines, tough-guy lines. After a firefight, as I put myself back together, I more or less reinvented reality, adjusting and modifying all the unmediated terror with an overlay of Vietnam lingo and Vietnam mannerism and Vietnam posturing and Vietnam psychic camouflage. The masquerade became the war. The war became the masquerade.

And then, miraculously, the war came to an end. I went home. Like Frederic Henry, I stripped off my uniform, put on civilian clothes, and kept on acting.

"I had the feeling," Henry muses, "of a boy who thinks of what is happening at a certain hour at the schoolhouse from which he has played truant."

Later still in *A Farewell to Arms,* as the events of Caporetto begin to bleach from memory in the way all worldly events must bleach, Frederic Henry's grasp on his war experience has become so tenuous that he can only say, "I'll tell you about it if I ever get it straight in my head." More tellingly yet, as events recede farther into the past, Henry says, "The war was a long way away. Maybe there wasn't any war."

At that point I'm back on the porch with my father, who blinks at me and says, "What war?"

———

And so, Timmy and Tad, that's what your dad sometimes thinks about when he goes quiet and seems to be drifting away from you. Not war, exactly. In fact, not really war at all. I guess it's old age. Each night, as I slip into my make-believe sleeping trench, I'm also slipping back to our "Row, Row" days, and to my own childhood, and to my vanished father, just drifting, merrily, merrily, and on those occasions, life is but a dream.

50

Getting Cut

For several years, the game of basketball has dominated our family's dinner table conversations. Timmy, in particular, is an encyclopedia of all things basketballish, and his enthusiasm for the game can turn a bite of meatloaf into a fifteen-minute disquisition on the lifetime statistical performance of a retired Bulgarian point guard. Tad, too, is an enthusiast, though his athletic interests are considerably broader than Timmy's, spread out among basketball, cross country, and tennis. Both boys dribble their way from bedroom to kitchen to living room; both spend hours playing Horse and practicing their three-pointers out in the backyard. Tad takes a carefree approach to this. Timmy does not. A determined earnestness—almost a grim earnestness—seems to drive the elder boy, each missed shot sending a surge of poisonous failure through his system. For Tad, air balls produce laughter. For Timmy, air balls produce apocalypse.

Back in grade school, Timmy had never been rated by his

coaches as an elite player. He was good but never good enough: too slow, too unaggressive. Even so, through seventh and eighth grades, the boy worked on his skills with the patient, slogging deliberation of a gravedigger—joylessly, it sometimes seemed—and by the time he reached ninth grade, he had willed himself into becoming a competent player, stolid if not flashy, smart if not wholly intuitive, a good shooter if not yet a deadeye gunner. He also grew. His voice deepened. At five feet ten inches, he now looks down on me with the eyes of a grown man, intensely private, a keeper of secrets, a deflector of emotion, a stubborn believer in himself, and a fiercely independent adjudicator of his own desires. He values things I never valued. He is confident in ways I am not. Without saying so, he wants me to back off—to stop asking questions about his homework, to stop monitoring his computer time, to stop telling him when to go to bed each night, and to stop offering amateurish basketball tips. In a sense, I suppose, he wants me to stop being a father.

And so . . .

Two days ago, Timmy was cut from his high school's basketball team. It hurt him, yes, but he stayed quiet. He didn't moan. He didn't complain. He blamed no one. He handled failure with a grace amounting to a controlled and elegant beauty.

"Are you okay?" I asked, many times, and in a flatly inexpressive voice, many times, he said, "I'm fine."

Did he cry?

I don't know.

Did he feel defeated? Did his faith in the power of perseverance collapse? Did he scream at the ceiling?

I don't know. Maybe briefly.

"Are you okay?" I kept asking, every day, and every day he said, "Fine."

He wasn't fine.

His bedroom door stayed more firmly closed than ever. He was silent at meals. He did his homework, shot baskets alone in the backyard, and plodded ahead with mulish, stone-faced resignation. But he wasn't fine. He still isn't.

———

Six more days have passed. Timmy's silence remains impenetrable. This morning, when I asked how he was doing, he said, "I probably wasn't good enough. But I don't want to talk about it."

"Not even a little?"

"No," he said.

"Okay," I told him, "but I'm here to listen."

"Thanks," he said.

Timmy was right: he probably wasn't good enough. Three or four ninth-graders in my son's school are superb basketball players, two of them rated highly in the state of Texas, and of course any number of upperclassmen are older, taller, stronger, faster, and more experienced than Timmy. Still, these boys are my son's friends—the kids with whom he eats lunch and does science projects and plays pickup games in the school gym—and part of what Timmy is enduring is a fourteen-year-old's pain at having been separated by decree from the people he hangs out with at homecoming and between classes. And for Timmy, I'm guessing, the separation must feel permanent. His pals will receive systematic instruction; he will not. They will get game experience; he will not. They will get better and better with intense coaching and extensive playing time; Timmy will have to improve on his own or not improve at all.

There is a strange and unfamiliar conclusiveness to this. Would a kid be cut from algebra or biology or history or English or Latin or art? Would a school wash its hands and say, "Get help somewhere else"? Maybe so. Maybe the school would flunk him out. In that case, Timmy, at age fourteen, has flunked his basketball dream.

What is most difficult for me and for Meredith is that we can only imagine the thoughts that now pass through our silent son's head. We whisper and speculate. We watch through a window as Timmy shoots and shoots and shoots until dark falls. We watch him do suicide sprints. We don't know what to say to him. Do we tell stories about our own failures? Do we shut up? Do we pry? Do we try to squeeze words out of him? Do we pretend that things are fine when things are not fine? Do we encourage him to take up dominoes or arm wrestling?

We're at wits' end. We have no clue. A kid dreams what he dreams, and you can't dream new dreams for him.

———

Another week and a half has gone by, and Timmy's spirit seems a trifle lighter, not exactly buoyant, not jolly by any means, but more and more inclining in that direction. He smiles again—not often but sometimes. He speaks now and then—not much and never about basketball, but he does speak. By default, the rest of us have taken the path of least resistance, seeking sunny topics of conversation, and even Tad, who will say anything to anyone, has scrupulously avoided not only the word "basketball," but also the word "game" and the word "bounce." True, there is no more dribbling from room to room, but at least there is occasional laughter in the gloom.

———

A few nights back, I asked Timmy if he wanted to watch a Celtics-Cavaliers game. He shook his head and walked away, but a half hour later, he joined me on the couch, gave me a kiss, and said, "There's nothing I can do except keep trying to get better. I won't stop, Dad."

"Okay," I said.

"I love you," he said.

To receive, unbidden, the words "I love you" from a fourteen-year-old boy makes getting cut seem a weirdly desirable outcome, a thing to be prized. Am I wrong, I wonder, to suppose that fathers everywhere crave what I crave, which is not basketball excellence, not aggressiveness, not speed, not skill, not physical virtuosity, but just a gentle kiss out of nowhere, a quiet "I love you" out of the tight-lipped teenage blue?

———

Except in fairy tales, failure is among the constants of human experience. Not every free throw drops. Not every kid is admitted to Stanford. Not every actor embraces Oscar. Not every love affair ends in wedding bells, and not every wedding bell peals through the years with lifelong happiness. As an example, when I was about Timmy's age, I'd been required to deliver a ten-minute speech before a hundred or so members of the local PTA. My topic had to do with civil war in Angola, where guerrilla forces were challenging Portuguese colonial rule, and my speech was liberally laced with the newly discovered word "chaos." That word, I later learned, was not pronounced *chows*. I used it five or six times. People stared at me. After a few minutes, muted laughter skidded around the room, succeeded by louder laughter. To my mind, as a ninth-grader who had plucked the word out of a copy of *Time* magazine, these parents and teachers seemed cursed with an extremely odd sense of humor, for I could see nothing funny about all that lethal chows raging across southwestern Africa. When I finished, I sat down beside my father, who, without looking at me, whispered, "Chaos, not chows."

Learning by mortification, I firmly believe, is learning for life. You do not forget.

Timmy, of course, is mortified at having been cut from his high school basketball team, just as a misleadingly spelled noun will forever mortify me. And for good reason. Mortification is failure exposed, failure gone public, failure that can gnaw on the spirit all the way to the grave and maybe beyond. While the upside of mortification is bone-deep learning, perhaps even bone-deep wisdom, the downside of mortification can be a future of excessive caution, excessive risk aversion, and psychological retreat. Plainly, Timmy had fled to a place inside himself, into isolation and silence. He no longer mentions his old basketball pals. He attends no high school games. He is mortified. He wants no pity, no consolation, no clichés, no pep talks, no encouraging slaps on the back, and certainly no advice from his father. I have plenty of my own humiliation stories to share with him, but Timmy and I both understand that stories will not undo failure or eradicate pain. Behind his bedroom door, I am almost certain, my son revisits his basketball tryouts, replaying blocked shots he never blocked, free throws that rattled around the rim but never fell, intercepted passes that he almost, but never quite, intercepted. Surely he indulges in this sort of if-only fantasy. Surely, too, there is recrimination, self-doubt, and—though this scares me—self-hatred.

Some nights, after lights out, I go to his bedroom door. I don't open it. I don't knock. I just stand and listen.

He wanted something so much.

He tried so hard.

He cared—and still cares—about putting large orange balls inside baskets. How sad. How preposterously human.

There is not a *Hoosiers* conclusion to this, but now, after the passage of two more months, Timmy is playing AAU basketball. His tryouts went well—well enough that he was selected by a good team. He is an improved player, especially his three-point shot, but speed, physical strength, and general aggressiveness remain problems. On defense, he too often reaches for the ball instead of swiftly shuffling his feet; on offense, he sometimes lets his team-mates take charge, waiting in a corner near the baseline instead of cutting to the basket or toward the action. He dislikes contact. He gets outmuscled under the basket. Still, he has begun to fight for rebounds now and then; he passes better, shares the ball, looks for the open man, and is a committed team player.

All in all, his relentless practice has paid off, and in six months, if he keeps at it, he may have a reasonable shot at making his school's junior varsity team. Will he be a starter? Probably not. Will he someday move up to the varsity squad? Hard to tell. Maybe—only maybe—by his senior year. But I fear it will be a terrible and continuing struggle. He will need to overcome—or somehow compensate for—his essential gentleness, his essential decency, and what appears to be a low dosage of natural, sponta-neous, genetic ferocity. Timmy is competitive, yes, but not fero-ciously competitive. He wants the ball, but not ferociously so. He likes to score, but not ferociously so. He likes to win, but not fe-rociously so.

For me, as a father who desires happiness for his son, there will be some tough times ahead. More failure is coming. And I'm helpless to prevent it. In a way, I guess, this funnels down to a pa-thetic and paralyzing recognition of the limits of fatherhood. I cannot *be* my son. As much as my muscles twitch when I watch Timmy on the court, I cannot jump for him or run for him or at-tack the basket for him. I cannot will ferocity into a gentle soul.

In this regard, Timmy reminds me of me. I am not naturally gifted at much of anything, including the making of these sentences, but, like my son, I do keep trying and trying, mostly fail-ing, and although the result may be infelicitous or plain abysmal in the end, I will not quit until this maybe book says what I need it to say. In any endeavor, I tell Timmy, trying and triumph are different things. Triumph without trying is sterile; trying without triumph is enriching. Not that I wish bad fortune for my son. Despite his struggles, I cannot stop yearning for a day — or even a moment — when Timmy's dreams come true. If not the bas-ketball dream, then perhaps a science dream or an art dream or a falling-in-love dream. Kids change. Kids grow up. And even if the odds are stacked against a career in the NBA, my son's stub-born persistence will surely serve him well as he dribbles his way into adulthood.

Only an hour ago, Timmy came into my study. "Back when I was a little kid," he said, "we used to play golf together. Do you re-member that?"

"Of course," I told him. "You didn't like it much."

"No, not very much," said Timmy, "but I think we should start doing it again. You and me and Tad. Maybe I'll get good at it."

"Okay," I said.

"That doesn't mean I'm giving up basketball. I love basket-ball."

"Fair enough."

My heart bubbled with delight. We have a tee time tomorrow.

51

Home School

Your assignment, boys, is to read a short novel called *Billy Budd, Sailor,* and then to talk to me about moral choice.

We will discuss these questions:

— If you were the captain of a British naval vessel in the mid-1800s, would you hang Billy Budd until he is dead for his purported crime?

— What exactly *was* Billy's crime? First-degree murder? Second-degree murder? Involuntary manslaughter? None of these?

— What does the word "crime" mean? Does it have different meanings in different contexts?

— When, if ever, should mercy intersect with military, civil, or divine law?

— What do the words "extenuating circumstances" mean? (Look this up online or in a dictionary.) In general, what kinds of things might constitute extenuating circumstances if you were to ignite a stink bomb in your teacher's waste-basket? Would the school principal be likely to find those circumstances extenuating?

— In your own lives, have you ever been in the position of having to make a choice like that of Captain Vere—a choice among competing possibilities, each of which has its own moral merits and moral deficiencies? For instance, have you had to choose between telling a kind lie and an unkind truth?

— Following our discussion, you will write a story organized around the dramatic principle of moral choice. Make the choice complicated, Timmy. Make it difficult, Tad. The most agonizing choices, both in stories and in the real world, are not always between right and wrong; some choices are between one cherished value and another cherished value. (Jack values his life of steadfast honesty, but he also values his two young children, and so one day his younger son steals a friend's . . . A Roman Catholic nun values her vow of chastity, but she also values her new-found love for Jack, a widower with two young children, and so one day she says to Jack . . . A warship captain named "Starry" Vere values order and discipline aboard his ship, but he also values fairness and justice and ordinary rectitude, and so one day a handsome young sailor named Billy Budd is falsely accused of inciting mutiny . . .) You get the idea, right? But I want each of you to invent your own story. If you get stuck, think back on the fairy tales of your childhood. Think about Huck Finn and Romeo and Juliet. Ask yourself: What would I do in those situations? And then ask: What *should* I do in those situations? My hope, of course, is that this exercise may help prepare you for what will eventually drop on your doorstep as you approach adulthood. You will have to choose. And your choices will sometimes involve what Reinhold Niebuhr calls "proximate solutions to insoluble problems." In these inevitably fuzzy circumstances, I may not always be available to offer advice, so I'll offer it now: Pretend your life is a story. Then write a good one.

52

Home School

I've looked at the first drafts of your stories, and a few problems need to be addressed.

1. Review the difference between "lie" and "lay." A good number of TV personalities, politicians, poets, recording artists, newspaper columnists, pediatricians, and crime writers should do the same.
2. Do not be terrified of emotion. Be terrified of fraudulence.
3. Stories are not puzzles. Puzzles are puzzles.
4. Information is not story. Information is information.
5. Pay close attention to the issue of simultaneity. In life, as in a good story, numerous things occur at the same time, even when your attention might be riveted on a rattlesnake coiled to strike. In other words, when you're writing stories, do not juggle only a single ball. (Single-ball jugglers rarely get hired twice to entertain at birthday

parties.) Fill your stories with "nice contradiction between fact and fact." Fill your stories with food and drink, the weather, tired feet, dental appointments, phone calls from out of the blue, upset stomachs, flat tires, pens that run out of ink, undelivered letters of apology, traffic jams, malfunctioning answering machines, forgotten birthdays, swollen bladders, and spilled coffee. These and other intrusions must be endlessly juggled as we make our way along the story line of our lives. Therefore, don't insulate your characters from the random clutter that distracts and infuriates and entertains all of us.

6. Similarly, do not let excessive plotting ruin your story any more than you would allow it to ruin your life.

7. Bear in mind that stories appeal not only to the head, but also to the stomach, the back of the throat, the tear glands, the adrenal glands, the funny bone, the nape of the neck, the lungs, the blood, and the heart—the whole human being.

8. You are writing not only for your contemporaries. You are writing also for a seventeen-year-old student who might encounter your story two hundred years from now, or for an old man in Denmark in the year 2420, or for a lonely widow sitting at a futuristic slot machine in the year 4620.

9. Also, believe it or not, you are writing for those who have preceded you—for Thomas Jefferson, for the children of Auschwitz, and for a father who may no longer be present to read your story.

10. Surprise yourself. You might then surprise your reader.

11. Do not fear (or deny) your own ignorance. It makes for curiosity.

12. Do not fear (or deny) ambiguity. Though the prose itself may be crystalline, good stories almost always involve people snagged up in confusing moral circumstances. Think of Raskolnikov. Think of Charles and Emma Bovary. Think of your dad.

13. Pay attention to every word. There are twenty-six letters in the English alphabet, plus a few punctuation marks. Those twenty-six letters, if poorly arranged, will result in mediocrity, infelicity, or plain gibberish. But from those same twenty-six letters, well arranged, come the sonnets of Shakespeare. The letters of the alphabet can be likened to the four chemical bases—adenine, guanine, cytosine, and thymine—that constitute the building blocks of all plant and animal DNA. The precise sequence, or order, of the bases determines whether an organism becomes a polar bear or a dachshund or William Shakespeare. Therefore, along the same lines, I suggest you do all you can to arrange the letters of the alphabet in exacting sequences.

14. Read your writing aloud. Does it make sense? Does it make music?

15. Timmy—I think you meant to write "décor" and not "decorum."

16. Tad—I think you meant to write "hunk" and not "honk."

17. Otherwise, great first drafts! Your second drafts are due on Thursday.

53

The Debating Society

Over the past week, I've had two irritating conversations with Timmy and Tad, each of which I will report here without comment, except to say I am not exaggerating. And except to wonder if other fathers have been able to deal with similar conversations without resorting to prescription drugs.

"So," I said to Tad two nights ago, "you haven't brushed your teeth. I asked you to do that, didn't I?"

"I guess so."

"You guess so?"

"Yes, but you didn't say *when*."

"When did you think I meant?"

"Well, I didn't know you meant right away. I thought you meant pretty soon."

"Tad, I asked you at nine o'clock. It's ten-thirty."

"That sounds pretty soon to me."

"Did you forget?"

"Not exactly. I got distracted."

"By what?"

"By everything else. There's a lot to remember when you're a kid."

"But just now, when I walked in here, you were playing Minecraft."

"It's not Minecraft, it's Clash Royale."

"Okay, but you were playing a game, right?"

"Not really."

"What does 'not really' mean?"

"I was watching *other* people play—these experts—they're amazingly good at it."

"And what about your teeth?"

"Teeth?"

"Isn't that what we're talking about? I asked you to brush your teeth and you didn't do it."

"But I was on my way when you came in here."

"On your way?"

"Pretty much."

"You were staring at your computer."

"Was I?"

"Go brush your teeth."

"Now?"

———

Two days earlier, on a school night, Timmy asked if he could watch the last quarter of an NBA playoff game.

"What about your *Fahrenheit 451* essay?" I said. "Is it finished?"

"Almost," he said.

"How close to finished is 'almost'?"

"I just have to write the conclusion. A few more sentences."

"Okay," I said, "go write six sentences—good ones. If you do that, I'll watch the last quarter with you."

An hour or so later, Timmy returned to the living room, turned on the TV set, and sat down beside me.

"Just to be sure," I said, "you did write six sentences, right?"

"Almost," he said.

"How many exactly?"

"Two and a half."

"Two and a half sentences in the last hour?"

"Well, that's really close to six," Timmy said.

"It's not even half."

"It's almost half."

"Yes, you're right. And so now you can almost watch the basketball game."

"What?"

"You can almost watch the game."

"That's not fair. You told me that on some days *you* can't write even *one* good sentence. Kids get writer's block, too."

"Turn off the TV."

"Maybe the game will inspire me."

"Turn off the TV."

"But what if my conclusion is already good?"

"How good can it be? Does a good essay stop with half a sentence?"

"Okay, but it'll get good."

"Turn off the TV."

54

Sushi, Sushi, Sushi

This one is Meredith's bite of sushi. I have no recollection of the incident, but my wife brought out an old notebook and pointed to a page dated October 2008:

"Last night I was putting Timmy down. We had read stories and turned off the light. Timmy asked if I would go get Daddy.

"I said, 'Why?'

"He said, 'Daddy's warmer.'

"I said, 'What?'

"He said, 'You're softer but Daddy's warmer.'

"So I went to get Tim, who climbed into bed with Timmy and said, 'What's this about Daddy being warmer?'

"Timmy said, 'You're warmer and Mommy's softer.'

"Tim said, 'Really?'

"Timmy said, 'Dad, it's like this. You're the blanket and Mom's the pillow.'"

Another tasty morsel from Meredith's notebook, also dated October 2008:

"Today Tad saw a plane flying overhead.

"He said, 'Mommy! A plane! A plane!'

"I said, 'Where do you think it's going?'

"Tad said, 'Umm . . . Africa.'

"So I said, 'What do you think they'll do when they get there?'

"Tad said, 'Land.'"

———

A block from our house is a small park where, for many, many hours, Meredith and I pushed the boys on a pair of adjacent swings. On an afternoon in 2009, when Tad was four, he watched his brother leap from his swing as it reached its highest point.

"Parachute!" Timmy cried.

Tad was transfixed.

Again and again, Timmy jumped and splashed down in a mix of sand and pebbles. "Parachute!" he kept yelling, mostly at Tad, who was plainly working up his nerve.

Eventually, Tad told me to stop pushing him.

He sat on his swing for ten minutes, motionless, two feet from the ground, then he released his grip and very carefully toppled into the sand and pebbles.

"No parachute!" he yelled at Timmy.

———

One morning, Timmy looked up at me while we were playing checkers. He was five years old. He said, "You know, I've been thinking. Why do bears live in the clouds?"

I blinked.

"I don't know why," I said.

"You should find out."

An entry from our babysitter's journal, July 3, 2007: "Tad went to the doctor and is supposed to work his way up to 20 words. Tad's words so far: Momma, Da-da, juice, Elmo, please, dog, mine, awake, Nemo, bye-bye, roar, blue, high, catch, uh-oh, shhh, yes, no, choo-choo, and *au revoir*." (Out in the dark, a man in a straw boater is hissing, "*Au revoir*, my ass.")

From the time they were three or four, Timmy and Tad received swimming lessons in our backyard pool. Meredith presided. I sometimes watched. For the most part, Tad took to the water like a guppy, but Timmy had serious trouble at first. (Even as a baby, he'd hated water.) One afternoon I watched him stand at the edge of the pool. He dipped a foot in. He yanked it out. "This water," he said, "is way too wet."

The boys used to build bedroom forts out of blankets, chairs, pillows, books, boxes, brooms, wastebaskets, curtain rods, cardboard, tennis rackets, window shades, and pieces of rope. One morning Timmy came to me and said, "Uh-oh. The fort fell down."

"What is it now?" I asked.

"A mess," he said.

———

And then an instant later Timmy is fourteen, deep-voiced, and he says, "Dad, I'm scared."

"About what?"

"About growing up."

55

Timmy and Tad and Papa and I (V)

Over the past month and a half, Timmy and Tad and I have spent time reading and talking about Ernest Hemingway's war stories. The boys did not care for them much.

After finishing one of them, "Now I Lay Me," Tad's most energetic comment was "Can I go play now?"

Timmy said, maybe perceptively, maybe not: "It was boring, but some of the boring parts were interesting."

"Which boring parts?" I asked.

"I can't remember," said Timmy. "I was trying to figure out how worms can climb into trees."

I owe the boys an apology. They are too young.

I had expected they might be curious about the things their father witnessed many decades ago as a young man at war. (They have yet to ask a single question.) I had also expected they might find common ground with the relative youth of Hemingway's characters. Hemingway himself, at age eighteen, was not much older than my sons when he was badly wounded and nearly killed on the Austro-Italian front. When I mentioned this, Timmy shrugged and pointed out that Hemingway had forgotten to write about getting wounded and nearly killed in the story I had assigned. "Nothing happens," Timmy said. "A wounded guy just lies around in a hospital, thinking about stuff. Nobody's fighting anybody."

Timmy's literary judgment, while severe, is not completely unfounded. The "war stories" of Ernest Hemingway contain almost no dramatic immersion in the sustained, slogging, minute-by-minute, here-and-now actualities of man killing man. By and large, the stories unfold well before or well after combat. We bump into Harold Krebs and Jake Barnes after, not in the midst of, their wartime horrors. In "Now I Lay Me," we spend time with a sleepless Nick Adams *after* his having been "blown up," and then, in the same story and in the space of a single combat-deleting sentence, we flash forward to rejoin Nick *after* he has been wounded once again. In "A Very Short Story"—a piece of writing I adore—and in chapter 6 of *In Our Time,* we get further glimpses of Nick *after* he has been wounded, but nearly without fail the terror and the pain and the physical experience of *getting* wounded are whisked well offstage. In "Big Two-Hearted River," we encounter Nick in the Michigan wilds, fishing and camping at some indefinite point *after* his war has come to an end. In "On the Quai at Smyrna," we see the refugees of war and the human costs of war, but the fighting itself is elsewhere. In one of his most affecting and enigmatic stories, "In Another Country," Hemingway's opening sentence bluntly declares for itself a separate peace: "In the fall the war was always there, but we did not go to it any more." Hemingway and his narrator are true to their word. The story does not go to war. In "The Butterfly and the Tank," the Spanish Civil War is located literally down the street from Chicote's bar, where the story's action unfolds and where people drink and gossip and trade rumors while the fighting occurs in another place, almost in another country. In "A Way You'll Never Be," we hear Nick Adams discussing an "attack" in which he'd participated, but the attack itself is never presented to us, nor is the killing, nor is the ugliness of battle, nor is the physical and emotional chaos of men killing other men. Nick's sympathies are entirely devoted to himself, to his own courage and comportment under fire, and not at all to the dead and maimed.

Similarly, in chapters 3 and 4 of *In Our Time,* Nick reports "potting" German soldiers as they try to climb a garden wall. The "potting" is accomplished at a distance of forty yards; Nick is not under fire himself. Like any reader, of course, I bring my own life to and into a piece of fiction, and like Timmy and Tad, I can't help but view the "potting" of enemy soldiers from a distance of forty yards as a pretty sterile and risk-free military enterprise. It is a far cry from what I remember as combat. To me, "potting" sounds like target practice, and Nick Adams does not appear to care, even a little, that his targets are human.

In *A Farewell to Arms,* we see Frederic Henry preparing for war, reflecting on war, injured by war, fleeing from war, haunted by war, and wearied by war, but only for a modest number of pages do we see much of Henry *in* the war, and even then he is located not in battle but rather on the outskirts of battle, listening to the thud of artillery off in the distance, watching troops plod grimly toward the front. Frederic Henry is removed from the ferocity of slug-it-out, kill-or-die combat; he is exempt from the commission of wholesale butchery; he does not spend his days and nights killing people. It is true that Henry sometimes finds himself in danger, and it is also true that he is seriously wounded, but he is wounded as a witness would be wounded, by freakish bad luck, by an artillery round fired from a great distance as he returns from seeking a topping for his pasta.

Along the same lines, in a story called "Night Before Battle," Hemingway's narrator tells the reader: "Below us a battle was being fought . . . [At] eight hundred to a thousand yards the tanks looked like small mud-colored beetles bustling in the trees and spitting tiny flashes and the men behind them were toy men who lay flat, then crouched and ran." Although at one point small arms fire strikes uncomfortably close to the story's narrator, he experiences warfare at considerable remove, enough so that tanks look like beetles and human beings look like toys, and the narrator complains that the combat he has been witnessing is "too far to film well." Again, Hemingway's protagonist is not *in* battle; he is a spectator to battle. He is a cameraman. Killing people is neither his job nor his spiritual burden.

To be sure, a notable exception to this sort of "distancing" occurs at the conclusion of *For Whom the Bell Tolls,* during which Hemingway's protagonist Robert Jordan is immersed in deadly combat. Jordan, however, is a specialist working on his own authority with a small band of partisans; he is physically removed from his own army; he is removed from the repetitive, merciless, day-by-day experience of the common soldier; he is subject only to such discipline as he chooses to impose on himself; he is free to spend his nights—and portions of his days—romancing young Maria; he sleeps not in a trench, not in a foxhole, but instead on earth that occasionally moves; he has been distanced, as few ordinary soldiers are, from the grueling and ceaselessly terrifying frontline duties endured by millions of young men in Flanders and along the Somme. For me, these consciously constructed circumstances, along with Jordan's Walt-Disney-at-the-Alamo final moments, combine to produce the impression of war as romance, both literal and figurative. It is an example of what Wilfred Owen called "The old Lie."

Hemingway's insulation of his characters from repetitive up-close combat—physical distancing, emotional distancing, the distancing of imagery, the distancing of time—cannot be accounted for by chance alone. A biographer, with a biographer's sometimes single-minded loyalty to biography, might argue that Hemingway, the man, the author, had not seen combat as a fighting and killing participant on the Italian front, and therefore, for biographical reasons, he may have avoided efforts to depict that which he did not intimately "know." Certain critics suggest that several of Hemingway's so-called war stories, including "Big Two-Hearted River" and "Now I Lay Me," are not fundamentally war stories at all. Literary historian Frederick Crews writes: "Nothing in [Hemingway's] subsequent conduct suggests that he returned from Italy with a subdued temper, much less a revulsion against killing or a grasp of the issues and ironies behind the war." In his consideration of "Now I Lay Me," biographer Kenneth Lynn also dismisses, or at least radically deemphasizes, the importance of Hemingway's wartime experience. "What counts supremely in the story," Lynn writes, "is not the northern Italian frame that has made so many readers regard it as a tale of war, but the childhood memories within the frame."

In any event, during his time on the Italian front, Hemingway had not shot people in the face. He had not advanced through mud under heavy machine-gun fire. At night, after performing his Red Cross duties, he had returned to the relative safety of the rear area, where he'd slept under a roof and enjoyed running water and hot meals and maybe a drink or two with friends — impossible luxuries for the common grunt. Although Hemingway had volunteered for duty, and although he had apparently comported himself with steady nerves, it is nonetheless true that he would be viewed by the frontline infantryman as a stalwart, honorable, but unmistakable noncombatant. He was a REMF.

And it was not just relative comfort that separated Ernest Hemingway from the grunts along the Piave River. He also retained considerable freedom of will. He could have chosen, without conspicuous dishonor, to retreat under fire. He could've hopped on his bicycle and pedaled for the rear. Not that Hemingway did. Not that he wanted to. But he *could* have. Hemingway had joined the American Red Cross, not the American army, and so he was not shackled to war in the way soldiers are shackled. In the moments before battle, the common grunt experiences a strange giving up of the self, an almost physical forfeiture of volition. Even in seemingly trivial ways, a soldier's freedom of will begins to shrivel into an impossible fantasy: to turn left or to turn right; to sit down or to stand up; to speak or not to speak; to advance under fire or not to advance. The young Ernest Hemingway, as an ambulance driver and canteen worker, enjoyed far greater individual agency than the men to whom he distributed his cigarettes and chocolate.

Finally, of course, Hemingway was excused as a young man from the burden of dispensing death. During his service in the Great War, and up until his disputed (and probably exaggerated) experience as a correspondent during World War Two, he was spared not only the killing but the lifelong aftershocks of killing. As a consequence, a peculiar and very narrow self-absorption runs through his stories set in wartime. He writes frequently and well about his heroes' fear of death and about the oppressively relentless atmosphere of death in a time and place of war—all that symbolic rain—but Hemingway writes rarely and not so well about *dealing* death, or about later dealing with dealing death. There is little sense of "otherness" in his so-called war stories. There is little guilt. There is no stunned amazement. There is no revulsion. There is no sick giddiness. There is precious little moral doubt or moral qualm or moral culpability. Abruptly and inexplicably, for instance, Frederic Henry pulls his pistol and shoots a fleeing Italian sergeant during the retreat from Caporetto. Why? Because the man is fleeing? If so, why not shoot the entire fleeing Italian army? Why not shoot the fleeing horses and the fleeing ambulances and the fleeing hangers-on? Why not shoot himself? (He, too, is fleeing.) More strikingly—rationality aside, rectitude aside, explicability aside—Frederic Henry may as well have shot a plastic duck at a carnival. "I opened up my holster, took the pistol, aimed at the one who had talked the most, and fired. I missed and they both started to run. I shot three times and dropped one." (That word "dropped"—so morally dull, so drained of human affect.) A few moments later, when one of Henry's companions attempts to "finish" the wounded man, the pistol doesn't fire and Henry says, "You have to cock it," and his companion cocks it and fires twice and the wounded man is no longer wounded, he is very dead, and Henry thinks nothing and says nothing, though he thinks and says a great, great deal about wartime death in general. "The sergeant lay in his dirty long-sleeved underwear. I got up with Piani and we started. We were going to try to cross the field."

I suspect that, for Ernest Hemingway, style trumped all in this murderous episode. The bewildering absence of emotion seems to me false. It is artifice. It is the famous iceberg, perhaps, but it is the iceberg of Jeffrey Dahmer.

More than that, I think a great and understandable fear drove Hemingway to shy away from the subjectivities of human emotion, subjectivities that may have seemed to him incompatible with the demands of realism. Sorrow is never hard and fast in the way a cocked pistol is hard and fast. Revulsion, as a state of mind, cannot be seen or touched. Pity cannot be held in the hand. The affective aspects of human consciousness swirl like gas, expanding and contracting, mixing with contradictory aspects, and they cannot be described with the exactitude a writer may bring to the description of rivers and rain and dust and cocked pistols. In fact, even when Frederic Henry reflects on his own wounding, his thoughts are almost entirely drained of emotion. And when Robert Jordan confronts his own death at the conclusion of *For Whom the Bell Tolls*, his final earthly thoughts emerge as weirdly stilted and pompously formal, as if perhaps he is struggling to keep his own terrors and uncertainties secret even from himself.

———

"So why," Timmy asked me, "do you make such a big deal about Ernest Hemingway? You don't even seem to *like* his stuff all that much."

"I hate it," I said, "and I love it."

"Both?"

"That can happen with stories. You can love some parts and hate other parts."

"But why do you *care*? Why make us keep reading all this stuff?"

"Because I want you to know me," I said. "Because Hemingway thinks about things I think about."

"Except you don't agree with him."

"Not always. Sometimes."

"Like when?"

"Well, like when Nick lies listening to the silkworms at night. When he thinks about leaving the world forever."

"Dying, you mean?"

"Yes."

"Oh."

Hemingway's literary ground zero—his obsession, his passion—is located not in warfare but in death itself: premonitions of death, brushes with death, meditations on death, dalliances with death, fear of death, hatred of death, mockery of death, resignation to death, and an abiding awareness of all those silkworms relentlessly munching away in the dark. For me, this is where the beauty of Hemingway's fiction resides. This is where I believe him.

True, I'm repulsed by what appears to be a pathological insensitivity to the man-killing-man aspects of warfare, but at the same time I'm spellbound by the subtlety, grace, immediacy, and reverence with which those same stories and novels treat the theme of human mortality. This, if anything, is Hemingway's subject. Not war. Not bullets, not bombs, not artillery rounds. Not the politics of war. Not the machinery of war and not the morality of war. For Ernest Hemingway, I'm pretty sure, war was most essentially an extension of the natural world, a world that promises only its own conclusion. He was *using* war, not just writing *about* war, as a means of exploring the fate of all living things, you included, your children included, the innocent and the guilty and the jury included. "Every man's life ends the same way," Hemingway wrote. He also wrote: "Madame, all stories, if continued far enough, end in death, and he is no true-story teller who would keep that from you." Famously, in *Death in the Afternoon*, he wrote: "The only place where you could see life and death, *i.e.,* violent death now that the wars were over, was in the bull ring and I wanted very much to go to Spain where I could study it. I was trying to learn to write, commencing with the simplest things, and one of the simplest things of all and the most fundamental is violent death." In the same book, which dwells in sometimes rhapsodic detail on the demise of bulls and horses and men, he wrote that he wished to study death "as a man might, for instance, study the death of a father." In *A Farewell to Arms,* he put into the mouth of Frederic Henry a poetic couplet by Andrew Marvell: "But at my back I always hear / Time's wingèd chariot hurrying near." In "A Natural History of the Dead" (the title makes my point) he wrote: "Let us therefore see what inspiration we may derive from the dead," after which the reader is treated to an exhaustive and anatomically enlightening survey of dead mules and horses and human beings, along with commentary such as: "The dead grow larger each day until sometimes they become quite too big for their uniforms, filling these until they seem blown tight enough to burst." Elsewhere, Hemingway wrote: "Before the war you always think that it's not you that dies. But you will die, brother, if you go to it long enough." He wrote: "The world is a fine place and worth the fighting for and I hate very much to leave it." After his grave wounding near the Piave River, he told a friend: "I died then. I felt my soul or something coming right out of my body, like you'd pull a silk handkerchief out of a pocket by one corner. It flew around and then came back and went in again and I wasn't dead any more." And about his own life he wrote: "When you go to war as a boy you have a great illusion of immortality. Other people get killed, not you . . . Then when you are badly wounded the first time you lose that illusion and you know it can happen to you. After being severely wounded two weeks before my nine-teenth birthday I had a bad time until I figured out that nothing could happen to me that had not happened to all men before me."

My eyes shift back to the preceding line, to the words "all men." Hemingway did not write "men at war." He wrote "all men." He was reaching beyond war. He was reaching into his youth and into his old age, and into your youth and into your old age, to rediscover the shocking certainty that what now exists will one day not exist, that for all of us the lights will go out and the café will close its doors.

What most of us wish to forget, Hemingway cannot help but remember.

What most of us press away, Hemingway embraces.

This, if only for me, is where the triumph of his best stories is found; his reach is inclusive; his subject is everyone and every-thing, the planet, the setting sun, the little girl with a brain tumor, the father contemplating a bottle of vodka, the silkworms munch-ing away in the dark.

In this regard, Hemingway's so-called war fiction seems to me indistinguishable from the greater body of his fiction, those nov-els and stories which on the surface are not in the least about war but which are nonetheless permeated by, preoccupied with, and wholly conscious of a crouching and pitiless finality—"The Capital of the World," "Indian Camp," "An African Story," "The Undefeated," "A Clean, Well-Lighted Place," "The Snows of Kili-manjaro," "The Killers," "The Short Happy Life of Francis Macomber," "A Day's Wait," "My Old Man," "The Faithful Bull," "An Alpine Idyll," "After the Storm," "Banal Story," "The Good Lion," "Fathers and Sons," *The Old Man and the Sea, Across the River and into the Trees, Islands in the Stream.* These stories and novels, some more than others, each in its own time-ticking way, are of a piece with Hemingway's "war fiction," reminding us of what we know but try so furiously, so hopelessly, not to know.

At its heart and in its governing passion, none of Hemingway's fiction is truly *about* warfare, or *about* bullfighting, or *about* fishing, or *about* shooting birds, or *about* drifting down the canals of Venice. To the extent that stories are ever about anything but themselves, Hemingway's great subject is the bizarre reality that reality will cease to be. It's a generalization, for sure, and one to which there are glorious exceptions, but it may help explain Hemingway's insistent focus on the dying, but not the killing, aspects of warfare.

Figuratively, but also literally, I'm quite certain that when Ernest Hemingway sat down to write in the early mornings, and as he slipped into the ballet of imagined events and imagined human beings, he was often engaged in something close to a dress rehearsal for his own coming extinction. He was practicing.

56

Into the Volcano

For the past two weeks, off and on, Tad has been working on an interdisciplinary school project that combines elements of sixth-grade history and mathematics. Along with a classmate, my son decided to focus on the construction of an imaginary Utopia, a world in which sixth-graders might live in peace and domestic tranquility.

Yesterday morning, with only mild and obligatory curiosity, I asked Tad to tell me a little about his project.

"Well," he said, "it's complicated. All the streets in Utopia have to make different angles. Like, Sweet Street has to be at a sixty-degree angle to some other street, and Bunny Boulevard has to make one side of a parallelogram. Like that, sort of."

"Sounds like fun."

"It isn't."

"And what about the history part?"

"Mostly we just make that up," Tad said, "but first we had to learn what Utopia is—I mean, what *other* people think Utopia should be like."

"Did you get some good ideas?"

"Well, no, but my own ideas were excellent. You want to hear them?"

"I sure do," I said.

And then, for ten or fifteen minutes, Tad described the building blocks of a sixth-grader's ideal world. Predictably, the streets of my son's Utopia were paved with Hershey bars, the shops offered unlimited free ice cream, the schools were in session only one day a week, summer vacation lasted eight months, and teachers were hired only if they were a lot, lot dumber than the students. "That's why everybody gets A's," Tad said.

"What else?" I asked.

"Robots do all the cooking and cleaning."

"Great idea."

"All the cars are self-driving. That way Mom isn't so stressed all the time."

"Makes perfect sense," I said. "What else?"

"Well, everybody who gets married has to have one boy and one girl. If you have two boys or two girls, you have to swap one boy for a girl or one girl for a boy."

"Swap your own kid?"

"That's the basic idea."

"So your mom and I would have to swap you for a little girl?"

Tad hesitated. "It's not real," he said. "It's Utopia."

"But aren't Utopias supposed to be good?"

"I guess so. Maybe you could swap Timmy."

"Well, look," I said. "In your Utopia, how old is a kid when the parents have to make the swap?"

"I don't know. Six or seven, I guess."

"Tad, do you want a new mom and dad?"

"What?"

"Where did you get this idea?"

"Nowhere. I thought it was cool."

"It *is* cool," I said quickly, "but it's a little . . . Did you mention this to a teacher?"

"I can't remember. Maybe not yet."

"You're happy here, aren't you? With me and Mom?"

Tad gave me a puzzled stare. "I think so, sure. Anyway, I forgot to tell you about the volcano."

"Volcano?"

"It's part of Utopia. What happens is, when people are about eighty years old, these guys take them up to the volcano and throw them in."

"Throw who in?"

"The old people."

"When they're eighty?"

"Yes," Tad said, "but if they want, they can *ask* to get thrown in when they're seventy, after they're too old to do anything interesting."

"Who throws them in?"

"Just these guys."

"Guys like you?"

"Pretty much. It's the most honorable job in the whole Utopia."

"Of course," I said. "It sounds honorable."

"Why are you giving me that look?"

"Tad, do you know how old I am?"

"You're not eighty, are you?"

"Not quite."

"So you don't have to worry. Besides, these guys are really good at it. They don't even burn their hands. And they get paid a fortune."

"Tad, do you know what a Nazi is?"

57

And into the Stew Pot

Today Timmy turns fifteen.

In about a week, Tad becomes a teenager.

Most often, these birthdays make me aware of the ticking clock, as if I'm running late for an appointment up on Tad's volcano. This morning, though, all seems well. I'm content. I'm glad another day is breaking. Years and years ago, when I jotted down the first sentence of these reflections, I would not have waged a nickel that at this point in my life I would still be alive, much less reasonably healthy, reasonably active, and reasonably cheerful in the face of slimming odds. True, I occasionally catch a whiff of sulfur; sometimes late at night I feel the heat. But for the most part the volcano seems to slumber, and I doubt that Tad will be tossing me into a fiery eternity before I've managed to tie up a few last threads.

Making my peace with Vietnam is one of those threads.

Looking up a couple of old war buddies is another.

And of course attaching the last period to this book is still another. I've been at it a long time, probably too long, but over the past week or so, I've begun to sense an approaching conclusion. Except for a few bits and pieces, I have said what I needed to say. Only thirty more pages. Maybe forty.

After that . . . no more early mornings.

The daily agenda will be simple: sleep until seven or eight, then a round of golf, then practice some sleight of hand, and then settle in to read the books I want to read. At my age, a certain selfishness seems permissible—doing the things I long to do and not what some preacherly internal voice tells me I must do. At the same time, though, I do not foresee a future of slothfulness. I imagine a diligent, determined, and altogether energetic immersion in old age. (If you have to do it, my dad used to say, do it with conviction.) And so with conviction, and maybe with pleasure, I will throw myself into the repose of the elderly, the lemonade and the hammock, the afternoon snooze, the contemplation of failure and error without all those remedial urges of youth. What is broken in my life will remain broken. What is regretted will remain regretted. Wisdom has eluded me for all these years, and I would be an idiot to think that even a modest sagacity might visit me in my decrepitude. Therefore, during what time is left to me, I expect no reconciliations, no revelations, no profundities, no beatific grace, and no peaceful resignation to the ways of the universe. I expect only diminishment and eradication.

Nevertheless, as I totter toward the grave, I find myself filled with a peculiar curiosity about what is soon to come. Will I go out kicking and screaming? Will I demand a good, fair fistfight with

God—no cheap miracles? Will I go dotty? Am I already dotty? Will I even recognize dottiness as I empty the mustard bottle on my final bowl of ice cream? On this birthday morning, especially, I'm struck by a mix of wonderment and awe at my proximity to life's close: the majesty of extinction, the spectacular finality of finality. It occurs to me, in fact, that Tad's volcano, with all its fireworks and Gestapo pageantry, is an appropriately magnificent, if somewhat brutal, metaphor for what awaits all of us.

Five decades ago, a similar combination of curiosity and awe had accompanied me through Vietnam, along with a great deal of terror, and now, in my old age, I'm back where I was in 1969. While I certainly do not enjoy old age any more than I enjoyed war, I do feel an intense, almost electric awareness of the physical world, as if everything on the planet has been magnified and brilliantly lighted. When you're almost dead, things sparkle. What is taken for granted in peacetime, as in youth, suddenly becomes so precious it makes you cry, and if there is any redeeming virtue to growing old, it is the pleasure I take in what had once seemed ridiculously ordinary. Butter on an English muffin. Sitting silently in a room with Timmy. Playing no-stakes Texas Hold'em with Tad. Singing "Happy Birthday" to a fifteen-year-old. Such pedestrian things seem swollen with meaning, even if the meaning mostly eludes me. During the war, the same sort of simple pleasure could be found in the smell of dawn after a night on ambush, or in a river turning muddy pink at the hour of dusk, or in looking up at a few billowy white clouds after some poor soul had lost his legs. All that is equally true of old age. You come to value things that never before had such crushing value.

————

Earlier this morning, as I cleaned up the kitchen, the usual bumble-bees of memory had been astir in my thoughts, busy little flashes of history. Oddly, one of those bumblebees is still buzzing inside me, and I can't seem to swat it away. It's a memory fragment from years ago, back when Timmy was five or six. He had been watch-ing Tom and Jerry cartoons, perfectly content, giggling, and then suddenly he was weeping. I asked what was wrong.

"Tom's dead!" Timmy half blubbered, half screamed.

I took the boy's hand and led him over to the TV, but he froze and jerked back and refused to take another step.

"Easy does it," I said. "We'll watch together. It's a cartoon, it's for kids—I'm sure Tom's not dead."

Timmy said nothing. His lips were trembling. He looked pale.

I ejected the disc from our DVD player, checked to be sure it was Tom and Jerry, and slipped it back in. For ten minutes or so, we stood watching Jerry taunt Tom in all the usual ways, which I found amusing, but Timmy was having none of it. At one point he put his hands over his face. "It's gonna *happen*," he whispered, peeking out at me. "I can't watch Tom die again."

A moment later, a new episode began. It was called "Heavenly Puss." After the first few frames, Timmy made a choking sound and bolted from the room.

Alone, still standing with the remote in my hand, I watched the episode from beginning to end. And, yes, Tom died. (Or so it would surely seem to any six-year-old.) The poor cat was flattened by a falling chest of drawers, slipped out of his body, and made his way to a golden escalator that ascended skyward, far beyond the clouds, ending up at the gates of cat heaven. For reasons I can't precisely recall, Tom was denied instant salvation—something to do with his nasty behavior toward Jerry—and the heavenly gatekeeper presented Tom with a deadline by which he must earn Jerry's forgiveness. Alas, the deadline expired, and Tom eventually tumbled through a trapdoor, heading for hell, finally splashing down in a boiling pot of fire . . . or was it magma? An evil-looking devil snarled and cackled and stirred the pot.

What Timmy had failed to notice—almost certainly because he was in tears—was that Tom eventually awakened from what was only a bad dream. (This was Hollywood's way, I suppose, of filing down the Pentecostal edges on its children's entertainment.) Still, that long golden escalator was pretty terrifying, as was the trapdoor, as was the cauldron of hellfire. Like many fairy tales, and like many TV evangelists, any of these images might easily condemn a kid to a lifetime of psychotherapy.

I turned off the DVD player.

A few minutes later, after searching the house, I found Timmy hiding under his bed. I coaxed him out, sat in a chair, held him on my lap, and tried to explain that Tom was perfectly fine—it was nothing but a nightmare.

"Tom's dead," Timmy said firmly. "He's in the stew pot."

"Stew pot?"

"That big black stew pot!" Timmy yelled. "It's where the dead people go!"

"Well, Tom's not an actual person. He's a cat, isn't he?"

"Okay—cats, too! But why does everybody have to go into a stew pot?"

"It was a cartoon. It was supposed to be funny."

"Stew pots aren't funny," said Timmy.

"Maybe not," I said.

For a moment or two, my son seemed to calm down, but then his eyes closed and his face collapsed and he was crying again. He pressed his head into my chest. "I'm scared," he said.

"I know you are. I know."

"I don't want you to go into a stew pot."

"Me?"

Timmy sat up and looked straight in my eyes. "Well," he said, "*you're* the old one."

"Right," I said.

"You are."

"Okay, I heard you."

What happened next has faded from my memory, but over the following decade, the term "stew pot" became a family mantra, those two simple words representing much more than the sum of the parts. The meaning is fluid, largely dependent on context, but "stew pot" encompasses danger and fate and consequence and fear and doom and mystery and finality and foreboding. Before a tough history exam, Timmy might say, "Uh-oh, here comes the stew pot." Or before one of Tad's basketball games, as we eye a formidable opposing team, Meredith might glance at me and mutter, "We're in trouble, time to get out the stew pot." For me, especially now in the early hours of this June morning, the words "stew pot" carry a stark visual clarity that makes me both queasy and resigned. For years, I've been on the fence about the whole cremation versus burial issue —neither makes me jump for joy—and I had been delaying the decision in the hope that more pleasant alternatives might pop to mind: grind me into dog food, maybe, or call in a taxidermist. But Timmy's stew pot, together with Tad's volcano, has settled the fire-or-ice conundrum once and for all. Fire it will be.

And thus another loose thread has been knotted.

———————

A few feet from me, my dad's urn—his own bronze stew pot— sits on a wide mahogany shelf filled with books, sixty or seventy of them, a resting place that is fitting for a man who so dearly loved to read. Perhaps like other sons, I sometimes talk to the ashes in the urn. I ask for advice. I tell secrets. I express my love. Although nothing ever comes back to me, I've grown accustomed to the silence and do not really mind, because my dad is here in this room, on a shelf, just a few feet away, and I know he wants to speak but simply cannot. It isn't his fault. He's dead. And whenever and wherever it is, a week from now or ten years from now, whether it's a volcano or a stew pot or a golden escalator moving through stardust, I hope Timmy and Tad will know in their bones that I want to speak to them, as sweetly and musically as I can, but simply cannot.

Now, the boys are awake. It's time to go wish Timmy a happy birthday.

58

Lesson Plans

In the event I'm no longer here in the summer of 2025, when Timmy is twenty-two and Tad is twenty, I invite my sons to write me a short letter, committing to paper a few thoughts about how the world is treating them and how they are treating the world.

As a purely imaginary illustration, Tad might write that he has delayed his freshman year of college and is raising bunnies on a farm in Peru. In his letter to a dead man, Tad might tell me about the farm, his daily routine, and the ups and downs of keeping rabbits alive. He might confess misgivings. He might explain to me that a single pet rabbit is fine but seven hundred rabbits are not, and that at night, listening to Andean panpipes, he wishes he were enjoying a pizza with friends in a dorm room in Massachusetts. Homesickness may have claimed him, or loneliness, or the realization that bunnies are a staple of the Peruvian stew pot. He might ask for my advice. He might not. If it were possible, which of course it will not be, I would probably counsel him to stick it out

356

a while longer, if only to discover what adversity might teach him, but I would also enclose, if I could, an airline ticket to the destination of his choice. (Among the lessons of adversity is the lesson that adversity sucks.)

In any event, I hope Tad and Timmy will also try what I sometimes try, which is to dispatch little mind-letters to my dad, even knowing that he won't be writing back. Yet I pretend otherwise. Pretending helps. Almost always, at least for a moment or two, I'll hear an indistinct sound in my head, like a voice murmuring in another room, but not a voice exactly, nor even a sound exactly, just the whispery vibrations that love might make if love could speak, the way we sense love's presence by some vague disturbance in a summer night.

I will try to make that soundless sound for you, Timmy and Tad. But if I can't, close your eyes and imagine it, and what you imagine will be your father.

———

If one of you is in possession of my urn, do not open it. Pretend that inside the urn is a smiling guy in a baseball cap. Pretend he is singing "Row, Row." Pretend he is kissing you good night. What we pretend always and forever *is*.

———

At some point in the year 2030, I hope you will revisit the house in which you grew up. I did this myself, not long after my own father died, and I was astonished at how each room still seemed alive with all that had occurred inside it. Timmy, I want you to stand before your closed bedroom door. Tad, I want you to peek into that tiny bathroom where you once took aim at a wastebasket. And both of you, please, I want you to spend a few minutes in the breakfast nook off the kitchen, a place where your mother and I wiped spaghetti sauce from your faces and laughed at your stories from school and watched you devour lobster tails on Christmas Eve. We had fun, didn't we? There was happiness in that house. The house will help you remember.

———

On Friday, June 20, 2031, please read Elizabeth Bishop's "One Art." I hope you will read this poem aloud, for you will hear the music of grief. As you wrap your tongues around the vowels of the poem, and as consonants ricochet off your teeth, take care to enunciate each syllable. Speak clearly and without inflection. Do not inject emotion into the poetry. Let the poetry inject emotion into you. Just as my father disappeared forever in 2004, so have I now disappeared, and it may help a little to utter aloud the last searing stanza from Bishop's villanelle:

> —Even losing you (the joking voice, a gesture
> I love) I shan't have lied. It's evident
> the art of losing's not too hard to master
> though it may look like (*Write* it!) like disaster.

In some ways, this assignment resembles our many home school sessions back when you were young, but my purpose in this case is different. I do not aim to educate. I aim only to offer you the companionship of others who have endured what you are enduring.

———

In the years between 2033 and 2036, you will be in your early thirties, grown men whose lives are full of all the strains and stresses of a thing called work. (Right now, I realize, the word is unfamiliar to you.) Whatever you end up doing, whether it's mind work or muscle work, I hope you will pursue it with the same grace, good humor, and patient focus that you once brought to the unicycle and to the hula hoop. As much as possible, make work play. If work stops being play, take a break or find new work.

Making this book for you has certainly been work, and I admit that at times it has been dispiriting, so much so that on several occasions I abandoned the effort entirely. The fun had vanished. But then . . . who knows why? . . . then the fun returned. For you, Timmy and Tad, I hope you stay in touch with those playful, adventurous qualities you brought to the basketball hoop and to the zipline in our backyard. Make your lives fun. Keep taking risks. Never abandon your openness to all that is new and untried and unexpected and mysterious. Hold tight to your who-gives-a-damn courtship of failure, your exuberance of spirit, your eagerness to climb trees in Switzerland and jump off docks in Connecticut.

Do not worry about accomplishment. Accomplishment will follow where playfulness takes you. Besides, you've already accomplished so much. You've delivered joy to a man who once believed there would be no more.

————

I have bequeathed to you, Timmy and Tad, a garageful of magic equipment, almost all of which came into your possession without instructions. If you decide to try your hand at mastering this stuff, I wish you lots of fun. Still, the odds are pretty good that one day you will stand awkwardly in the garage, not saying much, quietly surveying these glittery illusions with a blend of sadness and anxiety. One of you may finally murmur, "What do we do with all this stuff?" and the other will say, "Got me." Embedded in the next moment or two will be an important lesson. Do not feel guilt—or at least laugh at your guilt—when you rent that U-Haul trailer and take a long drive out to the city dump. You've already been plenty magical for your father.

————

In a world that seems riddled by an impulse for acquisition, I hope you will devote a portion of your lives to the opposite: giving without getting. As a little boy, Timmy, you once packed a grocery bag with gifts for a homeless man on 15th Street. And Tad: you were once asked what your perfect day would be, to which you replied: "Just make everybody feel good, especially bunnies."

And so, perhaps in the year 2038, please take the time to remember that these generous moments were among the happiest and most indelible of your dad's life. Then do something similar. Give without getting. Make me shine.

———

Right now, at 5:22 a.m. on July 23, 2018, we are in Paris. Your mom and I are having our first sips of morning coffee while you boys sleep off the exertions of yesterday's visit to the tomb of Napoleon, where you learned much more than you wanted to learn about the battle of Waterloo and the French army's retreat from the outskirts of Moscow. Altogether, both of you were remarkably patient, though you were also bewildered by your dad's fascination with a man who had been dead for a very long time. At one point, Timmy, you muttered something about the T-shirt I was wearing, which in large lettering bore the slogan "Make coffee, not war." I tried to explain—unconvincingly, I'm afraid—that it's possible to be transfixed by something you despise.

"Well," you said, "Napoleon sure didn't mind killing people. So why are we acting like we're in Sunday school?"

I nodded. The place had a hushed, solemn, and distinctly reverential atmosphere. Granted, we were in a royal chapel, but it was a chapel wholly dedicated to the enshrinement of fallen people-killers. Not only was Napoleon entombed here, but so too were numerous other heroes of France, all military men, mostly career officers, none of whose lives suggested the least aversion to slaughtering human beings in the name of who knows what.

"It makes me a little sick," you whispered to me, Timmy. "Why don't they build a place like this for somebody *nice*?"

"Good idea," I said. "Like Hugh Thompson."

"Who?" you said.

The answer to this question is among my lesson plans for the coming years. In the year 2031, I want you to read about Hugh Thompson. Visit his grave in Lafayette, Louisiana, where you will find a modest plaque in the earth, and then ask yourself: Who is the greater man, Napoleon Bonaparte or Hugh C. Thompson Jr.?

———

I will miss you, my dear sons. I already miss you. And at some indefinite point in the indefinite future, I will no longer be capable of knowing how terribly much I am missing you. With this in mind, I ask that we sometimes revisit one another in the only meeting places that will be left to us, which will be in dream, in memory, and in the pages of a book such as this one. Most powerful, of course, are memory and dream, and these will take care of themselves. I am worried, though, about our rendezvous in books. As your father, I cannot and should not burden you with long reading lists for the years ahead; already I've gone too far in that regard. My invitation to meet inside books must be tempered by your individual tastes and enthusiasms, and the best I can promise is that, should you decide to visit, I will be waiting for you in the nooks and crannies of "One Art" and amid the mustard gas and illumination flares of "Dulce et Decorum Est." If you open Turgenev's *Fathers and Sons,* and if you persevere to the end, you will witness firsthand the terror I have felt at the possibility of failing as your father. Likewise, while I certainly do not insist, I would be delighted if you were to spend a quiet hour or two with Ezra Pound's "Hugh Selwyn Mauberley." (You will need a good dictionary and a pile of reference books.) Pay special attention to a few of my favorite lines:

> These fought, in any case,
> and some believing, pro domo, in any case . . .
>
> Some quick to arm,
> some for adventure,
> some from fear of weakness,
> some from fear of censure,
> some for love of slaughter, in imagination,
> learning later . . .
> some in fear, learning love of slaughter;
>
> Died some, pro patria, non "dulce" non "et decor" . . .
> walked eye-deep in hell
> believing in old men's lies, then unbelieving
> came home, home to a lie,
> home to many deceits,
> home to old lies and new infamy;
> usury age-old and age-thick
> and liars in public places.

Though Pound is writing here about the Great War, the shout of futile fury in these lines could as well have come from the lungs of your father.

It is hopeless, I'm afraid.

We will never run short of things to kill for. We will never run short of lies. We will never run short of dead-sure, beyond-a-doubt liars in public places. We will never run short of fair cheeks and fine bodies, gallant believers learning later, and we will never run short of gentle-hearted Timmys and Tads who—fearing censure, fearing ridicule—join the parade of those who kill and die and cannot quite remember why. Was it falling dominoes?

It is hopeless. But pretend it is not.

———

And then there is the matter of my own books. I don't know what to say to you about that. Neither you, Timmy, nor you, Tad, have so far expressed even passing curiosity about what is inside those books, which surprises me, but please know that I will not be hurt or angry if you choose never to read a word. (I *will* be puzzled.) In any case, I hope you've come to know how much I love stories, especially those that contain a miracle or two. And I wish I had time to write one more maybe book about a father and two sons who will always be together, no matter what. Improbable, for sure. But a very cool story, don't you think?

59

Tad's Literary Advice

Today I told Tad that my maybe book may soon be finished.

He was silent for a while.

"Well," he said, "just put it in the homework bin and wish for an okay grade. That's what I do. But make sure your teacher is in a super-good mood."

60

One Last Lesson Plan

Dear Timmy and Tad,

On October 1, 2046, your dad's one hundredth birthday, I hope you will take time to play a round of golf, just the two of you. If you dislike golf, please do it anyway. Walk. Don't ride. Tad will get a kick out of telling golf jokes; Timmy will enjoy the autumn sunlight and the nineteenth hole. On that day in 2046, you will both be in your middle age, graying at the temples, doing God knows what with your lives, but I am confident you will have become the good men that your youth now promises. Tad—I hope you still have that devilish grin, that zany spin on the world, and I hope you're still cuddling bunnies at age forty-one, if only in your imagination. Timmy—stay stubborn, stay earnest, and keep crying for your fellow man.

Between shots, reminisce a little. Chuckle about how your dad keeps meddling in your lives even after he's gone.

Pretend I'm chuckling too.

Remember what you can.

Though it's hard to imagine, you may both be fathers in the year 2046, and, if so, you will certainly feel for your children what I now feel for you, which is a mixture of bedazzled love and the sadness of knowing that fathers cannot always join their sons for a round of birthday golf. I smile, though, at the picture of you lecturing your own kids about getting to bed on time or cleaning up their messes; I smile, too, when I imagine you immersed in the hurly-burly of paying bills, shopping for groceries, mowing lawns, vacuuming carpets, overseeing homework, and making sure the steaks don't burn. No wonder Peter Pan refused to grow up. In 2046, at the onset of your middle age, you will find yourselves worrying less about yourselves and more about those you love, your children in particular, and I am sure both of you will be doing your best in that regard, as I did, even if your best may only rarely be good enough.

Since October 1, 2046, will fall on a Monday, you may need to request a day off from work. Do so well in advance. (As kids, you had big problems with procrastination.) The good news is that on a Monday you will have the golf course pretty much to yourselves, no pressure to play quickly, and I hope you take pleasure in the October air and the feel of the earth beneath your feet and maybe one or two satisfying shots. On the twelfth hole, before you tee off, I ask that you recall a few lines from John Betjeman's "Seaside Golf":

How straight it flew, how long it flew,
It clear'd the rutty track

And soaring, disappeared from view
Beyond the bunker's back—
A glorious, sailing, bounding drive
That made me glad I was alive.

Although your drives may be less than glorious, I hope you grin at each other as you make your way down the fairway toward those unplayable lies in the woods.

I hope you're glad to be alive.

I hope you know your dad is happy that you are together today.

Although most of your youth will have been forgotten, and although your few memories of me will be jerky and inanimate, I'm also hopeful that this round of October golf will remind you of something powerful and irreducible, something independent of memory, like the smell of love, like the feel of an old man reading a book at midnight in a silent room.

On the thirteenth green, before putting, remember that dropping a small white ball into a hole is not the point of putting, no more than the point of writing stories is to earn a million dollars. The point is to strike an honest putt. And as you later address the ball on the fourteenth tee, remember that the point is not perfection, not outcome, but rather a relaxed awareness of your ball's brief passage, and your own brief passage, through time and space. In fact, now that I think about it, the point of golf is not golf at all, no more than the point of life is life. We are not bacteria. If the purpose of life were life, the human race may as well devolve into ragweed and be done with it. And so my lesson plan for October 1, 2046, has little to do with clubs and balls. It has much to do with reflection, quietude, and just being brothers on an autumn day. Therefore, as you approach the dangerous water hazard surrounding the fourteenth green, try to remember that no matter how bad your next shots may be, only the ball will drown.

Have fun. Chat about your kids. Commiserate. You'll have plenty of material.

For both of you in your middle age, it's likely that certain regrets will have accumulated, and I hope you won't be afraid to talk about those regrets while you're heading up the next fairway or two. In my own case, if I could be with you in 2046, I would surely express some heartache and contrition involving my father, Bill O'Brien, wishing I had known him better, wishing I had asked more questions, wishing we had played a last round of golf before his death, wishing I had slung my arms around him and pressed my face against his and squeezed a son's immense love into his muscles and bones.

After the golf, have a beer together.

Look at a few photographs.

Forgive what needs forgiving, laugh at what needs laughing, and then go home.

I loved you,
Dad

Acknowledgments

A shout of thanks to those who have contributed, knowingly or otherwise, to the making of this maybe book, among them Alex Vernon, David Krause, Bruce Nichols, Larry Cooper, Les Ramirez, Erik Hansen, Aaron Matthews, Ross Feeler, Robert (Buddy) Wolf, Bill Shapiro, Ivy Givens, Wyatt Prunty, Edward Miller, David Schmidt, Lucas Frank, Lynn Novick, Ken Burns, and the bewitching cast of our living room magic shows. To Tad and Timmy O'Brien: thank you for lending me your lives, which I now return to you. And to Meredith O'Brien: you insisted on children, you led with kindness and intelligence, you delivered peace and joy.

Notes on Sources

Chapter 11, "Home School"

In this chapter—and later, throughout these pages—I refer to 3 million Vietnamese dying as a consequence of the American war in Vietnam. The death toll is approximate and represents a compromise among several estimates. The Vietnamese government, in a 2008 publication, states that about 3.3 million Vietnamese died in total: 1.1 million in the North Vietnamese Army and the National Liberation Front, 250,000 dead and missing in the Army of South Vietnam, and 2 million civilian dead. The *New York Times* estimates that a total of "more than" 2.5 million Vietnamese died. The *BMJ* (*British Medical Journal*) cites a 2002–2003 World Health Organization survey in its estimate that 3.8 million Vietnamese suffered "violent war deaths" from 1955 to 2002; a 1991 study ordered by World Bank president Robert S. McNamara estimates that 2.36 million Vietnamese civilians and military personnel died from 1960 to 1975. It is unclear if these estimates include casualties incurred during the war's spillover into Laos and Cambodia. In some cases, it is unclear if the estimates include the Vietnamese military struggle against the French prior to the direct involvement by American troops. The most common estimate appears to be a total of 3 million, which is the number cited in the Florentine Films documentary *The Vietnam War,* first aired in 2017 on PBS. My thanks to Dartmouth University history professor Edward G. Miller and to Florentine Films researcher David Schmidt, both of whom provided generous assistance with this murky and disputed statistical issue. As Professor Miller pointed out in a January 6, 2017, email: "The numbers are all over the place. The three million figure is probably the most commonly cited, but that doesn't mean it's the most likely to be true." Similarly, David Schmidt stated in an email of the same date, "The only precisely accurate statistic for war dead is the American total, because each name has been individually counted." Finally, the Vietnamese government reports that 300,000 North Vietnamese and NLF soldiers are categorized as missing in action. Since more than forty years have passed since the war's conclusion, those 300,000 missing should probably be included in any realistic death toll. Among the sources I relied on were Philip Shenon, *New York Times,* April 23, 1995; Joseph R. Gregory, *New York Times,* October 4, 2013; Mike Ives, *New York Times,* December 24, 2015; "History of the Anti-American Resistance to Save the Nation," vol. 8, National Politics Publishing House, a 2008 Vietnamese government publication; Charles Hirschman, Samuel Preston, and Vu Manh Loi, "Vietnamese Casualties During the American War: A New Estimate," *Population and Development Review* 21, no. 4, December 1995; Robert S. McNamara, "The Post–Cold War World: Implications for Military Expenditure in Developing Countries," *Proceedings of the World Bank Annual Conference on Development Economics* (International Bank for Reconstruction and Development, 1991), pp. 95–122; "Fifty Years of Violent War Deaths . . . ," *BMJ* (*British Medical Journal*), June 26, 2008, https://www.bmj.com/content/336/7659/1482.

Chapter 23, "Home School"

The George Orwell quotation appears in "The Freedom of the Press," Orwell's proposed preface to *Animal Farm.* This eloquent, tightly reasoned essay is well worth reading in its entirety and is as pertinent to our circumstances today as it was more than seventy years ago. Written in 1945, the essay was discovered in 1972 among Orwell's papers and first published in the *Times Literary Supplement* on September 15, 1972. See: https://www.slideshare.net/belike_Abee/george-orwell-preface-to-animal-farm-or-the-freedom-of-the-press.

The Picasso quotation is from "Picasso Speaks," *The Arts,* vol. 3, May 1923, pp. 315–29, ed. Marius de Zayas. Reprinted in Alfred Barr, *Picasso* (1946).

The Marianne Moore quotation is from her poem "Poetry," which can be found at https://www.poets.org/poetsorg/poem/poetry.

Joseph Conrad's "the sitting down is all" is from a letter to Edward Garnett (March 29, 1898), who is credited with discovering and nurturing Conrad's literary genius. See https://www.williamlanday.com/2012/11/16/conrad-the-sitting-is-all, and "The Editor Who Pulled Joseph Conrad from the Slush Pile," at https://lithub.com/the-editor-who-pulled-joseph-conrad-from-the-slush-pile.

Chapter 29, *"Turkey Capital of the World"*

For information on the hanging of thirty-eight Sioux in Mankato, Minnesota, I consulted a fascinating and lavishly detailed contemporaneous account, originally published in the *New York Times* and reprinted in the *Minneapolis Star Tribune* on December 26, 2015. The account can be found online at http://www.startribune.com/dec-26-1862-38-dakota-men-executed-in-mankato/138273909.

For most of the demographic and statistical information about Worthington, Minnesota, I relied on the city's data website at http://www.city-data.com/city/Worthington-Minnesota.html. For information on Worthington's settlement by the white man, General Judson W. Bishop's "History of the St. Paul & Sioux City Railroad, 1864–1881" describes in striking detail his wagon journey across a "desolate prairie." The town of Worthington would soon be founded at a lakeside spot along the route Bishop had explored by wagon. Bishop's narrative can be accessed at http://lcweb2.loc.gov/service/gdc/lhbum/0866e/0866e_0436_0455.pdf. For background on Worthington's settlement by Scandinavian and German immigrants, I relied on *Nobles County History*, edited by Al Goff. A brief but enlightening overview of Worthington's early days can be found at http://www.noblescountyhistory.org/nobles-county-history. Other valuable information, both descriptive and statistical, appeared in a lengthy portrait of my hometown by *St. Paul Pioneer Press* writer Tad Vezner. Vezner's report, published in the *Pioneer Press* on September 17, 2011, and updated on February 3, 2017, is available at https://www.twincities.com/2011/09/17/worthington-minn-was-dying-then-enter-the-immigrants.

Information regarding the incident of alleged excessive force by Worthington Police Department officers was obtained from a variety of sources, including the city's newspaper, the ACLU of Minnesota, and Minnesota Public Radio. These sources can be accessed at http://www.dglobe.com/news/government-and-politics/4367954-citys-independent-investigation-still-underway-aclu-lawsuit; https://www.aclu-mn.org/en/press-releases/worthington-man-sues-local-law-enforcement-over-assault; https://www.mprnews.org/story/2017/06/22/aclu-calls-for-probe-of-violent-arrest-in-worthington; and https://www.aclu-mn.org/en/news/over-year-ago-i-was-assaulted-police-officer-im-still-waiting-justice. A video of the violent incident can be found at https://www.youtube.com/watch?v=UzrOobi5BRY&feature=youtube.

An example of how the nation's contentious immigration issues have spilled over into the small city of Worthington is available at http://www.citypages.com/news/worthington-father-of-four-ordered-deported-after-24-years-in-america/447754933.

Details about the inspiring life of my childhood friend Mike Bjerkesett can be accessed at http://www.startribune.com/obituary-mike-bjerkesett-a-pioneer-of-handicap-accessible-housing/412617083.

Chapter 30, *"Pride (III)"*

The Wendell Berry quotation is from his essay "The Failure of War," which can be found in Berry's book *Citizenship Papers*. The essay can also be retrieved at https://www.lionsroar.com/the-failure-of-war.

The Gandhi quotation can be found on several online websites simply by typing the quotation into a search engine. However, I was unable to locate a precise citation. Although the quotation may prove unattributable, or apocryphal, I have included it anyway, for obviously someone has expressed a thought I wish had been my own.

Chapter 32, *"Timmy and Tad and Papa and I (II)"*

For information and opinion about the presumed connections between "Cat in the Rain" and Hemingway's personal life, I relied on Kenneth Lynn's *Hemingway;* Carlos Baker's biography, also titled *Hemingway;* Jeffrey Meyers's *Hemingway: A Biography;* Carlene Brennen's *Hemingway's Cats;* and Simon Lavery's analysis at http://tredynasdays. co.uk/2013/10/ernest-hemingway-cat-rain-critique-pt-ii.

Chapter 33, *"Home School"*

Calculations of war deaths, even in contemporary times, are at best approximate. Statisticians do not stroll with their calculators through ongoing battles or into burning jungles and cities. Even if war deaths could be accurately counted, categorized, and reported, little such effort has been expended over recorded history. Numerical evidence is thin and suspect. Estimates of fatalities can vary, as in the case of World War Two, by as many as 30 million people. And there is frequently no way of retrieving or evaluating methodologies used to compute war deaths that were reported in ancient, medieval, and some modern textual sources. Still, as a starting point, I consulted an online website that attempts to estimate "all deaths that are either directly or indirectly caused by war," including "the deaths of military personnel which are the direct result of military wartime activities" and including the deaths of civilians that have resulted from "war-induced epidemics, diseases, famines, atrocities, genocide, etc." The web site can be accessed at https://en.wikipedia .org/wiki/List_of_wars_by_death_toll#Works_cited.

Information gleaned from Wikipedia, in my experience, is not uniformly trustworthy, therefore I consulted the relevant references cited there for each of the wars mentioned in chapter 33. Where I had reason to question either the accuracy or the verifiability of any range of estimated deaths in a particular war, I reported only the lowest available estimate. I reported no estimates that could not, in some way, be independently justified. But in a certain sense, the precise number of wartime casualties is irrelevant. To a grieving father, one is a large number.

Chapter 34, "Home School"

I am indebted to Mark A. Nichipor of the National Park Service, whose knowledge, wisdom, and encouragement were invaluable, and who cheerfully responded to my barrage of naïve questions about the battles at Lexington and Concord. I also wish to acknowledge a privately printed work of scholarship, *We Were There,* by Vincent J. R. Kehoe. Rich in human detail, this two-volume work offers a compilation of British and American accounts of the battles on April 19, 1775, including diaries, letters, and after-action reports. I found many of the quotations in chapter 34 in Kehoe's compendium. Among other sources consulted: Allen French, *The Day of Lexington and Concord* and *A British Fusilier in Revolutionary Boston;* Arthur B. Tourtellot, *Lexington and Concord;* National Park Service map of the British expedition's route of march; *Journals of the Continental Congress,* vol. 2; and Richard Frothingham Jr., *History of the Siege of Boston and of the Battles of Lexington, Concord, and Bunker Hill.* It was also instructive to spend a day walking a considerable distance along what is now called Battle Road. Though I was burdened only by my clothing, the hike soon lost its romance.

Chapter 39, "Timmy and Tad and Papa and I (III)"

The Andrea Pitzer quotation can be found in her biography *The Secret History of Vladimir Nabokov.* Pitzer's superb book offers a reminder that Nabokov flatly dismissed the work of Hemingway, whose prose style could not have stood in greater contrast to his own. Hemingway, perhaps with Nabokov in mind, issued his own famously dismissive comment: "Prose is architecture, not interior decoration, and the Baroque is over." It is interesting to note that both writers had taken instruction in boxing. How entertaining it might have been to sit ringside as these two ironed out their aesthetic differences.

The quotation from Erich Maria Remarque's novel *Arch of Triumph* appears in a Random House e-book edition translated by Walter Sorell and Denver Lindley.

Chapter 43, "War Buddies"

Beyond anecdotal evidence, I was able to find very little precise data regarding the moral and political judgments of present-day Vietnam veterans looking back on their war. A handful of studies shed oblique light on the matter, however, and the following sources were helpful: Jonathan D. Klingler and J. Tyson Chatagnier, "Are You Doing Your Part? Veterans' Political Attitudes and Heinlein's Conception of Citizenship," http://journals.sagepub.com/doi/abs/10.1177/0095327X12471932; Farai Chideys, "This Election Is Testing the Republican Loyalties of Military Voters," https://fivethir tyeight.com/features/what-impact-will-the-military-vote-have; Frank Newport, "Military Veterans of All Ages Tend to Be More Republi-

can," https://news.gallup.com/poll/118684/military-veterans-ages
-tend-republican.aspx; and Rebecca Burgess, "After Johnny's Marched
Home," *American Interest,* https://www.the-american-interest.com
/2015/11/11/after-johnnys-marched-home. My thanks to Lucas
Frank at Florentine Films for locating three of these sources. The letter
to the editor mentioned in chapter 43 appeared in the *Austin American-Statesman,* April 30, 2016.

Chapter 49, *"Timmy and Tad and Papa and I (IV)"*

The quotation from Remarque's *The Night in Lisbon* appears in a Random House e-book edition translated by Ralph Manheim.

Chapter 55, *"Timmy and Tad and Papa and I (V)"*

The Frederick Crews quotation is from Matthew C. Stewart's "Ernest
Hemingway and World War I: Combatting Recent Psychobiographical Reassessments, Restoring the War." An abstract of the article is at
https://www.questia.com/library/journal/1G1-63045302/ernest-
hemingway-and-world-war-i-combatting-recent.

Kenneth Lynn's opinion about the internal focus of "Now I Lay Me"
appears in his biography *Hemingway.*

A contentious, occasionally vituperative, and highly entertaining exchange of opinions about the literary importance of Hemingway's World War One experience appeared in the *New York Review of Books,* October 22, 1987: https://www.nybooks.com/articles/1987
/10/22/pressure-under-grace-an-exchange.

My reference to Jeffrey Dahmer in chapter 55 is neither casual nor
flippant. Antisocial personality disorder, which incorporates elements of
the now out-of-favor terms "psychopath" and "sociopath," is typically
diagnosed by a number of clinical factors that include absence or paucity of remorse and shame, egocentricity, impoverished major affective

reactions, absence or paucity of empathy and compassion for others, superficial charm and good intelligence, and inadequately motivated antisocial behavior. In the comrade-shooting episode in *A Farewell to Arms,* Frederic Henry exhibits all but one of these traits. (He is not particularly charming, except perhaps in the presence of Catherine.) Without compelling evidence to the contrary, including evidence drawn from the behavior and thoughts of Hemingway's character, a reader may reasonably conclude, as I do, that there is little or no emotion to report, and that Frederic Henry is in fact coldly and abnormally indifferent to killing, either by nature, by iron volition, or as a result of battlefield trauma and desensitization. Also, on a personal level, which is the level on which stories and novels are received, I cannot discount my own wartime experience, which contains no examples of actual human beings who displayed anything close to the profound, dense, and relentless absence of affect exhibited by Frederic Henry and Hemingway's other martial protagonists. The only such examples that come to mind, in fact, are those I've encountered in cartoons, horror movies, murder mysteries, fairy tales, and YouTube interviews with war criminals and incarcerated serial killers such as Jeffrey Dahmer and Arthur Shawcross. (When asked about empathy for his victims, Shawcross said, "It's not there . . . Something inside me is weird.") Finally, it should go without saying that I do not direct these reflections at Ernest Hemingway, but only at the writer's fictional wartime heroes. Though I am not a psychiatrist, I would certainly be uneasy if Frederic Henry were to step out of a novel and buy the house next door. See Martha Stout, *The Sociopath Next Door;* James Fallon, *The Psychopath Inside: A Neuroscientist's Personal Journey into the Dark Side of the Brain.* Fallon discusses in depth the "sliding scale" by which psychologists measure the presence and severity of antisocial personality disorder. As a neuroscientist, he also discusses relationships between physical brain abnormalities and behavior that laymen call sociopathic and psychopathic.